A Christian Engineer Explores Evolution

An Even-Handed Guide to the Science

David Korotney

Rick,

Thanks so much for reviewing a first draft of my book. You provided the engineer's perspective, while another provided a writer's view, another a biologist's view, etc. You caught some things on tone and perspective that I changed.

Thanks again,

David

ISBN 978-1503071056

To my sons Jared and Alec, who kept asking me
"So is your book done yet?"
and to my wife Abby, who is just happy
that I have a hobby

A Different Kind of Book on Evolution

There are a lot of books out there about evolution, and the Biblical account of creation, and how the two might, or might not, fit together. But with few exceptions, it seems that authors generally take a position at one end of the spectrum or the other. On the one hand you have those who are convinced that there's nothing to evolution at all. It's completely false in every respect, and the Biblical account of creation is literally true in every respect and is the only story that can be trusted. On the other hand you have those who are absolutely convinced that evolution has been proven to be true, and that there is no room for, nor need for, God in the story of the rise of life on Earth. It's the classic example of religion versus science, and the two sides often don't get along very well.

But the older I get, the more I am convinced that few Christians fall into one of these two camps. Many think that there is something to evolution, though they might not know where to draw the line between what God might have done and what might have occurred through natural processes.

There are, of course, people who have made an effort to find the middle ground, and have laid out how various aspects of evolution might fit in with the Biblical story of creation. But in many of these cases, I still sense an undercurrent of distrust of scientists who study evolution and champion its ideas.

If you are one of those who think of themselves as being somewhere between the two extremes, then this book is for you. Or, if you simply haven't thought about the issue much and want to know what all the hubbub is about, this is for you as well. Or if you are currently at one of the two extremes but are willing to at least consider what the other side has to say. Or you were assigned the topic for your debate class. Or you broke both legs in a skiing accident and this is the only book within reach.

But be warned: This isn't a book about the correct answer. Not the politically correct answer, not the religiously correct answer. This is a book about the science at issue in the theory of evolution. What the science says and what it doesn't say. Where the uncertainties are. What scientists know for sure, what they have some reason for believing, and what they are merely guessing at. It's a book about the facts, as well as I can understand them and as objectively as I can convey them.

I love science. Over the years I have read books on physics, cosmology, psychology, and mathematics, just for fun. I enjoy the process of figuring out how things fit together and the process of generating new ideas from a jumble of facts. This might explain why I studied engineering in college, and why I am forever tinkering with some project in the basement.

I am also a Christian. A Christian nerd, thank you very much.

I did not become a Christian until I was 21, so up until that point religion had no opportunity to influence how I viewed science. And since becoming a Christian, my views on science haven't really changed much. I have more or less viewed the Bible as a means for understanding the truth about God and our relationship with Him, and science as a means for understanding the truth about the physical universe. It always struck me as strange that anyone would find the two in conflict.

More recently, however, I've been able to see how and why there is a conflict when it comes to the subject of evolution. I still don't think there needs to be a conflict, but I understand why it's there. In this book I hope to diffuse some of that conflict by being clear about what, exactly, is at issue, and how different people view the same data and information differently.

There's a lot to the science of evolution, and many great minds have spent many, many years investigating the issues. As I researched evolution for purposes of writing this book, it became clear to me that there is an enormous amount of detail in the science, and I doubt that anyone will ever write a book that covers it all. Even the scientists that work in evolutionary biology, paleontology, and the like tend to specialize in particular areas: ankle bones of extinct ungulates, whale skulls, bacterial flagella. I suspect that even among them, few really know everything about every scientific issue involved in the theory of evolution.

So, this book is necessarily an overview. It touches on every major scientific topic in evolution, and every significant area of contention between those who believe in evolution and those who don't or who are suspicious of it. I've done my best to dive into the science in enough detail to provide a reasonably clear picture of where the disagreements are, and to give you the tools you need to make a rational decision about evolution.

But this isn't a textbook. I haven't covered every single issue and every single argument. I'm fully aware that this will irk folks on both sides of the debate, who will think that I have given too much credence to some argument in support of the "wrong" side and have missed some critical argument that would favor of the "right" side. Moreover, I have made every attempt to be objective about everything and to describe why each side sees things the way that they do. This, too, will upset some folks. Since I can't make everyone happy with a book intended to provide an objective view of the science, the most I can hope for is that I upset every side equally. So, my apologies ahead of time.

Some things to note about the book's organization:

The first several chapters are a prelude of sorts to set the later discussion of the science in context. While this is primarily a book about the science, you simply can't be objective about it without recognizing the various biases that we all have, and why those biases are there. To this end, I discuss some of the ugly fallout from the theory of evolution, but also some of the conundrums with the Biblical creation story. To make sure we're going into the science with our eyes wide open, I also spend some time discussing the less-than-stellar treatment of science by the church over the last 2000 years and the difficulty of using science to explain miraculous events. With any luck this discussion will help you to appreciate both the complexity of the issue and our limitations in sorting it all out correctly. As Thomas Edison once said, "We don't know one-millionth of one percent about anything."

A quick look at the chapter titles will make it clear that most of the book is spent discussing the science behind evolution rather than alternative theories. I recognize that some Christians will view this fact alone as evidence of bias on my part, but really this is just a reflection of the fact that most of the debate about evolution has to do with whether the science is really strong enough to make the claims that it does. In my experience, alternative theories of the emergence and diversification of life on earth (in particular creationism and its less overtly religious cousin intelligent design) generally include less detail than the science behind the theory of evolution, and thus there is less to discuss. That said, I do provide some discussion of these alternative theories in Chapters 17 and 18.

CONTENTS

A Christian Engineer Explores Evolution

Acknowledgments

A number of people provided helpful feedback on the first manuscript, including Drew Collins, Shannon Gordon, Sarah Rassoul, Rick Rykowski, Larry Singer, Betsy Williams, and Sue Willis. Those folks called me out on such things as tone, bias, the use of Christian jargon, bad jokes, and yes, even errors, both factual and grammatical. The final product is most certainly better as a result of their input.

A Christian Engineer Explores Evolution

Chapter 1

Is Genesis Clear? Not So Fast

By and large this book steers clear of trying to find a way to fit evolution into the Biblical story of creation in Genesis chapters 1 and 2. Others much smarter than I have made attempts to do that over the last two hundred years. Nevertheless, since the conflict between religion and evolution is rooted in the Biblical story, it's important that you recognize something about the Biblical story before we go on:

> *No matter how you interpret the creation story in Genesis, you are going to run into problems matching what you read with what you know about the world.*

It doesn't matter if you are reading the creation story in the most literal way possible or the most metaphorical, figurative, symbolic way possible. The creation account in Genesis raises awkward questions for which there are no easy answers.

Now, some of you might be wondering how a good Christian can say such things. So, before we go on, let me say this:

I believe the Bible is the inspired word of God. I believe that what it says is the truth. I believe that the story of creation in the book of Genesis is true.

But, at the same time, I've come to recognize that the truth isn't always simple. Have you ever studied biochemistry? You might say that biochemistry is the truth about chemical reactions that occur in living things. It's anything but simple, but it's still truth. I think that the same goes for the creation story in the book of Genesis. It's the truth, but that doesn't necessarily mean it's simple.

Let's start with the most literal reading of the creation story, which is the most straightforward way to read it. In this approach, God creates everything from nothing in six 24-hour days. Earth and sky, sun and moon, plants and animals, all pop into existence fully formed. It certainly seems simple, and in some respects it is.

But let's look a little closer.

God creates light on the first day, separates the light from the darkness, calls the light "day" and the darkness "night." But He doesn't create the sun and stars until the fourth day. How could the world have light before the sun was created? And how can there be any measure of day and night for the first three days of creation without the sun rising and setting?

Speaking of the sun being created on the fourth day, why would God create all the plants on the third day if there was as yet no sun to help them grow? I suppose the plants could survive for a day without any sunlight, so there's no serious problem here. It just seems strange.

On the second day, God inserts a space between "the waters" to separate the water on the earth from the water in heaven. Does this mean that heaven was originally made out of liquid water?

In Genesis Chapter 2, the whole creation story is repeated, but now some of the events seem to be out of order. When placed side by side, the creation accounts in Chapters 1 and 2 look rather different:

Chapter 1: Plants → animals → Adam and Eve

Chapter 2: Adam → plants → animals → Eve

Although not directly related to the creation story, I'll throw in one more strange thing from Genesis Chapter 3. Although the serpent is commonly understood to be Satan, he is described in two places as a physical animal, as if he was just one of many that God created, albeit more clever and crafty.

There are some other strange things about the Biblical creation story that aren't obvious unless you think about them for awhile. For instance, if God's original intention was that the earth be completely free of sickness, suffering, and death, then there would be no carnivores. Lions would never eat lambs, and spiders would never eat flies. Such a world is not merely different from the one we live in today, it is fundamentally different at the most basic biological level. For a lion to eat plants instead of animals, his mouth would need to be full of crushing molars instead of flesh-tearing incisors and canines. The biochemistry of his digestive system would need to be very different as well to digest the cellulose of plant material instead of the protein and fat in meat. If spiders ate fruit instead of flies, they would not need to build webs and would not need their venom either.

And here's another strange thing. Presumably every creature that God created during the first six days was intended to live forever, and their descendants would live forever. God commanded all creatures to be fruitful and multiply and fill the earth, so He clearly wanted the number of animals to increase. But if no animal ever dies, wouldn't earth quickly be filled with animals?

Let's play with this idea for a moment.

Imagine God creates two frogs on the fifth day of creation. Frogs typically produce hundreds of eggs each year, but today the vast majority never reach adulthood because they succumb to disease, drought, and predators. But what if one hundred frog eggs grew to be adult frogs in the first year? And what if in the second year, those one hundred frogs each laid one hundred eggs, so that there would be ten thousand frogs at the end of the second year? If you do the math, it turns out that it would take less than nine years for frogs to fill the earth. Literally. Every square inch of ground in the entire world would be occupied by a frog.

And that's just frogs. What if you throw in lions and tigers and bears? Oh my!

All of these strange things in the creation story in Genesis can be explained in various ways, but it takes some creativity to do so. In fact, it requires that we deviate from a purely literal reading and treat some things (like an aquatic heaven) as more metaphorical. Thus, no matter how literally you want to read Genesis, you're stuck doing some interpretation and in the end you may be left with some questions that simply can't be answered.

Sometimes Christians wonder how evolution could possibly fit into the Bible's creation story. Their concern is that the Bible's version of creation story must be contorted, twisted, and re-interpreted in order to fit evolution, and that doing so is tantamount to changing the Word of God to say what you want it to say. This was also a big concern in Galileo's time, as described in Chapter 4. But if you conclude that evolution can't be true because it doesn't fit into the Biblical story of creation in a straightforward way, remember that the most literal reading of Genesis isn't straightforward either. You're going to face the trouble of interpretation no matter how you approach Genesis. Choose your pain.

So, if you wanted to fit evolution into the Genesis story, how would you do it?

Good Christians have been talking about this for two centuries. Even before Darwin's *Origin of Species* was published in 1859, the emerging field of geology and its cousin paleontology were picking up speed, and serious proposals were published in which the six days of creation in Genesis Chapter 1 were interpreted as corresponding to much longer epochs of time. So, for instance, instead of all the plants popping instantly into existence on the third 24-hour day, plants arose more slowly over millions of years, but that period of time could still be called a "day." Similarly for fish on the fifth "day" and land animals on the sixth "day," all living things would arise over a long period of time.

But even this requires some fudging, because the plants could not have arisen over millions of years in total darkness - remember that the sun was not created until after all the plants, according to the Bible story. And, if you believe the fossil record, all life began in the oceans, not on land, which seems to run in the opposite direction to the order in Genesis Chapter 1 where land plants arise on day three and ocean life appears on day five.[1]

The Bible's description of creation presents another problem for anyone attempting to fit evolution into the Genesis account. In several places in Chapter 1, it says that living things will produce offspring "of the same kind," suggesting that seeds from an oak tree will only produce new oak trees, not apple trees, and a cow will never give birth to a goat. Some have interpreted this language as saying that all the species of plants and animals originally created by God in the first six days of creation are fixed in form and that no new species will ever arise. Thus, they reason, if evolution says that species can change over time to produce new species, then evolution cannot be true since it seems to run afoul of the statement in Genesis that living things only produce offspring of the same kind.

If you are inclined to try to fit evolution into the Genesis account, there are of course other ways to interpret "of the same kind." For instance, while it is true that species change over time under the theory of evolution, in no way does the theory say that a parent can be a different species than its own offspring. A cow will always give birth to a cow. But according to evolutionary theory the baby cow will differ from the mama cow in extremely minor ways at the genetic level. It is only through successive generations, typically over many thousands if not millions of years, that a new species might arise. Given this, even evolutionary theory could be seen as being consistent with the Bible's statement that all living things have offspring "of the same kind."

Another approach is to treat the word "kind" as referring not to species of plants or animals, but rather broader groups of related organisms. In the discipline of biology, similar species are grouped together into a genus, similar genera (plural of genus) are grouped together into a family, and so on. Within a genus or family, there are different species, but they all share certain characteristics. For instance, the horse, donkey, and zebra are

---

[1] Chapter 17 discusses Noah and the Great Flood, which some believe provides an explanation for why the fossil record appears to show a different order for the emergence and diversification of life than Genesis.

separate species, but they are all in the genus Equus. Under this approach, then, God created an animal on the sixth day that was the first in the genus Equus, and which over time and many generations differentiated into the three separate species horse, donkey, and zebra through an evolutionary process. Since there's nothing in the Bible to indicate whether "kind" means species or one of these broader groupings, this is at least a potentially legitimate interpretation.

The bottom line is that none of the traditional approaches to interpreting the creation story in Genesis are simple or straightforward. And because of that, we should feel a certain sense of freedom to at least consider whether evolution, or some aspect of it, might be true.

Chapter 2

The Wide Range Of Views
Among Christians

The dominant views of Christianity on the subject of evolution have largely been established by those with the loudest voices: those in the pulpit, those who write books, and those who teach. To many outside of the church it may seem that Christians have a more or less unified position against evolution. In reality, there is a wide range of viewpoints among Christians about the biggest questions in the evolution debate, such as:

* How old is the earth and how old are fossils?
* How did life get started?
* Once started, how could life have evolved from tiny microorganisms to the vast array of plants and animals we have today?
* Did humans evolve from some sort of ape-like creature?

This book is designed to provide enough information so that you can make an informed decision about these questions and many others as well. Assuming, that is, that you feel the need to actually make a decision about where you stand on evolution. It is my opinion (one of the very few you will find in this book) that it is legitimate to remain agnostic on the issue of evolution and still remain a faithful Christian (see more discussion of this in Chapter 20).

Because there is such a wide range of views on evolution, it may be helpful to see where you are currently in relation to the full spectrum of viewpoints, from the strong Creationist viewpoint on one end to the strong Evolutionist viewpoint on the other. Below is a diagram where I've attempted to define seven different "paradigms." There are probably other paradigms as well, with finer nuances that fall between those I've identified. But most people should be able to identify primarily with one of these seven.

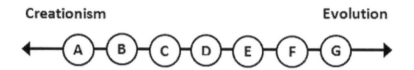

Paradigm A
The creation story in the book of Genesis should be taken literally, with each of the six steps occurring in a series of 24-hour days. Earth and all life were created all at once approximately 6,000 years ago. Not one aspect of biological evolution is true.
Paradigm B
Earth may be billions of years old, but God created all life within six 24-hour days about 6,000 years ago. Not one aspect of biological evolution is true.
Paradigm C
Earth is billions of years old. God created all life over billions of years in such a way that it corresponds to the fossil record. However, there was no evolution. God brought every species into existence fully formed, but in a sequential manner instead of all at once.

> *Paradigm D*
>
> Earth is billions of years old. God created the first microorganisms, and over billions of years they evolved into all the plants and animals we know today. However, humans did not evolve. God created humans separately.

> *Paradigm E*
>
> Earth is billions of years old. God created the first microorganisms, and over billions of years they evolved into all the plants and animals we know today, including humans.

> *Paradigm F*
>
> Earth is billions of years old. The first microorganisms came to exist naturally out of chemicals, and over billions of years they evolved into all the plants and animals we know today, including humans. However, God directed the process of evolution at every stage because it would not have occurred otherwise.

> *Paradigm G*
>
> Earth is billions of years old. The first microorganisms came to exist naturally out of chemicals, and over billions of years they evolved into all the plants and animals we know today, including humans. God did not direct the process of evolution, but simply created matter and energy and the universe to work in this way.

Of course, there is also one more paradigm which I didn't include in my list. Call it Paradigm H: Evolution is a fact, and there is no God. But if there is no God, then the Bible is irrelevant, there is no need for any debate over evolution, and this book is pointless. I'm assuming readers of this book are at least sympathetic to the idea of God, and there is no need to bother any further with Paradigm H.

The viewpoints we hold on the theory of evolution are the results of how we were raised, what we've heard in church or other Christian venues, what our friends think, what facts and information we have been exposed to, and which experts we trust.

If you grab any two Christians at random, odds are good that their views of evolution won't be exactly the same. They'll probably disagree about a whole lot of other hot-button Christian issues as well.

Unfortunately, many times we don't give our fellow Christians the freedom to have their own opinions on evolution. Let me show you what I mean. First identify which of the seven paradigms above most closely describes your own viewpoint. Now consider the paradigms to the left of yours, towards the creationism end of the spectrum. Would you use any of the following words to describe people holding such views?

- Religious fanatic
- Anti-science
- Narrow-minded
- Ignorant

Now consider the paradigms to the right of yours, towards the evolution end of the spectrum. Would you use any of the following words to describe them?

- Anti-Christian
- Irreligious
- Un-Biblical
- Gullible

When it comes to discussing evolution with those who hold different views than your own, none of these labels is particularly helpful. Whether you say them out loud or not doesn't matter. It's the attitude that kills meaningful dialogue, and potentially meaningful relationships as well. In the context of discussing evolution, loving your neighbor means respecting their viewpoint even if it differs from yours and even if you are sure you are right.

That's not to say that all viewpoints are all equally correct. Most certainly one of the paradigms I've listed above is more correct than the others, and maybe one of them is 100% correct and the others are complete nonsense. But because the issue is complicated and we are all coming at it from different directions, it's important to recognize that people can legitimately hold different positions. Given this, we need to focus more on how we are treating the people with whom we are discussing evolution, and less on the issue itself.

I know that sounds silly for me to say, given that I'm writing a book on evolution. But as much as I love science, people are simply more important. This book is intended to open dialogue in a way that strengthens relationships rather than creating more dividing walls.

One more thing. I have avoided using the words "creationist" and "evolutionist" in this book because they are loaded terms that come with a certain set of expectations, and many people wouldn't classify themselves as one or the other. But I still need some way to refer to the different points of view that people have. So as you go through the book, you'll notice that I sometimes refer to Theistic Paradigm and Organic Paradigm. Theistic Paradigms are those that tend towards the creationism end of the spectrum, though they may contain some elements of the evolution viewpoint. Organic Paradigms are those that tend towards the evolution end of the spectrum, though they may contain some elements of the creationism viewpoint. Wherever you fall on the diagram above, you can treat the Theistic Paradigm as representing those views that are more creationist than yourself, and the Organic Paradigm as representing those views to that are more evolutionist than yourself.

Chapter 3

Evolution's Ugly Side

All sides agree that the theory of evolution has had some very real, very ugly consequences in the 150 or so years since Darwin's *Origin of Species* was released. If there is going to be honest dialogue about evolution, it is only right that we get all of that ugliness out in the open.

The first area of ugliness will matter only to Christians and others who believe in a loving, omnipotent, omniscient God. It is the fact that some people, on hearing a description of evolution, conclude that there is no room for God in a natural, seemingly unguided process wherein simple forms of life gradually develop into more complex forms over time. They conclude either that God isn't necessary for life on Earth, or that He doesn't exist at all. Their faith weakens or disappears altogether. You might call this "deconversion."

While it's sad to see, I understand how it might happen. With a Theistic Paradigm approach, there is still some mystery in how life came to be. And where there's mystery, it's easy to declare that "God did it." But in an Organic Paradigm approach, the mystery is less obvious and it is correspondingly more difficult to see the fingerprint of God on the universe. For someone who is already questioning his or her faith or the existence of God, evolution could be the thing that pushes that person over the proverbial edge.

If this is a fair description of your own experience, be encouraged. There are many Christians who have some level of belief in evolution. And, as discussed in more detail in Chapter 20, our faith in God should be influenced more by the story of Jesus than anything else.

The second area of ugliness is closely related to the first, and involves God's role in establishing absolute morality. Just as the theory of evolution might lead an individual to conclude that God was not involved in the appearance and diversification of life on earth, it could by extension lead him to conclude that God is not involved in human affairs today. A God who is not involved in his creation is a God who can be ignored, along with whatever opinions about right and wrong that he might have. Without a God-given set of principles for what constitutes right and wrong, the only alternative would be to distinguish right from wrong on the basis of societal conventions which are ultimately the product of faulty human opinions. If you and I have a disagreement about something, neither of us can appeal to any absolute morality since your opinion about what is right and wrong is no more valid than mine. Morality becomes purely relative.

To be fair, some of the greatest moral failures in history have occurred exactly because of appeals to religion to establish morality: anti-Semitism, the Crusades, and the Spanish Inquisition come to mind. While these examples represent serious and significant failures to apply the moral precepts of the Bible appropriately, many Christians nevertheless fear the deterioration of morality in our society if the theory of evolution continues to arouse disregard for absolute standards of right and wrong.

The third big area of ugliness associated with evolution is something that should matter to everyone regardless of your belief in God. You might refer to it as artificial selection among humans or social Darwinism. This will take a moment to explain.

In the theory of evolution, the fittest individuals in a group of organisms are more likely to survive, and thus are more likely to reproduce. Those individuals who are less fit (those who are weaker, more susceptible to disease, less able to run from predators, etc) tend to die off. In essence, nature is continually "selecting" individuals who are more fit over those who are less fit, and as a result the group as a whole is continually moving towards greater fitness, greater health, better adaptation to its environment, etc. I go into greater depth on the subject of natural selection in Chapter 10.

But in humans, this natural selection process doesn't happen. We take care of the sick, the weak, and the mentally or emotionally handicapped. We protect and provide for those that can't protect or provide for themselves. As a result, it is not the case that only the fittest of humans can reproduce - every human has a more or less equal shot at reproducing. If there is any truth to the process of natural selection among other animals, it certainly doesn't apply to us modern humans.

At various points in history, some people have concluded that this is a bad thing. The human race, they concluded, has stopped evolving, and in fact is devolving. By allowing less fit individuals to reproduce (where "less fit" is of course defined by those who consider themselves to be "more fit"), the human race as a whole is made weaker and less capable. People with this frame of mind have decided that, since natural selection isn't doing its job, artificial selection must be encouraged. In other words, those who consider themselves to be "fit" must actively work to ensure that the "unfit" do not reproduce. In more extreme forms, this attitude includes not just ensuring that the unfit do not reproduce, but also that the unfit do not consume limited resources. In other words, the unfit simply must be done away with.

The best-known example of the wide-spread use of artificial selection was during the German Nazi era of the 1930's and early 1940's. With clear references to Darwinian evolution and its extrapolation to humans, Nazi philosophy theorized about a "master race" that could be attained only through the deliberate and systematic elimination of inferior humans. Anyone with what Nazi's considered to be obvious shortcoming was targeted. This included the mentally and emotionally disabled, people with deformities or birth defects, and of course whole races such as the Jews. Scientific research on such people, if you can call it science, was intended to find out more about why such people were "defective" so that their entrance into the human race could be more easily prevented.

Lest you think that such large-scale artificial selection happened only far across the Atlantic, let me tell you a troubling story about the eugenics movement here in the United States.

In 1883, a half-cousin of Charles Darwin named Sir Francis Galton formulated the concept of eugenics. In its most basic form, it simply means any effort to improve the genetic quality of future generations of humans. In practice, it meant making a determination about what sorts of genetic qualities were undesirable, and then developing plans to reduce the likelihood that those undesirable qualities would be passed on to future generations. The primary means to accomplish this was by implementing policies to control immigration of "undesirables", prohibiting interracial marriages, selective breeding, and forced sterilization.

In the early decades of the 20th Century, a well-coordinated and active eugenics movement developed in the United States. Official organizations and offices formed around the country. Eugenics was widely accepted in the academic community, and many universities taught eugenics classes. Supporters of eugenics included Alexander Graham Bell, Winston Churchill, and Margaret Sanger.

Most proponents of eugenics had racist tendencies, and used the philosophical arguments of directed human evolution and artificial selection to legitimize various racist policies. For instance, most American eugenicists believed that social mobility (i.e. being wealthy) was indicative of one's genetic fitness, and that poverty was a characteristic of genetic inferiority. Since most wealthy people were Caucasian and most African-Americans were poor, this approach allowed eugenicists to deem whites as "fit" and African-Americans as "unfit."

Many laws were passed in the U.S. under the banner of eugenics. For instance:

- In 1896, Connecticut enacted a law that prohibited anyone who was an epileptic, an imbecile, or feeble-minded to marry.

- In 1927 a Supreme Court case legitimized the forced sterilization of patients at a Virginia home for the mentally retarded.

- Under North Carolina's eugenics program which was in operation as recently as 1977, an IQ of 70 or lower meant sterilization was appropriate.

- In the state of California, about 20,000 involuntary sterilizations were performed between 1909 and 1963, the most of any state.

In all, 32 states had eugenics programs of one sort or another.

It is not clear if these public policies and laws would have existed if the theory of evolution had not provided the underlying rationale that legitimized them. Any time a scientific theory has a profoundly negative impact on society, it is appropriate to take a step back and ask whether there is something wrong with that theory. After all, if a scientific theory is true, one would expect it to produce positive results rather than negative ones. On the other hand, many good things have been used for evil: Christians have justified war, torture, and slavery with appeals to the Bible; God created sex to be good, and yet sex has been used for atrocious things throughout history. If we are going to approach the theory of evolution fairly and objectively, we need to be wary of rejecting it outright because of the evil that has been done in its name.

Chapter 4

Religion, Science, And The Story Of Galileo

Conflicts between science and the Bible have existed for centuries. While evolution is probably the most recent and most well-known example, another case that is almost as well-known is that of Galileo and the idea that earth travels around the sun. Since there are many parallels between that case centering on astronomy and the issues surrounding evolution, it's worth taking a short detour to see what we can learn from the Galileo case.

Galileo Galilei was born in 1564 in Pisa, Italy. This was about 40 years after the Protestant Reformation had begun, and more importantly right about the same time as the Roman Inquisition began. Thus Galileo grew up at a time when fervor in the Catholic Church against heretical teachings was growing at a fast pace. It was arguably the wrong time to be born if you had a penchant for questioning commonly held beliefs about the nature of the world.

Galileo had a natural talent for science and loved investigating various aspects of physics. However, science wasn't a typical approach to making a living at that time. He had considered entering the service of the Catholic Church at one point, but his father, recognizing his son's intelligence and wanting him to learn a trade, sent him to university to become a physician instead. This didn't last very long, however. He simply wasn't as interested in medicine as he was in science and math. So, eventually his father pulled him out of the university to live at home where he could study science at his leisure.

Galileo became well-known as a creative mechanical genius, and started making a living by designing and building various devices for individuals who submitted orders for them. He also lectured on science and abstract mathematical principles. It was these public lectures that initially brought him into conflict with others who were trained in Aristotelian abstract reasoning. These others dismissed the idea that actual experimentation was the proper way to determine how the world operates, and instead believed that pure reason could get one to any truth. Galileo's personality didn't help matters, as he had a tendency to challenge every assertion, even statements made by Aristotle which was regarded as almost blasphemy. By today's standards he would be considered merely an inquisitive skeptic whose mind was never satisfied with traditional answers to complicated questions. But back then this approach was both atypical and, to some, insulting. Why couldn't he just accept that certain things are true without challenging them?

Nevertheless, his scientific work and the mechanical devices he designed and built did gain him a lot of positive attention. This led to him being invited to Rome to make presentations to various church officials, and he was even extended goodwill by Pope Paul V. At this point he had many good friends and admirers in Rome.

The trouble started innocently enough, when Galileo built a telescope and began making observations of sunspots, the moon, and other planets. At this time the prevailing opinion was that earth was the center of the universe, and that the sun, moon, stars, and planets all revolved around earth. Some 80-plus years earlier, Nicolaus Copernicus had developed an alternative idea in which the sun was at the center and the earth and all planets moved in orbits around the sun. The "Copernican view" was generally regarded as an interesting concept on abstract theoretical grounds, but one that could not, in reality, be true.

Galileo's observations led him to conclude that Copernicus had been correct. He began describing his observations in lectures and writings, and stating his conviction that the Copernican view of the earth traveling around the sun was not merely an interesting idea but was true in reality. While many found his arguments convincing, opposition arose from others who argued that the Bible was clear that the sun moved around the earth and not the other way around. Galileo, being the argumentative sort, felt compelled to put his views of the matter in writing. In short, he said that the Bible was not intended to teach science, and that it used certain phrases to get certain points across without intending to provide a description of how the physical universe was structured. In other words, the Bible might say that the sun moves, but it doesn't really move.

Galileo's writings were widely circulated, and started a rather fierce debate. Galileo had deigned to step into theology, which at that time was the jurisdiction of the Catholic Church alone. In 1616 Rome issued an order to Galileo forbidding him to teach on this topic. The order expressed the position of the church in this way:

> *"The proposition that the sun is the center of the world and does not move from its place is absurd and false philosophically, and formally heretical because it is expressly contrary to holy scripture."*[2]

Off the record, some church officials indicated that Galileo would probably not have been censured if he had only expressed his views as a hypothesis rather than a fact. But this was simply not how Galileo the scientist thought.

Still, rather than face formal correction, Galileo agreed to keep quiet about his views. But in the years that followed, he continued his work in astronomy, focusing more on how ocean tides are connected to the movement of the moon around the earth. These studies provided additional evidence that the Copernican view was correct, and he slowly began letting his research and conclusions be made known again.

In 1632, about 16 years after the church first censured Galileo, he published a new book in which he gathered all the evidence he

---

[2] Giorgio de Santillana, <u>The Crime of Galileo</u>. University of Chicago Press, 1955. pp. 306-310.

had collected and, through a dialogue between three fictitious characters, presented his arguments supporting his position that the earth spins on its own axis, and also orbits the sun. In response, the church formally passed judgment, saying that he had disobeyed the order to maintain a hypothetical stance on the issue, and restating its position that the Copernican view is false.

Galileo was 70 years old when he was hauled before an Inquisition committee. In failing health and beset with anxiety, with failing eyesight, and being threatened with torture and imprisonment, he yielded on all counts and recanted all his views. He was charged with heresy, and forced to recite a scripted statement of repentance while kneeling before the committee. The church in Rome sent copies of the final judgment to the churches in all surrounding areas, and placed limits on where Galileo could go, where he could speak, and on what topics. Humiliated, Galileo never wrote or spoke again of his studies of the Copernican view.

No matter what your views of evolution are, your reaction to this story is probably the same as mine. The church was so dreadfully wrong, and its treatment of Galileo so horribly unjust. But rather than merely dwell on the negative, I want to make sure we are taking some lessons from it.

First of all, the church leadership of the day was convinced that the Copernican view was wrong for the simple and very understandable reason that it was contrary to a literal reading of the Bible. Any scientific theory, they reasoned, that could not be aligned with Scripture in a straightforward and unambiguous way could not possibly be right.

Something to think about: Do you think about evolution in this way? Have you rejected the idea of evolution because it does not appear to be consistent with the Bible?

Second, it didn't really matter much to the church leadership what the scientific evidence was that supported the Copernican view. Either the evidence itself was wrong, or Galileo's interpretation of it was wrong. Never mind that the Inquisition committee that charged Galileo with heresy never really bothered to study the evidence or its interpretation. From their point of view, there was simply no need to do so. They already knew what the answer was.

Something to think about: How closely have you looked at the evidence of evolution? Or have you decided that there's really no point in looking at it, because you already know that evolution isn't true?

Third, Galileo's opinion that the Bible is not intended to teach anything about how the physical world works may have been correct (at least, on the issue of whether or not the sun moves around the earth), but by voicing that opinion he made the mistake of stepping into the church's business, interpreting Scripture and determining what's to be taken literally and what's to be taken figuratively.

Something to think about: Does the idea of interpreting the Bible differently than you have in the past, or differently than Biblical experts, make you nervous? Do you think that a different approach to Bible interpretation could open the door to all sorts of crazy ideas that lead people away from God?

I'm guessing that many, maybe even most, of us Christians are at least a bit suspicious about science when it comes to the theory of evolution. And the reason is pretty obvious: there seems to be a lot at stake. If you feel this way, it might be worth reading Chapter 20 before moving on to Chapter 5.

Let me give you something else to think about.

Many years after Galileo, when it finally became clear to the leaders of the Catholic Church that the Copernican view was in fact correct, do you think that their faith in God was shaken? Do you think that they slumped in their chairs, sullenly wondering if the whole Bible was false? Did this revelation about how the earth and sun really move cause a mass exodus from the church?

Of course not. But the revelation about the movement of the earth and sun did remove some of the mystery behind how God operates the universe. No longer would Christians simply say, "God makes the sun and earth move by His power." Now they say, "God makes the sun and earth move through gravitational forces acting on masses that orbit around one another." God still does it, but now we understand a bit more about how it works.

Just like Galileo, we humans are an inquisitive bunch. We love to discover things. Life isn't very interesting if you never learn anything new, never experience anything new, never see anything new. And scientists are just normal people who have made the hunt for new insights into how our world works into a vocation. From that point of view, you might say that science is really just another way of searching for truth. Not moral truth or spiritual truth, but truth about matter and energy and the nature of time and space. Science is all about learning more about how the physical universe operates. There's a real joy in the search for truth of this sort, at least for nerds like me.

I understand that anything that removes some of the mystery of how God brought life to be, anything that makes it appear as though it was "merely" a biological process, might make you nervous. The same was probably true of the church leaders who condemned Galileo. Of course they probably would not have admitted to being nervous, and neither would we. Instead we call it faithfulness to scripture, or even faithfulness to God. But God is bigger than science, and faith in God need not depend on what science does or doesn't tell us.

Chapter 5

Science And Miracles

Science as we know it today is quite different than the study of philosophy from which it emerged. What started out millennia ago as an effort to understand the nature of reality through pure reasoning and speculation slowly incorporated observation, then categorization and direct measurement, and eventually more active techniques for testing theories. Today the "correct" approach to science is taught to all of us in grade school under the heading of the "scientific method." Here's how it is typically described:

- Start with a hypothesis about the way the world works

- Based on the hypothesis, make a prediction ("If I do X, then Y should result")

- Design and conduct an experiment to test the prediction

- Make observations about what actually happens when you do X

- Draw conclusions: Did Y happen when you did X?

- Confirm or refute the original hypothesis

In short, we are taught that science is all about designing experiments and using the results of those experiments to formulate laws about the way the world works.

In reality, however, science isn't always about experimentation. Experiments play a prominent role in such areas as physics and chemistry, but are less prominent or even absent in areas such as astronomy, geology, and archaeology where theories are both based on and evaluated by observations. While there are some aspects of evolution that lend themselves to experimentation, for instance in the context of artificial selection or genetic studies in bacteria, for the most part evolution is an observational science rather than an experimental one. Insofar as the theory or any of its components must be tested, this is typically accomplished through more observation.

The scientific process is also much messier than we are taught in grade school. There are lots of false starts and results that are murky. Limits in time or money often mean that shortcuts must be taken, which might call into question the accuracy of the results. And the uncertainty inherent in any experiment often means you must repeat the experiment multiple times and apply complex statistical algorithms to make any sense of the data.

But putting all that messiness aside, the goal of science is simple: to understand the universe. Sometimes there is hope that there will be some sort of payback, like for instance the study of fusion or genetic engineering. In such cases, scientists may be employed by companies who know that, if they can just understand something better, they can exploit it and develop a new product or service.

But in many other cases, science is more about the thrill of discovery. Think about the search for life on other planets or the mating habits of spiders. What's the point, really, of investigating such things? Like many others, I'm fascinated by various NASA missions to other planets, and I enjoy watching the occasional nature show as well. But I don't think anyone really expects this sort of science to have any practical impact on how we live.

The study of evolution falls mostly into this second category. While there are some advances in the area of genetics and biochemistry that are linked to the study of evolution and have the potential to result in new medical treatments, new diagnostic methods, and even the preservation of endangered species, the study of evolution is really just an inquisitive mind's pursuit of the story of how life on earth arose and developed.

The pursuit of understanding the universe is a bit like putting together a puzzle without the benefit of the box showing what the picture is supposed to look like. Scientists gather bits of data one by one and try to fit them together like the pieces of a puzzle. Over time, a picture emerges. There are still lots of missing pieces, and it's not certain that all the pieces are in the right place, but you can still make out the basic idea of the picture. As the picture emerges, scientists can better design the next experiment or identify the next observation to find the next missing piece of the puzzle. In theory, the picture will become clearer and clearer.

Here's an example. Imagine that someone has walked through a sandy field and left some footprints. However, only a few footprints are easily visible.

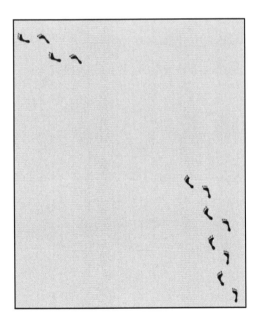

Based on what you see, you try to reconstruct the path that the person took. With little else to go on, your reconstruction would probably look like this:

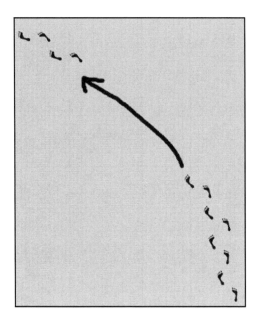

But then, on examining the ground a bit more closely, you find some additional footprints that were hidden behind some tall grass.

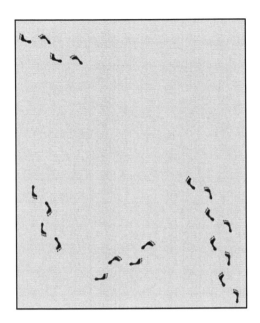

Based on this new evidence, you modify your reconstruction of the path that the person took through the field.

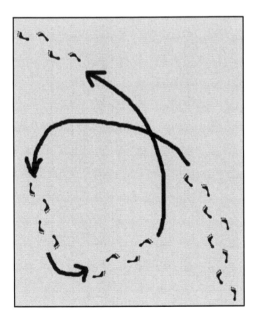

Every new piece of evidence allows you to develop a better guess as to the path that the person took. At some point you may run out of direct footprint evidence, and to make any further progress you need to look for indirect evidence. Is it possible that the person was going around looking at flowers? Are there swampy areas that the person might have been avoiding? Is there some matted down grass that looks like someone might have walked over it? Your reconstructed path may never be perfect, but as the information gaps get smaller and you are creative about how you draw conclusions, you can have reasonable confidence that your reconstructed path is more or less accurate.

And so it is with science. You look at evidence, try to create or dig up additional data to fill in the gaps, and develop an ever-more-accurate picture of how the world works. The picture that you develop, analogous to some sort of generalized scientific theory, is based on the sum total of all the evidence you have to date. It's probably never going to be perfect and there is always going to be some data that doesn't seem to fit the general rule. As a result, scientific theories are always subject to revision.

It's worth noting that the above description of science is generally accepted by both the Theistic and Organic Paradigms, with one important exception. What if the person who walked through the sandy field actually showed up? Now you have the one true authority on the matter, and have no need to reconstruct the path. Instead, he can tell you exactly what path he took. No scrounging for bits of data, no need to guess. You now know the answer, completely and unambiguously. All is well, unless...

Unless the path that this person claims to have walked bears no resemblance to the data in front of you. For instance, imagine that he tells you that he took a somewhat twisty path through the sandy field, like this:

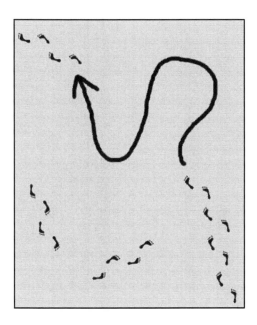

Now you have a dilemma. The authority on the matter seems to be saying that some of the footprint evidence you have collected is wrong. Either you mistook something for a footprint that was actually something else, or it's a forgery. Moreover, the path he claims to have walked goes through an area for which there is no footprint evidence at all. What are you going to do? Trust the data and your own reconstruction of the path, or trust the authority standing in front of you?

I hope it's obvious that I am speaking about the fundamental disagreement between the Theistic and Organic Paradigms on the subject of the theory of evolution. What is the definitive source from which you will draw conclusions about the origin and diversity of life on earth? Is it the data and the reconstruction of earth's history based on that data, or is it the rather different account of earth's history provided by the author himself in the Bible? As I said in the Introduction, this book is not about choosing sides, but about how and why the two sides see the science behind evolution the way that they do.

Science has both its pros and cons, things it does well and things it doesn't do so well. The first and most important thing to remember is that science is about understanding the what and the how of the physical universe: what happens under these circumstances, how does this work, what is this made of, how did this get here, etc. Science provides a very good process for finding patterns and repeatable processes in nature and allows us to zero in on the laws that govern matter and energy. In short, science is observational and descriptive.

But science is never going to provide an answer to the question "Why?" Any time a scientist says something like, "Here's why this chemical reaction occurs" what he is really saying is "Here's how this chemical reaction works." He can't tell you why a chemical reaction works one way rather than a different way. He can't tell you why the universe operates the way it does rather than some other way. He can't tell you why chemicals exist, or why scientists exist who study what chemicals do, or why anything exists at all.[3]

"Why" is an existential question, and is wrapped up in our pursuit of meaning and purpose in life. That's why "Why" questions are the purview of philosophy and religion. Science can't delve into such questions.[4]

When it comes to the use of scientific principles and methods to study evolution, there are several broad, overarching concerns raised by the Theistic Paradigm:

1. Evidence for evolution isn't proof of evolution
2. Evolutionary scientists are biased
3. The science behind evolution presumes uniform processes at all times and places

Of course these aren't the only concerns raised by folks in the

---

[3] There has been some recent theoretical work in physics aimed at explaining how something (the universe) could arise from nothing based on principles of quantum mechanics. Whether the "nothing" of which physicists speak is truly nothing, however, is debatable.

[4] Or rather, it shouldn't. We humans view the world subjectively, and this subjectivity often leaks over into science which should, in theory, be strictly objective. But this problem is no different for folks in the Theistic Paradigm than it is for folks in the Organic Paradigm.

Theistic Paradigm. Later chapters will deal with many of the concerns with specific pieces of evidence or specific conclusions reached by scientists. Here I address only the more general issues with the scientific method as it is typically applied to evolution.

Concern #1: Evidence for evolution isn't proof of evolution

This is an absolutely true statement. However, it's true about nearly everything, not just evolution. Proofs only exist in mathematics, and even in mathematics there are things that cannot be proven. If you have a bent towards mathematics, do a quick internet search on Gödel's incompleteness theorems and you'll see more on this than you'd ever wanted to know.

What happens if you demand proof for everything before you will accept it as true? Well, for one thing you won't believe in the Bible. There's certainly evidence for who wrote which parts of the Bible and when. Josh McDowell has compiled an enormous amount of evidence for the authenticity of the Bible in his two-volume set *Evidence That Demands a Verdict*. But as compelling as it may be, it's still just evidence, not proof. The only way that you could have proof that, for instance, Paul wrote two letters to the church at Corinth is if you were there when it happened, watching him write. The only way you would have proof that Jesus rose from the dead is if you were there, watching it happen. And then that proof would only be valid for you. Anyone who wasn't there could dismiss your testimony about what happened as a delusion or a lie.

For a moment, let's think more about this business of evidence versus proof.

Supposedly there is a country called Japan. However, I've never seen Japan. I've met people who claim to have been there, and I've seen pictures purporting to show places in Japan, and I've seen maps of the world that include a country on them called Japan. But none of this is proof, at least not to me. It's just evidence. Until I actually see Japan with my own eyes, I feel fully justified in doubting its existence.

There is also something commonly called the law of gravity. If you think that gravity has been proven, you are sadly mistaken. Yes, scientists have measured the gravitational constant repeatedly and it appears to be constant at 6.67×10^{-11} Newton-meter^2/kilogram^2. Yes, gravity seems to have the same strength at every location and at every time that it has been measured. On the other hand, gravity has never been measured at the North Pole, so how do I know that it works the same there? In fact, there are many places all over the earth where gravity hasn't been measured. How do we know for a fact that gravity really works the same everywhere if we haven't actually measured it everywhere? How do we know that the next time we measure gravity, we won't get a different answer than 6.67×10^{-11} Newton-meter^2/kilogram^2? Maybe the law of gravity should really be the theory of gravity since we have lots of evidence, but no proof.

Just for the record, I believe in both Japan and gravity. I believe in them because the weight of the evidence leans strongly in one direction, and because I can propose tests of their validity that anyone can conduct and be expected to get the same answer. Conceptually it's no different for anything else in life. At some point, you need to take the weight of evidence in front of you and make a decision. Some things are going to have lots of evidence, while other things will only have a little bit of evidence. Some things can be tested directly (anything that exists now or is a process that can be observed happening), while other things can only be evaluated indirectly (things that existed or occurred only in the distant past or processes that occur so slowly that it is difficult to observe them directly). Depending on your particular bias concerning the issue at hand, you may demand more evidence than the average Joe before you accept something as being true. If you are faced with a new idea that is at odds with what you have always thought to be true, you will demand lots of evidence before you are willing to change your mind (Carl Sagan's statement that extraordinary claims require extraordinary evidence comes to mind).

Which brings me to another point. Believe it or not, your views on evolution, or anything else for that matter, are probably based less on the evidence itself and more on who is presenting that evidence to you. Say you go to the doctor with an ailment, and he prescribes some medicine. Do you demand to see all the clinical trials and statistical analyses of the data before you accept that the medicine is going to do some good? Probably not. A truly objective, proof-demanding person might, but I've yet to meet such a person. We trust doctors, and we tend to believe them when they tell us that medicine X will help us. On the other hand, if your lawyer offers you the same medicine, you might feel compelled to investigate it a bit more before actually taking it. We don't trust lawyers to give us good medical advice.

The science behind the theory of evolution can be messy and involves lots of details that few Christians really understand. While I attempt to summarize much of it later in this book, the fact of the matter is that I'll never know as much as a scientist who actually works in this area. As for you, you're only exposure to the science behind evolution might be this book. So, I'm looking for sources that seem trustworthy as I assemble this book, and you are trusting that what I am writing is accurate. We're both accepting certain things as being true mostly because we trust the sources.

Which brings me to the last point. One of the tests you can use to determine if all the evidence considered together reasonably supports a theory is by asking how many experts support that theory (let's assume that "experts" are folks who are well versed in all aspects of the theory, and are not merely folks who have strong opinions about it). If the experts tend to agree that a theory is supported by the evidence, then those of us who aren't experts can have greater confidence that we are on safe ground in believing the same. Of course this approach isn't foolproof, and there are lots of historical examples of laypeople following the consensus of experts with tragic results. Think about past theories for the causes of autism (bad mothering), or the safety of Thalidomide to treat nausea during pregnancy (which caused serious birth defects), or evidence of witchcraft (unusual moles on the skin). Ultimately agreeing or disagreeing with any idea is a matter of conscience. But if you are unsure, siding with the majority opinion among experts is often the best route in the absence of any other way to make a decision.

With regard to the science behind evolution, there is indeed strong and wide-ranging agreement among those who would be considered experts in the field that the theory of evolution is by and large true. Most of the disagreements (and there are many) tend to be in the details rather than in the broad mechanisms. But there are also experts who strongly believe that the sum total of all the evidence does not support the theory of evolution. In terms of sheer numbers, these experts are clearly in the minority, but their arguments are well thought out and shouldn't be dismissed out of hand. As many in this minority have said, just because many people believe something doesn't make it true. And they are right.

Concern #2: Evolutionary scientists are biased

Are evolutionary scientists biased? Of course they are. So are you, and I, and everyone else on the planet. Despite what the authors of Skeptic Magazine might think, there is really no such thing as a truly objective person.

Think back to the scientific method discussed earlier. You start with a hypothesis, and through experimentation you end by determining whether your original hypothesis was right or wrong. But what happens if you are really, really sure that your original hypothesis was right, and yet your experiment demonstrates that your hypothesis is wrong? A perfect scientist would simply reject his original hypothesis and move on. But most real scientists don't relinquish their grasp on their hypotheses easily. They will scrutinize their experiment looking for flaws. They'll repeat their experiment, maybe multiple times. They'll play with the statistical analysis of the data, looking for alternative ways to view the results. They might even find a way to reason that the conclusions don't disprove the hypothesis, but instead are an exception. And a very few unscrupulous sorts might even fudge the data, convincing themselves that doing so isn't really lying, it's just helping the world to understand the importance and relevance of their original hypothesis that, for whatever reason, they are sure is correct.

Thankfully, there are checks and balances designed to keep any sort of funny business to a minimum. For instance, scientists are often in a publish-or-perish mode of existence, where publishing their results in a well-known scientific journal is important to their career. Such journals always include a review process by other scientists who, truth be told, get giddy when they find a flaw in someone else's work. Outside the review process for scientific journals, there are also broader forums of conferences and debates that force every scientist to defend his findings under the scrutiny of others who know the same subject area as well or better. Of course none of this is a guarantee of scientific integrity, and there have been charges of discrimination throughout the history of science by those who felt that their work and ideas were being systematically suppressed by those more powerful and influential than themselves.

With regard to evolution, the primary bias-related accusation brought against evolutionary scientists is that they are biased against any consideration of supernatural causes, but will instead only consider natural causes. This accusation has always confused me for two reasons. First, highlighting supernatural causes for things we observe in the universe implies that there is no reason to study the issue any longer. Why bother looking for an answer if you already know the answer? But whether a supernatural cause is involved or not, scientists (including the Christian ones) will still want to know how it happened. It's that spirit of discovery that we all have that motivates them to keep investigating and learning.

Second, supernatural causes, unlike natural causes, can't be verified through a scientific process because the tools that science uses are natural tools: test tubes, hammers, chemicals, etc. There's no such thing as a supernatural test tube or a supernatural hammer with which you could poke around at a supernatural cause. Supernatural causes are simply out of reach of science. You could, for instance, assert that the half-life of radioactive materials used to date rocks and fossils was different in the past than it is today due to God's miraculous work in creating the earth. But there is no scientific test that will prove or disprove such an assertion because the only half-lives we can measure are those that exist in rocks today. See Chapter 8 for more on the issue of half-lives.

It might surprise you to know that some scientists have considered supernatural causes for various aspects of the theory of evolution. But considering supernatural causes - and even accepting them - is about as far as they can go as scientists. Once you have "considered" a supernatural cause, are you then required to stop investigating the issue? Of course not. If that was the approach taken to everything we didn't understand, little scientific research would ever get done.

If we are being honest with ourselves, we will acknowledge the possibility that science may eventually uncover the underlying, natural mechanisms behind things which today have no clear explanation. I base this statement on the fact that science has done this many times in the past. For instance, at one time supernatural causes were assumed for lightning and thunder, the aurora borealis (northern lights), earthquakes, procreation, disease, the movement of the planets, and rain. It might seem strange to us now, since we understand the physical mechanisms behind each of these things pretty well. But while they remained mysteries, with no natural explanation in sight, the only way to make sense of them was to attribute them to some unseen, unfathomable supernatural force. Such mysteries have shrunk in number over time due to the diligent work of scientists who, whatever their beliefs might have been regarding ultimate supernatural causes, continued their research to better understand the natural mechanisms involved. Over time, such work has resulted in a steadily shrinking collection of things that are explained by supernatural causes alone.

The promise of science is that the number of things for which we have no clear natural explanation will continue to get smaller and smaller over time. With regard to the theory of evolution, there are some scientists who believe that the emergence and diversification of life on earth will eventually be so thoroughly explained by science that all mystery will be removed. And there are, of course, other scientists who disagree. As the saying goes in the stock market, past performance is no guarantee of future performance.

One of the sources of conflict between the Theistic and Organic Paradigms regarding supernatural causes is the idea that the natural and the supernatural as two separate things. Some in the Theistic Paradigm may charge scientists with bias against consideration of supernatural causes because they think that a scientist focusing on natural causes must necessarily be ignoring or excluding supernatural causes. Certainly some scientists think this way, but by no means all. Moreover, there is nothing stopping us Christians from adding supernatural causes on top of the natural ones. The Bible is very clear that certain natural things for which science has given us great insight nevertheless have a supernatural cause. For instance:

> *Procreation*: "For you formed my inward parts; you knitted me together in my mother's womb." (Psalm 139:13)

> *The rising of the sun and rain*: "For he makes his sun rise on the evil and on the good, and sends rain on the just and on the unjust." (Matthew 5:45)

> *Weather*: "He it is who makes the clouds rise at the end of the earth, who makes lightnings for the rain, and brings forth the wind from his storehouses." (Psalm 135:7)

In fact, I can go one step further. Some of the miracles in the Bible appear to have natural causes, or at least some sort of a natural process. A good example is Moses and the parting of the Red Sea:

> *Then Moses stretched out his hand over the sea, and the Lord drove the sea back by a strong east wind all night and made the sea dry land, and the waters were divided. (Exodus 14:21)*

The waters didn't instantly split apart like you might see in the movies. It took all night for it to happen, and in some strange way wind did the work. It's still a grand supernatural miracle, but one that apparently also involved some sort of natural process. Other examples of miracles that appear to also involve some sort of natural process include the following:

> *Now the Lord God appointed a plant and made it come up over Jonah, that it might be a shade over his head, to save*

him from his discomfort. (Jonah 4:6)

And he took the blind man by the hand and led him out of the village, and when he had spit on his eyes and laid his hands on him, he asked him, "Do you see anything?" And he looked up and said, "I see people, but they look like trees, walking." Then Jesus laid his hands on his eyes again; and he opened his eyes, his sight was restored, and he saw everything clearly. (Mark 8:23-25)

One last thing about bias among evolutionary scientists. While in general bias does not appear to be problematic in the sense of influencing the validity of data that has been collected, there is one particular form of bias that is nevertheless common. The vast majority of evolutionary scientists extend their belief in the evolution of plants and animals to a belief in a natural mechanism for the origin of life on earth. As discussed more fully in Chapter 19, the issue of the origin of life is not, strictly speaking, part of the theory of evolution. While there are many interesting theories for how life may have originated on earth, and a fair amount of experimental evidence for how certain steps might have occurred, no one has been able to generate life from non-life in the laboratory. Despite this, most evolutionary scientists do believe that a purely natural mechanism will eventually be discovered, or at least invented. They see no reason to believe in a supernatural cause for the origin of life on earth for the simple reason that science has a good track record of finding natural explanations for other things if enough time and effort are put into it. In short, they are biased against a consideration of a purely supernatural cause for the origin of life despite having little evidence for a natural cause.

Maybe a natural explanation for the origin of life on earth will be discovered someday, but it seems clear that any such discovery is a long way off. In the meantime, any Christian would be on relatively solid ground if he said that, in the absence of a clear natural mechanism for the origin of life, it is only reasonable to attribute the origin of life to an act of God. Perhaps more importantly, if scientists did create a plausible step-by-step natural process for the origin of life, it would still be legitimate to say that God directed the process in the same way that he directed the wind to produce the grand miracle of the parting of the Red Sea. It was natural, but also supernatural.

Concern #3: Evolution science presumes uniform processes at all times and places

To appreciate why this concern exists, I first need to take a short detour.

How would you define a miracle? If you aren't the spiritual sort, you might simply refer to something extraordinary or unusual as a miracle. You get the job even though you flubbed the interview. You drop a glass onto a granite countertop and it doesn't break. Christians may even use the same language from time to time.

But there is a category of miracles that is altogether different: miracles that seem to be not only against all odds, but also against the laws of nature. Pretty much all of the healings that Jesus did in the Bible are of this type, simply based on how quickly they occur. If Jesus had laid his hands on a blind person and he slowly regained his sight over the course of the following month, many might doubt that a miracle had really occurred. But for a blind person to regain his sight in a matter of seconds, at the exact time that Jesus commands his eyes to be healed, is something altogether different.

What does science have to say about miracles? Nothing. Zilch. As I said before, science is the study of the natural world, and simply has no tools for delving into the supernatural. Miracles are the exceptions, bending or suspending the laws of nature. Miracles are neither predictable nor repeatable, so they can't be studied through anything like the scientific method. Miracles are the oil to science's water.[5]

Earlier I used the example of the law of gravity as something that is generally assumed to be true at all times and places on earth

---

[5] I'm an engineer, not an English major, so my metaphors are bound to stink.

even though it hasn't been measured at every time and place. All the data gathered on gravity has shown the same pattern, so we can have a high degree of confidence that gravity works the same at all times and places.

The problem is, I know of one example of a time and place where gravity didn't work the way it is supposed to. It occurred on Lake Tiberias around the year 32 AD. Jesus had sent his disciples on a boat ahead of him, and during the middle of the night he came out to them, walking on the water. We don't know the mechanism behind this particular miracle. Maybe gravity was suspended at that one particular spot for a few minutes. Maybe Jesus became weightless. Maybe the water under his feet was solid even though it was still liquid. Maybe angels were holding him up. No matter. The point is that something happened that made it appear as though gravity wasn't working the way it is supposed to. But the law of gravity is still a natural law that we can trust to operate at all times and places. I suppose you could caveat this natural law with a footnote saying "The law of gravity does not apply if God decides to do something different," but then you would have to caveat everything that way.

While God created the universe and established the laws that govern all matter and energy, He is not limited by those laws. He can suspend them, or go around them, any time He pleases. He can stop the pull of gravity, walk through walls, change one chemical into another (e.g. water into wine), and tell a storm to clam up. And when He does these things, the natural laws that govern gravity and chemistry and weather don't change. Instead, they are temporarily inapplicable.

As I said earlier, much of science is about using a limited set of data to develop a broadly applicable theory of how the universe works. By necessity, such theories assume that miracles have never happened, can't happen, won't happen. This isn't anti-Christian, or even anti-supernatural. It's simply a function of the fact that science can only consider the natural world. If science could not rely on the premise that natural phenomena work the same way at all times and places, and that miracles won't interrupt those natural phenomena, there would be little use in pursuing science at all.

With that admittedly lengthy introduction, let me now address the concern that the Theistic Paradigm has raised about uniform processes.

Evolutionary scientists have based many of their conclusions on the premise that the natural mechanisms they are studying worked the same way in the distant past as they do today. This includes such things as the movement of continents, fossil formation, the decay rates of radioactive elements, and DNA mutation rates. In all of these cases, scientists have determined how these processes occur today based on observation and experiment, and have made the assumption that those processes worked the same in the distant past as they do today. This is a perfectly reasonable assumption given that there is no direct evidence to indicate that this assumption is wrong, and any other assumption would be arbitrary anyway.

The problem is, miracles are real. Insofar as a miracle may have affected such things as the movement of continents, fossil formation, the decay rates of radioactive elements, or DNA mutation rates in the distant past, there would be no way to know.

When God created the universe, the earth, and all life, it was most certainly a miracle. However, we don't know the details of that miracle. Was it something that could be explained by purely natural processes, like the rising of the sun or procreation? Was it some sort of combination of a natural process and supernatural direction, like the parting of the Red Sea? Was it a natural process that just occurred very very fast, like one of Jesus' healings? Or did plants and animals pop into existence fully formed, without any natural process whatsoever? No one knows for certain because no one was there to see it happen.

But some of these possibilities have the potential to invalidate the assumption that the natural processes we observe today worked the same in the distant past. Here's a simple analogy. Say you have a 12-inch ruler, and with it you determine that the height of a coffee mug is 4 inches. Then you see a news article from the manufacturer of your ruler saying that it was made of a peculiar type of plastic that has been discovered to shrink over time. So is the mug really 4 inches tall? If the ruler has shrunk, then maybe the mug is actually 4½ inches tall even though you measured it to be 4 inches. There's no way to know if your measurement of the height of the mug is accurate if you can't trust the ruler to be accurate.

So it is with some evolutionary science. If the "ruler" used by scientists (for instance, the rate of sedimentary rock formation) is different today than it was in the past, then any conclusions they draw using that ruler could be wrong (in other words, sedimentary rocks would seem old even though they are actually quite young).

Evolutionary scientists extrapolate their data to other places, conditions, and times because there really isn't any other choice - as I said before, science has no way to account for miracles, and is forced to assume that natural processes always work the same way. Christians can legitimately point to the fact that the miracle of creation may not lend itself to scientific inquiry[6], and that as a result the conclusions reached by evolutionary scientists may be wrong. However, we can't do much more than say it's a possibility. There really isn't any way to determine the answer one way or the other.

For the rest of this book, I am treating the science behind evolution at face value. In other words, I am treating it as if the miracle of creation involves natural processes that do in fact lend themselves to scientific inquiry. Because if this isn't the case, if the emergence and diversification of life on earth is completely disconnected from natural processes, there's really no reason for me to write any more, and I can go make something in my woodshop instead.

---

[6] By analogy, physicists tell us that the properties of the universe immediately following the Big Bang are "undefined," meaning that they would not have followed classical laws of physics, and thus we do not have the tools to probe into the nature of the universe at that time in its life.

Chapter 6

An Overview Of Evolution

Before we get to biological evolution, it's worthwhile looking at evolution in other contexts, since evolution has many of the same features no matter where it appears. Knowing how evolution works more broadly will provide you with some understanding for why scientists biological evolution the way that they do.

In the most general sense, evolution is just change over time. In this sense, you can have evolution in just about any context:

- Political ideologies
- Cultures
- Languages
- Art
- Technology
- Fashion
- Medicine
- Music

One of the hallmarks of evolution is that it doesn't necessarily have a direction towards bigger and better, or more complex, or smarter. In some cases it does seem to do this, as with technology or medicine, where changes are largely directed by humans with specific goals in mind. But in other cases the thing evolving is really just changing from one form to a different form without anyone directing the changes, and without the newer version necessarily being "better" (whatever that means) than the previous version. For instance, take languages or music. In these cases, humans aren't trying to make them accomplish something better, or more efficiently. Humans are certainly involved in the changes, but it's not like there's a goal in mind, and there's no obvious advantage of more recent versions compared to the older versions. And yet, you can look back at the history of music, or language, or even fashion, and you can see trends as thing X morphed into thing Y which then transitioned into thing Z.

But just because evolving things don't always get "better" doesn't mean that evolution is meaningless and random. On the contrary, anything that evolves is becoming more suitable as judged either by its environment or by people. This means that the newer version is a better fit in some way, or is more acceptable than the older version. As soon as something tends towards being less suitable over time, it's likely to simply disappear or be replaced by something else. People don't tolerate things that get less suitable over time, and neither does nature.

A few examples should help underline the point that evolution is about changes that make something more suitable, but not necessarily better:

- Ask any fashion designer, and he can point to a new style that disappeared almost as soon as it arose. There was an attempt to do something different, to be creatively experimental, but it just didn't fly. It didn't impress the fashion police, so it died. But something else new and creative thrived. Why one new fashion trend survived while another died is largely a mystery. All you can really say is that the one that survived was more acceptable to consumers than the one that died, but you can't really say it is "better."

- In technology, there are always winners and losers. The Segway scooter was expected to be wildly successful, but it never caught on even though it was viewed as an advanced form of personal locomotion. Laserdiscs and video calling first appeared in the 1980's and seemed like such great ideas, but people just weren't that interested. You might say that each of these things represented an advancement of some sort, and were better in some ways than their predecessors, but they nevertheless failed.

- I've heard some really bizarre music that, according my kids, is currently very popular. I'm not sure I would say that it's better than music from the 1970's[7], but I can say that music certainly has evolved in the last several decades. So have the clothes worn by the most popular musicians, again not necessarily for the better.

- The philosophical ideas behind Nazism evolved over several decades and grew into an incredibly powerful force. At the time, those ideas were accepted by many Germans because they appeared to have the power to solve many of their societal ills (real or perceived). In this sense, Nazism was deemed to be more suitable to Germans than alternative ideologies available at the time. But while those ideas certainly did evolve, I think most of us would agree that they weren't for the better.

These examples should also make it clear that evolution is really only obvious in retrospect since it's very difficult to know ahead of time what changes might be most suitable. The world is simply too complex for anyone to really know what changes are going to fly and which ones are going to die. As we'll see later, this is also true for biological evolution.

The fundamentals of biological evolution

Biological evolution has a lot in common with these other forms of evolution. The basic idea is still change over time, those changes are undirected and don't have a specific goal in mind (under the Organic Paradigm), and only those changes that provide an adaptive advantage endure. It seems simple and logical, and at

---

[7] Which, by the way, is the best music of all time.

this most basic level it is. But one conclusion that appears inescapable is that the most complex and advanced organisms, including us, were not inevitable. To put it another way, under the theory of evolution, humans are just a happy accident. This is one of the implications of the theory of evolution that is most disturbing for those in the Theistic Paradigm, and which leads them to believe that something in the theory must be terribly wrong. A process that appears at first glance to be random, with no guarantee that humans would ever arise, seems to run exactly counter to the notion that God wanted humans to exist.

However, biological evolution is not a purely random process, at least not in the sense that we usually think of the word. Biological evolution is the result of a process in which species either become better suited to their environment over time and thrive, or they become less well suited and languish. Both possibilities may be equally likely, and that is the random part of the process. But if a species is changing in such a way that they are becoming more likely to thrive (in the parlance of science, they are becoming more fit or better adapted), they will also be more likely to reproduce. And if they are more likely to reproduce, they are more likely to show up in the fossil record. On the other hand, a species that is changing in such a way that they are becoming less well suited to their environments are less likely to reproduce, less likely to endure, and thus will be less likely to show up in the fossil record. When scientists look back over time and see what appears to be the evolution of one species into another, what they are seeing is primarily the result of changes that were adaptive since changes that were not adaptive leave little or no trace in the fossil record. As a result, the history of evolution as evident in the fossil record appears to show a process that is not random.

To anthropomorphize this process a bit, nature "chooses" between individuals in a group based on small differences that make one individual ever so slightly better adapted to its environment than another individual. If you look closely enough at any group of organisms of the same species (for example, a herd of zebras), you will notice that they are not all identical. Not only do they have small differences in their appearance (like different patterns of black and white stripes), but there are also small differences in personality, physical aptitude, etc. Some zebras are a little faster than average, some zebras are a bit more aggressive than average, and so on. Such variations were one of the primary pieces of evidence that Charles Darwin focused on in his 1859 book *Origin of Species*.

Not only are there small differences between individuals in a group, but changes also occur from one generation of organisms to the next because the biochemical processes that pass genetic material from parents to offspring aren't perfect. Sometimes there are glitches in the process, and these glitches can affect anything in or about the organism, for better or for worse. These glitches are called random genetic mutations.

Both the natural variations between individual organisms in a group at any given moment, and the small changes that occur over time are both a result of how our DNA operates. Together they ensure that all the organisms are not equally suited to their environment. Some can escape predators a bit better than others, some have slightly better camouflage than others, some have slightly better eyesight than others and so can more easily spot food, some have thicker fur and so do better in the winter, etc. In many cases these differences will be so subtle that they would not be obvious to the casual observer, but they will always be there. Sometimes the differences will only matter a little bit or not at all, and other times they might matter a lot.

Given these differences between individuals in a group, it stands to reason that those individuals that are, on average, slightly better adapted to their environment are more likely to live long enough and be healthy enough to reproduce. When they do reproduce, whatever made them better suited to their environment will be passed on to their offspring. Likewise, those individuals that are, on average, slightly less well adapted to their environment are less likely to live long enough and be healthy enough to reproduce. Over multiple generations, then, a group should always be tending towards becoming better adapted to its environment if that group continues to exist at all. If it ceases to exist (i.e. extinction), it's because the inherent variations between individuals in the group and changes that occur through genetic mutations during reproduction simply couldn't keep pace with a changing environment (for instance, the environment is getting colder, or dryer, or a new predator enters the ecosystem, etc).

The entire theory of evolution can be summed up with a simple equation:

Genetic variation + natural selection = evolution

Chapters 9 and 10 unpack these two important elements of evolution in more detail.

Is evolution a fact or a theory?

The big problem with this question is that scientists often define these words differently than the rest of us. To a scientist, a fact is something for which the evidence leans strongly in one direction. In other words, a fact is something that anyone can observe and is reproducible, but it can still can be proven wrong if new and different evidence is discovered. A fact is something that's true, but it's nevertheless true provisionally. For non-scientists, however, a fact is never provisional, but instead is something that is absolutely, positively, actually 100% true, and won't and can't ever be proven false.

Similarly, the word theory is often defined by us non-scientists as meaning anything that is less certain than a fact. It may have some evidence to support it, but it still has some noteworthy uncertainties and so hasn't risen to the level of a fact. For many scientists, however, a theory is a conceptual picture of how something appears to work based on a collection of facts (which, as I said, are only provisionally true). For scientists, theories involve descriptions of processes and relationships that result from the interpretation of collections of facts.

So, depending on your definitions of fact and theory, you could categorize evolution as either or both. If you have your doubts about evolution, and so refer to it as "only a theory," just be aware that scientists typically think of theories as being true rather than being merely an abstract idea that may or may not be true in reality.

Diction aside, the question "Is evolution a fact or a theory?" is really meant to get at the question of whether the evidence in favor of evolution outweighs the evidence against it, or alternatively whether the uncertainties drown out the facts. It turns out that the answer to this question depends heavily on the degree of evolution you are talking about. Many Christians think of evolution as one species changing into another, but in fact this type of evolution is only the most complex form. The simplest levels of evolution have been directly observed, while the bigger and more complex levels have not. As a result, the evidence for the simplest levels of evolution is stronger than the evidence for more complex levels. Chapter 11 gets into the different degrees of evolution in more detail.

Chapter 7

The Evolution Of Language
(Yes, It's Relevant)

You may think that the evolution of language should have little bearing on the question of whether plants and animals evolve. And you would be right. But the evolution of language is surprisingly similar to the theory of biological evolution, and also provides important insights into how we modern humans read the story of the Tower of Babel in the book of Genesis.

Unless you have lived in a cave all your life, you will know that languages change over time. For instance, all of the so-called Romance languages (French, Spanish, Italian, Portuguese, Romanian, and others) descended from Latin, while the Indic languages (Hindi, Punjabi, Urdu, and others) descended from Sanskrit. The language you are reading right now descended from Middle English, which was itself descended from Old English. William Shakespeare wrote his plays just as Middle English was transitioning to modern English, which is why people today can more or less understand his writing even though it seems strange and archaic (or, to engineers like me, simply indecipherable).

All languages are changing all the time. I have a book on my shelf entitled *The Elements of Style* by Strunk and White. First printed in 1959, it describes the rules of proper English grammar and composition. It's written in a rather clear-cut, commanding style, as in "do this" and "never do that". But even today some of those "rules" are falling behind the inevitable changes that all languages undergo. Given enough time, none of the "rules" it contains will be relevant.

For languages that have a written form, studying the evolution of language is not unlike the study of fossils. Better, actually, because fossils preserve only bits and pieces of the history of life on earth, whereas written languages lay out in fine detail how they arose and operated and changed over time. Of course, the further back in time you go, the less complete the record of past languages is. But particularly in cases in which a language was used in some type of religious or sacred text, the record can go back thousands of years.

It's actually quite striking just how similar the evolution of language is to biological evolution. For instance:

- All languages descend from previous languages. Languages don't pop into existence fully formed.[8]

- Languages often sprout variants called dialects, not unlike a species sprouting subspecies.

- Over time, several dialects of a single language can become so different that they become distinct languages. Geographical isolation is believed to play a strong role in this process, just as it is believed to operate in the generation of new species from subspecies.

- A language can go extinct.

- Changes in a language over time are hardly detectable in human life spans. They are really only obvious when you compare writings from different time periods of what are believed to be related languages. This is similar to observing changes in the forms of organisms by comparing fossils from different time periods.

---

[8] I'm ignoring the fact that there are also "constructed" languages that have been created by humans in an attempt to circumvent the crazy grammar, pronunciations, and inconsistencies that are inherent in all evolved languages.

- Linguists can make logical guesses about languages for which no written record exists by comparing known languages that are believed to have descended from the unknown language. For instance, linguists have theorized that a language called "Proto-Indo-European" was the precursor to all European and west Asian languages, including both Latin and Sanskrit.

Of course there are features of the evolution of language that are less like biological evolution. Languages evolve in a way that tends towards greater simplicity and efficiency. For instance, sounds that are not accented (like the first syllable of "goodbye") tend to weaken over time (think how we say "g'bye") and eventually drop off entirely ("bye!"). Words typically said together can morph into a single word ("goodbye" actually started out as "God be with you"). The development of slang vocabulary and pronunciation can be driven as much by sociological factors between generations as it can be by mere unguided drift. There are also fewer restrictions on how a language may change compared to how a particular species might change. For instance, one language can borrow words from another language even if the two languages are very different. I don't know of any zebras that have borrowed DNA from a giraffe.

So what conclusions can we draw about whether, and to what degree, biological evolution is true based on a study of the evolution of language? Not much. Despite the surprising and profound similarities, they are really two different animals, and to my knowledge no one has ever made any attempt at this.

However, the evolution of language and biological evolution do have something very important in common. Both have stories in the book of Genesis that we must somehow fit into the real world evidence we have discovered. For language, the relevant Biblical story is the Tower of Babel.

At the beginning of Genesis Chapter 11, it is made very clear that at one time there was only a single language in the entire world, and that this somehow aided humanity in their efforts to build monuments to their own pride. God looks down, sees this is a problem, and decides to arrange things so that they cannot understand one another's language. This disrupts their plans and forces the people to scatter all over the world.

If you take the story at face value, all languages appeared more or less instantly. Two guys were sitting next to each other chiseling out stones for the big monument, talking about the weather or what their wives packed for their lunches, or whatever. The next thing you know, they don't understand each other. One guy starts speaking French and the other guy is speaking Urdu. First each thinks the other is just messing around, then they get angry, then they get scared. All work on the monument stops as every man sets out to find someone who can understand him. In short order, the French speakers get together, pack their bags, and head off to start a new city somewhere else. Same with the Urdu speakers, the Swahili speakers, and the Pig-Latin speakers.

The point is that there isn't any hint in the Biblical story that all languages descended from a single language through an unguided evolutionary process that occurred over many generations. And yet, that's what the scientific evidence tells us, at least as far as written languages go (since we can't directly study purely verbal languages that have gone extinct). This presents us with a conundrum not unlike that with the theory of biological evolution. Interestingly, I have never heard anyone declare that the evolution of language is merely an unproven theory because it is inconsistent with the Tower of Babel story. Why is the evolution of language treated so differently from biological evolution when the two present more or less the same problem in terms of interpreting the related Bible stories?

One possibility is that there is a clear indication of the passage of time in the creation story in Genesis Chapter 1 (events unfold over six days), whereas the Tower of Babel story does not contain such a clear indication of the passage of time. Even so, the Tower of Babel story implies that God's work to form many languages took place in a relatively short period of time: the people living in the city of Babel were forced to stop building the city because they could not understand one another. At a minimum, it takes several hundred years for one language to split into two, but the event that took place at Babel seems to have occurred in a much shorter timeframe than this.

We can also look at the Tower of Babel story from the perspective of what we know about the language in which it was written. Most scholars believe that the story of the Tower of Babel would have been originally written (probably by Moses) in what is now called "Biblical Hebrew" somewhere during the middle of the second millennium BC. Linguists have traced the evolution of Biblical Hebrew based on a combination of ancient texts as well as a reconstruction based on other languages that existed at the same time and in the same geographical region as Biblical Hebrew. As a result, it appears that Biblical Hebrew formed alongside Aramaic, Arabic, Phoenician, and several others, all of which arose from a previous language that has been termed Semitic. The Semitic language had itself developed alongside Egyptian, and both Semitic and Egyptian appear to have evolved out of an even earlier language that we call Afro-Asiatic.

But of course, Moses would not have known all this when he wrote the Tower of Babel story. At that time, there would have been no concept of the evolution of language. As far as he knew, the languages that existed at that time had always existed in their (then) present form. In his efforts to tell the story of the history of humanity, then, how would he explain the fact that there was a single language spoken by Adam and Eve and many languages in Moses' time? The answer was a story in which God was the inventor of all the languages on the earth.

Note I am not saying that Moses merely made up a story to fit the facts as he knew them at that time. It's certainly possible that the Tower of Babel story was dictated from God to Moses verbatim exactly as we now read it. But if so, we must face the fact that the picture it paints - languages popping into existence fully formed - does not fit very well with the scientific evidence that the languages of Moses' time had descended over many generations from previous forms.

I have no intention of solving this dilemma. Any reasonably smart person can come up with a variety of possible explanations for how the Tower of Babel story and the evolution of language fit together. For instance, you might decide that languages only began evolving after the Tower of Babel. Prior to that, there was only a single language, and God intervened exactly as it is written in Genesis Chapter 11 to instantly divide that single language into many. Or you might decide that the Genesis 11 story is a summary of what actually occurred over several hundred years. Regardless, the solution is going to require some creativity, either in how you interpret the Bible or in how you interpret the science, or both. This is the same sort of creativity that would be required if you were to try and fit the theory of biological evolution into the Genesis account of creation. Hopefully this fact will provide you with some freedom to evaluate the science behind the theory of biological evolution without feeling an a priori need to reject the theory because it doesn't seem to fit with the Biblical story of creation.

Chapter 8

Measuring The Age Of Very Old Things

For most of the last two millennia, it had been assumed that the earth was only a few thousand years old, 10,000 at most, based on a study of the successive ages of people in the first several chapters of Genesis. Early in the Nineteenth Century as the field of geology began, however, many scientists could not envision how the structures they saw in rock could have formed in so short a time. While there was no precise way to date individual rock formations, the general consensus among geologists was that the Earth was at least millions of years old, and potentially much older. Since the age of the earth and the theory of evolution seemed to be linked even before Darwin's *Origin of Species* was published in 1859, the true beginning of the disagreements between the Theistic and Organic Paradigms probably started with debates over the age of the earth.

Some creative ways to measure age

Nearly all methods used to estimate the age of very old things are based on the idea that the way in which something changes over time is more or less constant. That is, the rate at which some process occurred in the distant past is the same as the rate of similar processes that we can measure today. For instance, the movement of modern day glaciers has been measured at an average of about a foot a day. A few glaciers move much faster, but they are the exception. Based on this data, we can make estimates for

71

how long it took glaciers to move across North America during the last ice age. Those estimates could certainly be wrong, but if appropriate caveats and uncertainties are also included with the estimates, most scientists feel comfortable trusting them.

In the last 200 years, scientists have developed some very creative ideas about how to measure the age of rocks, fossils, and the earth. Some of these ideas turned out to be quite flawed, such as the time it would take the seas to turn salty or the time it would take for a molten earth to cool to its present state. Others may be more trustworthy, but are rather limited in how far back in time they can reach. These ideas have included coral growth cycles, annual clay deposits in glacial lakes, and measuring tree rings.[9]

One process that can be measured today is continental drift. For instance, the continents of South America and Africa are moving away from each other at the rate of about 1.5 inches per year. There is little disagreement between the Theistic and Organic Paradigms that this is occurring because we have sensitive instruments that can measure it. There is also good reason to believe that South America and Africa were actually connected at some point in the past, meaning that there was no ocean between them. When looking at a globe, most people notice that the east coast of South America and the west coast of Africa have complementary shapes. Even more interesting is the fact that certain fossil finds in South America actually line up with discovery of the same fossils in Africa. This strongly implies that the two continents were once a single landmass.

---

[9] The "Laboratory of Tree Ring Research" at the University of Arizona was an actual, deadly serious effort to date archaeological sites.

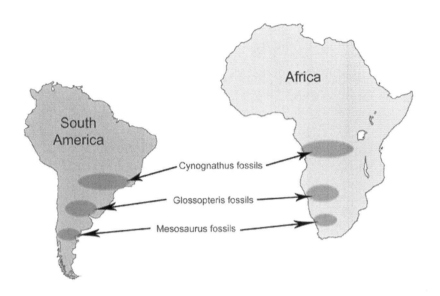

The calculation for how long ago these two continents separated is pretty simple: just rewind the clock. Moving at a rate of 1.5 inches per year, with a current average distance of 3000 miles, it would have taken about 130 million years for the two continents to get to their present positions from an initial state of being connected together.

Of course we don't know for a fact that the rate of continental drift has been constant over time. In fact it must surely have varied. However, among all measurements of current continental drift that scientists have been able to make, the fastest rate that has ever been measured was about 4 inches per year, and most measured rates were much lower. Using this faster rate, the amount of time that has passed since South America and Africa were the same landmass would be reduced to about 48 million years, still a far cry from the 10,000 years that some in the Theistic Paradigm believe is the maximum age of the earth.

Could the continents have moved much faster in the distant past than they do today? The short answer is yes, but there are some problems that would have to be overcome. First, there is no known geologic mechanism that could result in a rate of movement fast enough to bring the two continents to their present positions in only 10,000 years (which would be about 20,000 times faster than the current rate of continental drift). It would have taken an act of God to make it happen. Second, if the continents were to move that fast, it is likely that the enormous energies released would have created worldwide earthquakes, tsunamis, and volcanoes so numerous and severe that earth would have uninhabitable during the period when the continents were moving. On the other hand, if God superseded natural forces to make the continents move to their present positions in 10,000 years, presumably he could also have intervened to ensure that life was not threatened by the energies released in the process.

While using the rate of continental drift does provide a means for estimating the time required for certain continents to arrive at their present position, this method does little more than set a minimum age of the earth. To accurately measure the age of the earth, as well as rocks and fossils, you need a clock that is much more accurate and can reach all the way back to when earth was formed.

Radiometric dating

Most people know something about radioactivity. Plutonium and uranium have been used in atomic bombs and nuclear reactors. Radon is a radioactive gas that can seep into your house from the surrounding ground. About 60 radioactive compounds exist in nature, and many more can be produced in a laboratory.

In essence, a radioactive element is one that is holding too much energy. It's unstable and wants to shed the excess energy. When it does shed the excess energy, it is said to "decay." However, the rate of decay depends on how unstable the atom is, and each type of radioactive element is unique in this instability. Atoms that are more stable will take longer to shed their excess energy than atoms that are less stable. For instance, an atom of lithium-8 is very unstable, and is likely to decay in about one second, while an atom of barium-130 is very stable and will likely not decay for more than a trillion years. Think of a tall stack of ice cubes and an equally tall stack of wooden blocks. Both are unstable and could topple at any moment. But the ice cubes are slippery and thus less stable than the wooden blocks. Being less stable, the ice cubes would be more likely to topple sooner.

There is no way to predict when a single radioactive atom is going to decay. It's true that the more unstable a particular atom is, the more likely it is going to decay sooner rather than later, but that's about as specific as you can get. The exact timing is driven by quantum mechanics, and thus the decay of a single atom can only be described by a messy mathematical function called a probability distribution.

Luckily, when you have a very large number of atoms, a very clear pattern emerges for the proportion of atoms that will decay within a certain amount of time. This is based on a mathematical principle called the law of large numbers. Thus, for instance, we know with great precision and certainty that 50% of a sample of carbon-14 will decay within 5,730 years, and the other 50% will decay in greater than 5,730 years.

It is possible to derive a mathematical function that describes exactly what proportion of the original sample of a radioactive element will decay within a certain amount of time. I'm going to save you the aggravation of reading the full derivation and just jump to the punch line:[10]

$$F = e^{\ln(0.5) * (t/a)}$$

F represents the fraction of radioactive material that remains radioactive (i.e. has not decayed) after a period of time t has passed. The fraction of the sample that has decayed would then be 1 - F. The constant a is the "half-life" of a radioactive material, which represents the time it takes for half of the radioactive material to decay. It is unique to each type of radioactive element.

The function for F is a bit easier to understand in graphical form:

---

[10] You're welcome.

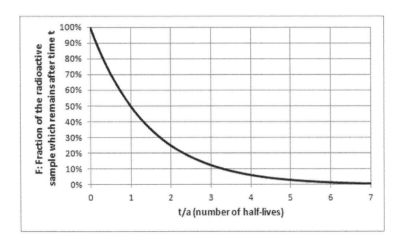

Notice that for each additional half-life, the amount of the original radioactive sample that is still left is cut in half. So, after one half-life has passed, only 50% is left. After two half-lives, 25% is left. After three half-lives, 12.5% is left. The shape of this curve has been verified experimentally to match how all radioactive materials decay, and there is essentially no disagreement between the Theistic and Organic Paradigms on this.

When radioactive elements decay, they shed either some energy or some subatomic particles, and in the process the original element turns into a different element. The table below shows some of the elements most commonly used in radiometric dating, along with the "daughter" elements that they decay into.

This radioactive element (the "parent" element)	...decays into this element (the "daughter" element)
Carbon-14	Nitrogen-14
Samarium-147	Neodymium-143
Uranium-235	Thorium-221
Potassium-40	Argon-40
Rubidium-87	Strontium-87

The fact that you end up with a different element after the decay occurs is the key to using radioactivity to determine the age of very old things.

In practice, the decay rate equation is rearranged to give you the value of t (the age of a rock) for a given value of F (the fraction of a radioactive parent element that has not yet decayed). The value of F is based on measurements of a rock containing some radioactive material. The calculation of F works like this:

$$F = \frac{Mass\ of\ parent\ element}{Mass\ of\ parent\ element + mass\ of\ daughter\ element}$$

In order to fully understand how radiometric dating is used, it may be helpful to go through an example.

Imagine that you have a rock that you determine contains 10 grams of potassium-40. There's no way to know how old the rock is based simply on this fact. However, you also determine that the rock contains 5 grams of argon-40. Since argon-40 is the decay product of potassium-40 (see table above), it's a safe bet that some of the potassium-40 decayed over time and made the argon-40. In other words, the argon-40 used to be potassium-40 at some point in the past. Putting the two measurements together, you surmise that there were originally 15 grams of potassium-40 and no argon-40 in the rock, way back when the rock was originally formed. The balance looks like this:

	Today	When the rock originally formed
Potassium-40	10 grams	15 grams
Argon-40	5 grams	0 grams

The 10 grams of potassium-40 that currently exists in the rock is 67% (10 divided by 15) of the original mass of potassium-40 that existed when the rock first formed. This 67% represents the proportion of the original potassium-40 that has not yet decayed, and thus is the value of F in the equation above, or on the vertical axis of the graph. You can then back-calculate that the number of half-lives (t/a) is 0.584 (67% on the vertical axis of the graph corresponds to 0.584 on the horizontal axis). Since potassium-40 has a half-life of 1.277 billion years, you can calculate the age of the rock as follows:

$$t/a = 0.584$$
$$t = 0.584 \times a$$
$$t = 0.584 \times 1.277 \text{ billion years}$$
$$t = 746 \text{ million years}$$

So, based on the measurement of the amount of potassium-40 and argon-40 that exists in the rock today, and an assumption that there was no argon-40 in the rock when it first formed, you estimate that the rock is 746 million years old. That's radiometric dating in a nutshell.

Of course there's no way to prove that a rock is 746 million years old. Oog the caveman did not chisel the date into the rock so that we would have a convenient way to test the accuracy of radiometric dating for very old things. However, one type of radiometric dating has been proven to work for materials that are a few thousands of years old: carbon-14 dating, also called radiocarbon dating.

By and large, radioactive elements are not created anywhere on earth. Most of the radioactive elements that exist on earth were created either at the time that the earth formed or at some earlier time such as in a supernova explosion. They have been decaying ever since. Even when new rocks form, such as when a volcano spews out lava that cools and hardens into rock, any radioactive elements trapped in that new rock were there all along, since the beginning of the earth.

However, carbon-14 is different. It is formed regularly in the atmosphere as cosmic rays from space strike nitrogen molecules in the atmosphere, converting nonradioactive nitrogen into radioactive carbon-14 (i.e. the cosmic rays add energy to nitrogen to make it radioactive, the opposite of what occurs when a radioactive element decays). This carbon-14 is a radioactive version of the more typical, non-radioactive carbon-12. Once formed, the radioactive carbon-14 quickly reacts with oxygen floating around in the air to form carbon dioxide (CO_2). Thus while most carbon dioxide in the atmosphere contains non-radioactive carbon-12, a small amount of carbon dioxide will contain radioactive carbon-14.

Most plants breathe in carbon dioxide and through photosynthesis use the carbon to build all the carbon-based structure of plants: starch, cellulose, lignins, sugars, oils, etc. Since some of the carbon dioxide in the atmosphere contains radioactive carbon-14, all plants also have a certain amount of carbon-14 as part of all their cells. The ratio of this radioactive carbon-14 to the non-radioactive carbon-12 in plants is the same as the ratio of carbon-14 to carbon-12 in carbon dioxide in the air. Moreover, since animals eat plants, all animals likewise have the same ratio of carbon-14 to carbon-12 in their tissues as the ratio that exists in plants and atmospheric carbon dioxide.

Note that radiocarbon dating using carbon-14 uses the same principle as every other kind of radiometric dating (the time it takes for a radioactive element to decay), but the calculation of F is different for radiocarbon dating. For most radioactive elements, F is based on the measured amounts of parent and daughter elements in a rock. For radiocarbon dating, in contrast, F is based on the measured amounts of carbon-14 (the parent element) and carbon-12. Although nitrogen-14 is the daughter element resulting from the decay of carbon-14, nitrogen-14 is not used to calculate the age of materials. It turns out that it is much easier to measure the amount of carbon-12 than it is to measure the amount of nitrogen-14, since newly formed nitrogen-14 tends to form ammonia which dissipates quickly.

Even though the carbon-14 in a plant or animal is decaying to nitrogen-14 according to the decay function described earlier, it is simultaneously being replenished all the time as the plant breathes in new carbon dioxide from the atmosphere, or as the animal eats plants. As a result, the ratio of carbon-14 to carbon-12 in all plants and animals remains the same over the life of that plant or animal, and moreover this ratio remains the same as it is in the atmosphere. But when a plant or animal dies, it stops taking in new carbon. The decay of carbon-14 to nitrogen-14 still occurs, but now the amount of carbon-14 begins to decrease since it is not being replenished. This is the key to measuring the amount of time that has passed since the plant or animal died. By measuring the amount of carbon-14 in any dead plant or animal material and comparing it to the amount of carbon-12 in that same plant or animal, you can use the decay function and the carbon-14 half-life of 5,730 years to determine its age.

Radiocarbon dating has been verified by comparing ages calculated using carbon-14 to ages known from other sources (archeological finds, ancient writings, and counting tree rings). Here are some of those verified samples:

4900 years old
Wood found in the subterranean brick structures of the First Dynasty tombs of Hemaka and Zet in Egypt

4600 years old
Acacia wood from the tomb of the pharaoh Zoser

3792 years old
Part of the deck of the funeral ship placed in the tomb of Sesostris III of Egypt

2928 years old
Sample from one of the largest redwood trees ever cut

2624 years old
Wood from the floor of a palace in Persia

2020 years old
Linen wrapping of one of the Dead Sea Scrolls

1880 years old
Carbonized bread from a house of ancient Pompeii

Despite these successes, there have also been a number of notable failures with carbon-14 dating. The commonly cited ones are for living freshwater snails and mollusks. Since these organisms are still alive, carbon-14 dating should indicate an age of zero (or near-zero, within the typical uncertainty estimates). But in some cases carbon-14 dating has suggested that these living creatures are thousands of years old. On further study, it was found that these organisms do not gain carbon in the same way that most other living things do, from the air or from eating plants. In some cases, the carbon in their shells is derived from carbonates in the water that have been present in underground aquifers for hundreds or thousands of years, shielded from cosmic rays. In other cases, the organisms were feeding on humus, the remnants of decayed organic material that can be thousands of years old. Either way, the carbon that was incorporated into these organisms had a much lower carbon-14 concentration than that existing in the air. If an organism isn't getting its carbon from the carbon dioxide in the air, radiocarbon dating isn't going to work.

There have also been some radiocarbon tests on coal that measured small amounts of carbon-14, on the order of about 0.2% of that found in the air. According to the decay function, this corresponds to about nine half-lives, or about 50,000 years old. Coal is what's left over after plants die and are compressed over millions of years. If coal is truly millions of years old, it should contain absolutely zero carbon-14. There are a number of theories about why these coal samples contain some carbon-14, but they cannot be directly tested. As a result, those who believe that the earth is no more than 10,000 years old point to these tests on coal as proof. In response, those who continue to believe that the earth is billions of years old point to the fact that there are other coal samples that do in fact contain zero carbon-14, and thus the coal samples containing measurable levels of carbon-14 are simply atypical, "outliers" in the parlance of statisticians.

Regardless of whether explanations exist for such unexpected results in radiocarbon dating, they raise the specter of unknowns that we don't know are unknowns. In the case of the tests on snails and mollusks, the actual age was known, and thus scientists were compelled to conduct further studies to find out why. In the case of tests on coal, scientists knew that there should have been zero carbon-14, though they can do little more than theorize why this wasn't the case. But in most cases of radiocarbon dating there is no way to know if some odd circumstance, something unforeseen, has caused the age estimate to be biased in one direction or the other. In other words, the age estimate might be wrong, but you would not know that it's wrong. This is one of the legitimate concerns of those who do not trust radiometric dating in general.

Nevertheless, radiocarbon dating has by and large been accepted as a reasonable means for dating dead plants and animals by most people in both the Theistic and Organic Paradigms. While radiocarbon dating cannot be used to date rocks, its demonstrated successes provide strong evidence that radiometric dating using other radioactive elements is at least on solid ground conceptually.

When disagreements arise between the Theistic and Organic Paradigms about the value of radiometric dating, those disagreements generally center around one of four assumptions critical to the accuracy of these techniques:

- *Constant half-life*: The half-life of the radioactive elements is constant over time and is not impacted by any environmental conditions.

- *Initial concentrations*: The amount of the parent and daughter elements that existed at the time the rock formed can be determined experimentally.

- *Contamination and leaching*: No amount of parent or daughter elements have been added to or removed from the rock since it initially formed.

- *Detection limits*: The radioactive materials used in dating a rock must be chosen so as to avoid the extreme ends of the decay curve where element concentrations are very low and laboratory instruments can give erroneous results.

A failure in any of these four assumptions can make radiometric dating uncertain or even downright untrustworthy. Those who believe that the earth is no more than 10,000 years old point to these things as reasons not to trust radiometric dating. Below I provide a discussion of each of these four assumptions.

Issue #1: Constant half-life

Scientists have studied the atomic mechanisms through which radioactive elements decay and now understand them very well. On theoretical grounds, radioactive decay should be essentially independent of environmental factors. In other words, half of a sample of potassium-40 should decay in 1.277 billion years regardless of pressure, temperature, the chemical environment, or electromagnetic radiation. Testing on many different radioactive elements has confirmed that this is true to a large extent, though some tests suggest the possibility of at least some small dependence on environmental factors (less than 1%).

Of course, experiments designed to measure the constancy of decay rates can only examine the entire decay curve for radioactive elements that have very short half-lives, on the order of a few months or less. Otherwise the experiments could take many years which simply isn't practical. Unfortunately, the radioactive elements that are useful for dating rocks and fossils have half-lives in the millions to billions of years, so any testing of the decay rate can, practically speaking, only examine the first tiny part of the decay curve. Any deviations from the expected decay rates in this first small part of the decay curve can be extrapolated to the rest of the decay curve, but all such extrapolations by definition assume that the regions that cannot be studied directly will have the same characteristics as those regions that can be studied. In other words, an assumption about the long-term decay rate for radioactive elements used to date rocks and fossils is inevitable.

Nevertheless, the disagreement between the Theistic and Organic Paradigms on the issue of constant half-lives usually does not focus on the effects of environmental factors. Instead, the focus is on how God's work to create the earth may have caused half-lives at the beginning of earth's history to be much shorter than they are today. If they were indeed shorter way back when, there would be no way to know by looking at modern half-lives or the atomic mechanisms through which decay occurs, so this idea is untestable. But that doesn't mean it's wrong. If the creation of the earth were a miraculous event occurring in only six days, you could imagine lots of things happening during those six days that were unlike any of the natural processes that we can observe today. If miracles were flying around left and right, with rocks popping into existence and moving around the globe in a matter of days, why wouldn't the fundamental atomic processes that drive radioactive decay also be very different than they are today?

An example might help you see how this could create a problem with radiometric dating.

Suppose that the half-life of potassium-40 were only 6 days long at the beginning of earth's creation instead of the 1.277 billion years that we measure today. During the six days of creation, then, half of any potassium-40 in a rock would decay to argon-40. Suppose further that on the seventh day of creation the half-life of potassium-40 jumped from 6 days to 1.277 billion years. Over the course of the next 10,000 years, the amount of potassium-40 in that same rock would only drop from 50% to 49.9997% due to the much longer half-life. If the age of the rock were then determined from a potassium-40 half-life of 1.277 billion years and an amount of potassium-40 that is 49.9997% of its original value (as determined from the amount of argon-40 in the rock), we would come up with an age of 1.277 billion years instead of 10,000 years.

$$F = e^{\ln(0.5) \, * \, (t/a)}$$
$$49.9997\% = e^{\ln(0.5) \, * \, (t/a)}$$
$$t/a \approx 1$$
$$t = 1 \times a$$
$$t = 1 \times 1.277 \text{ billion years}$$
$$t = 1.277 \text{ billion years}$$

In other words, the rock might really only be 10,000 years old, but because you think that the half-life has always been 1.277 billion years, the decay equation would not be calibrated properly and the rock would look much older than it is.

As described in Chapter 5, science can tell us essentially nothing about miraculous events such as sudden jumps in the half-lives of radioactive elements. To put it another way, if such a jump did occur, there is no scientific way to verify it. We can, however, calculate the heat released from radioactive elements as a function of the type of decay and the half-life. It turns out that if all radioactive elements had much shorter half-lives at the creation of the earth than they do today, the amount of heat that they would have produced collectively would have been enormous, so much so that life on earth might have been impossible. Of course, if the half-lives were shorter because of the miraculous events occurring at earth's creation, those same miraculous events could have kept earth's temperature in check as well.

Issue #2: Initial concentrations

In the example above, the value of F in the decay rate equation was determined to be 49.9997% based on a measurement of the amount of both potassium-40 and argon-40 in the rock:

$$F = \frac{Mass\ of\ potassium - 40}{Mass\ of\ potassium - 40 + mass\ of\ argon - 40}$$

However, this calculation is only valid if there was no argon-40 in the rock when it formed. What if there was? That would mean that some, but not all, of the argon-40 that we measure in the rock today came from the decay of potassium-40. But since you weren't there when the rock formed, how could you possibly know how much of the argon-40 is from potassium-40 decay and how much was simply present when the rock formed?

This would seem to be an insurmountable obstacle to radiometric dating, but it isn't. There are several different ways around this problem.

When scientists conduct radiometric dating on rocks, they don't pick just any part of the rock at random. Instead, they identify crystals of specific types of minerals, such as feldspar or mica. They do this because each mineral retains characteristic amounts of different radioactive elements when it forms, based on a long history of experimentation on mineral formation. For instance, it is now well known that argon-40, being a gas, will tend to bubble out of any molten rock, whereas the potassium-40, being a metal, will not. Thus when minerals form under high temperatures, experiments have shown that most of the argon-40 actually leaves the rock more or less immediately. Of course there is some variability in this - it is not true that 100% of the argon-40 always bubbles out of the molten rock. Trace amounts of argon-40 are known to sometimes stay in rocks when they form. This is why rocks produced in recent volcanic eruptions, including rocks tested from the 1980 eruption of Mt. Saint Helens in Washington State, have been shown to contain some argon-40. But since this is known to occur, scientists make efforts to take it into account when calculating the value of F. It usually appears as a measure of uncertainty. For instance, a rock's age might be listed as 500 million years ± 5 million years, where the ±5 million years accounts for the possible presence of argon-40 that was already in the rock when it formed.

Experiments on the formation of minerals don't always yield results that are as clear as those with argon-40. In some cases, both the parent element and the daughter element may be equally likely to stay in the rock when it is forming. In these cases, scientists can use "isochron analysis" in which they analyze the concentration of the same radioactive element in multiple minerals that formed in the same piece of rock. Since all the minerals in a given rock solidified out of some molten goo at the same time, the different ratios of parent to daughter elements in each of the minerals can be used to calculate the amount of daughter element that was present when the rock formed. Rather than ending up with a single value for F, you generate multiple values for F that can be mathematically analyzed to determine the most likely concentration of the daughter element in the rock when it originally formed. The math used in isochron analysis is a bit messy, but there is little disagreement between the Theistic and Organic Paradigms that it is a valid approach.

Finally, there's the simplest method: Just use multiple radioactive elements. For instance, you could use all of the following common dating methods on the same rock sample:

Samarium-147 → Neodymium-143

Uranium-235 → Lead-207

Potassium-40 → Argon-40

Rubidium-87 → Strontium-87

Since the chemical properties of all of these elements are different, the elements incorporate into a mineral's structure at different rates. As a result, it's unlikely (though not impossible) that the same error would occur in all of them due to the presence of some daughter material when the rock initially formed. So, if all the methods give approximately the same age, you can have pretty high confidence in the result.

An illustration of the use of this approach is shown below for a rock from western Greenland that is among the oldest ever dated.

Method	Age (in billions of years)
Rubidium-87 / Strontium-87	3.70 ± 0.12
Lead-207 / Lead-206	3.80 ± 0.12
Uranium-235 / Lead-207	3.65 ± 0.05
Thorium-232 / Lead-208	3.65 ± 0.08
Lutetium-176 / Hafnium-176	3.55 ± 0.22
Average	3.64 ± 0.30

Since the five different methods yield ages that are very similar, we can have confidence that the final estimate of 3.64 billion years is reasonably accurate.

There are also cases in which this approach does lead to different results for each method. One example is some tests done on rocks from one of the deepest layers in the Grand Canyon.

Method	Age (in millions of years)
Potassium-40 / Argon-40	842 ± 164
Rubidium-87 / Strontium-87	$1{,}055 \pm 46$
Lead-207 / Lead-206	$1{,}250 \pm 130$
Samarium-147 / Neodymium-143	$1{,}330 \pm 360$

When different radiometric dating methods give results with this much variability for the same rock sample, something is amiss. Scientists would typically launch an investigation into what may be causing the problem. In some cases, they may find a clear reason. In other cases, they may have little more than plausible theories.

For those who believe that the earth is no more than 10,000 years old, variable results such as these are evidence that radiometric dating is not trustworthy. How can you be confident of any radiometric dating results if some are so obviously wrong? A common reaction from the Organic Paradigm is that, even if you assume that the lowest age measurement is the most accurate of the four in the table above, and even if you assume that the true age is at the low end of the range of uncertainty, the resulting age of the rock is still many times larger than 10,000 years. So the Organic Paradigm would agree that radiometric dating can't always give you the precision you want, but that this does not entirely invalidate its use to determine the age of rocks.

Issue #3: Contamination and leaching

Just like the initial concentration of the parent and daughter elements when a rock forms, any radioactive elements that have somehow gotten into or seeped out of a rock between the time it formed and when it was tested can also throw off any attempts at radiometric dating.

Minerals have a crystalline structure, which generally makes it difficult for external elements to enter into the crystal or for elements that were within the mineral when it formed to get out. But it does happen. Since the initial development of radiometric dating, a lot of work has gone into studying the properties of the most common minerals, including their propensity to permit elements to move through them. This work has resulted in databases of "diffusion coefficients" which indicate the rate at which a specific element X can move through a specific mineral Y. In general it is the smallest and most inert elements, such as helium, that are most likely to move through the crystal structure of a mineral. The larger and more reactive elements, which are more important in radiometric dating, are much less likely to move through minerals. Studies of mineral properties have also made it clearer how environmental conditions can affect diffusion, such as temperature, pressure, whether the mineral crystal has any tiny cracks, and the nature of the rocks surrounding the crystal. All this information on minerals can help a scientist determine the likelihood that the parent and daughter elements within a mineral have changed due to diffusion since the mineral first formed, and to account for this when calculating the uncertainty (the plus-or-minus that always follows an age estimate).

But even with all this information on diffusion into and out of minerals, it's still possible that you won't be able to determine with precision the amount of parent and daughter elements that may have entered or exited a mineral since it was formed. In many cases, the tools that are available for determining the initial concentration of the elements can also be used to work around any potential contamination or leaching. This includes isochron analysis and the use of multiple radiometric dating methods on the same sample. Of course these techniques aren't foolproof, and there is always the possibility that an age estimate can still be significantly wrong.

A considerably bigger problem is contamination that occurs during the process of preparing a mineral sample for radiometric dating. Often the measurable amounts of the parent and/or daughter elements in the sample are so low that the amounts of those same elements that normally exist in the air, water, and objects around us can significantly throw off the measurements. For this reason, there are very specific guidelines for how to clean samples, and the laboratories where radiometric dating tests are done are "clean rooms" (picture a brightly lit, all-white laboratory and scientists wearing blue cloth booties and face masks). Because of the high risk of contamination, radiometric dating has become a highly specialized science which takes significant expertise. Tests that yield ages that are significantly different than what one would expect can often be traced to contamination. Even if a source of contamination cannot be specifically identified, some scientists will nevertheless cite contamination as a likely cause of an unexpected result, particularly if subsequent repeat tests yield ages that are more in line with expectations.

Issue #4: Detection limits

Radiometric dating only works if the amounts of parent and daughter elements in a sample are large enough for a laboratory analyzer to measure precisely. While the equipment used to measure these substances is always being improved, it still has limits. This means that you need to stay away from the two extreme ends of the decay curve if you want to minimize the experimental uncertainty.

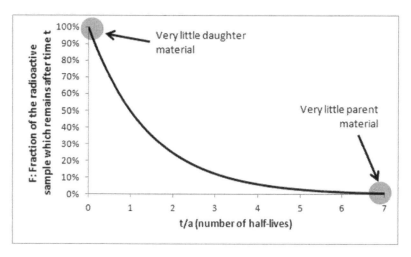

The practical result is that someone wanting to determine the age of something using radiometric dating must choose the types of radioactive elements he is going to measure in such a way that the two extreme ends of the decay curve are avoided as much as possible. Awkwardly, this means he needs to have in mind a general idea of how old the material might be so that he can choose a radioactive element with an appropriate half-life. If he chooses an element with a half-life that is wildly different than the age of the material he wants to date, he will be at one of the two extreme ends of the decay curve, and he is more likely to get incorrect results.

Time for another example.

Your buddy gives you a rock and asks you to date it. You decide to use rubidium-87, which has a half-life of 49 billion years. When you analyze the rock, you discover that there is 99.99% of the parent element rubidium-87 and 0.01% of the daughter element strontium-87. Based on the decay curve, you calculate that the age of the rock is 7 million years old.

Then your buddy reveals that the rock was actually formed from a volcanic eruption that occurred just a few years ago. The rock is, in fact, much younger than 7 million years. How could the radiometric dating have been so wrong?

The answer is that the instrument used to measure the radioactive elements cannot precisely measure very low levels of the daughter element strontium-87. 0.01% may seem like a small number, but the true number was actually 0.00000001%. The instrument could see that there was some strontium-87, but it reported a quantity higher than the real number. The result was a calculated age that was much larger than the true age.

Because of these types of errors, any measurements that are at or near the detection limits of the equipment being used are generally treated with suspicion, and a follow-up test is typically conducted using a different radioactive element with a different half-life.

The age of the earth

Using radiometric dating techniques, scientists have concluded that the earth is about 4.5 billion years old. This age comes from the study of minerals called zircons. The crystal structure of zircons typically contains lots of uranium, but experiments have shown that it does not incorporate lead from the surroundings when the zircon initially forms. Therefore, all the lead that appears in zircons must be the result of uranium decay, and the uranium-238 / lead-206 method works particularly well.[11] There is little disagreement between the Theistic and Organic Paradigms about this.

However, there is another aspect of zircon dating that has been more controversial. When uranium-238 decays, it emits a proton. This proton can combine with a free electron floating around inside the zircon to produce a helium atom. Thus, even though helium is not the direct decay product of uranium-238 (uranium-238 decays directly to thorium-234), helium is nevertheless formed during the decay process, not as a daughter element, but through a tangential side reaction. Being small and inert, these helium atoms would be expected to move through the crystal and leave the zircon in a relatively short period of time. Over the course of many millions of years, all the helium atoms formed through the decay of

[11] Uranium-238 actually decays through a series of 14 steps, each of which produces another radioactive element. The very last step in this series is the production of lead-206.

uranium-238 should have left the zircon, and there should be essentially no helium in the zircon crystal at the time it is tested.

But there have been tests on zircons in which substantial helium is found. The presence of helium does not change the fact that the zircons are dated at 4 billion years using the uranium-238 / lead-206 method, so those in the Organic Paradigm are generally not alarmed by the unexpected presence of helium, and theorize that the helium is simply the result of contamination. They also point to other tests on zircons in which no helium was found. Those in the Theistic Paradigm, however, have suggested that the presence of helium would be consistent with changes in the half-life of uranium-238 over time. If the half-life of uranium-238 was much shorter in the past than it is today, then the zircons could be only 10,000 years old even though they appear to be 4 billion years old, and the presence of helium in the zircons could be explained by the fact that 10,000 years is not long enough for the helium that was created in the decay process to seep out of the crystal.

Chapter 9

Genetic Mutations

The two primary pillars of the theory of evolution are genetic variation and natural selection. So, to understand evolution, there's really no way to avoid at least a shallow dive into the gene pool.[12]

How DNA works

Most people know that the basic code of all life, the blueprint from which all biological organisms are built, is DNA - deoxyribonucleic acid. With almost no exceptions, every cell of your body, every plant cell, every microorganism, contains DNA. The structure of DNA is basically a twisted ladder with many rungs called a double helix. The rungs are made of pairs of relatively simple molecules called nucleic acids, or nucleotides.

---

[12] I made a funny.

Amazingly, there are only four kinds of nucleotides, commonly referred to as A, T, C, and G (standing for adenine, thymine, cytosine, and guanine). But since DNA can be very long - the human DNA ladder contains some 3 billion "rungs" - there are an incredible variety of patterns that can be created from just these four nucleotides.

The primary function of DNA is to provide the template from which proteins are made. A series of nucleotides defines a gene, and one gene provides the blueprint for the construction of one protein. Proteins then go on to help with building everything else that your body is made of. The organization of DNA can be summarized like this:

DNA is organized into chromosomes
↓
Chromosomes are composed of genes
↓
Each gene is composed of nucleotides
↓
There are four nucleotides typically
identified as A, T, C, and G

The process through which DNA is used to make proteins is not unlike someone building a house. The first step would be to go to a library, find a blueprint for the house you want to build, and make a copy of that blueprint. Then you would take the blueprint copy to the construction site where fellow workers would read the blueprint. Using typical construction tools like saws and hammers, they would then put raw materials (boards, nails, glue) together in the proper sequence.

Here's the parallel process for building a protein:

- An enzyme called helicase "unzips" the DNA stand by breaking each rung of the ladder (which is composed of a pair of nucleotides) into two separate nucleotides. The unzipped DNA looks like this:

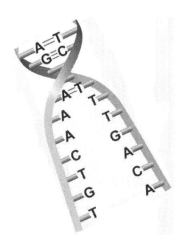

- An enzyme called RNA polymerase reads the sequence of nucleotides in one of the separated strands of DNA, and builds a string of "messenger RNA" to match the nucleotide sequence that it is reading. Messenger DNA is essentially a duplicate of a single gene in DNA. (*You've just made a copy of the blueprint for building the house*).

- The messenger RNA detaches from the DNA, and goes looking for a protein-making factory called a ribosome. (*You've taken the house blueprint out to the construction site*).

97

- When it finds a ribosome, the messenger RNA attaches to the ribosome.

- The ribosome then starts its work of making a protein. First the ribosome reads a sequence of three nucleotides from the messenger RNA. This sequence of three nucleotides is called a "codon." The codon tells the ribosome which type of amino acid to look for. (*The construction workers read the house blueprint and take note of the first step*).

- The ribosome grabs the correct amino acid from the soup of chemicals floating around it. This amino acid becomes the start of the protein. (*The construction workers grab the first board from a pile of wooden boards, and lay it in the proper position on the ground*).

- The ribosome then reads the next codon from the messenger RNA, and again goes looking for the amino acid that matches that codon. The protein is now composed of two amino acids. (*The construction workers grab a second board and nail it to the first board*).

- The ribosome keeps this up until it has constructed the complete protein, which then separates from the ribosome. (*The construction workers keep reading the blueprint and adding pieces to the house, one by one and in the correct order, until the house is built*).

- The newly formed protein gets some help from other specialty molecules to fold itself into the correct shape, and goes off to do whatever work it was designed to do. (*Decorators come in and make the house truly livable.*)

This is the primary process through which an organism's particular DNA (its genotype) determines its structure, form, functions, and activity (its phenotype).

Before I go on, take a moment to memorize the two words genotype and phenotype. I use them a lot in the rest of the book.

You may have heard it said that the DNA of humans and apes is 99% the same. This is a true statement.[13] It is sometimes used in arguing that humans and apes are related, meaning that they both evolved from a single common ancestor in the recent past ("recent" meaning 6-7 million years ago). But this particular type of evidence for evolution is actually rather misleading. If the genotype of an organism determines its phenotype, then it stands to reason that two organisms having a similar phenotype should also have a similar genotype. Likewise, two organisms that look and act very different should have rather different genotypes. An eagle and a hawk have very similar DNA, which shouldn't be surprising given that they are both birds, and similar types of birds to boot. A fish and an elephant have rather different DNA, which also shouldn't be surprising. With regard to evolution, then, the most you can say is that the similarity of genotypes for similar phenotypes is consistent with, not evidence of, the theory of evolution.

Speaking of misleading statements, there's something else that's important to know about genetics. For all our understanding of what DNA is and how it works, it's easy to get the impression that scientists have a detailed understanding of how genotypes create phenotypes. It's true that scientists know how genes lead to the production of proteins as described above. They know the structure of DNA in detail, and have mapped the full sequence of nucleotides in humans and many other species. They know that DNA is grouped into chromosomes, that each chromosome contains two copies of every gene (each of which is called an allele), and that small differences in alleles produce the dominant-versus-recessive traits that we learn about in high school biology (eye color, tongue rolling, dimples, etc). Scientists have also been able to connect some specific genes with particular phenotypic traits.

Notwithstanding all this knowledge, our understanding of how

---

[13] Sort of. This estimate is typically based either on genes in humans and chimpanzees that serve similar functions, or on genes that code for proteins. In fact some researchers have discovered that, if you look at all parts of human and chimpanzee DNA, the similarity could be as low as 70%.

genotypes create phenotypes is actually rather poor. For instance, it turns out that the vast majority of DNA in the most complex organisms, including humans, doesn't actually code for proteins. No one is really sure what it does or why it's there. As a result, it's commonly referred to as "junk DNA" which, as one researcher put it, is a dangerous term for something we don't understand. One theory is that it is leftover DNA from the evolutionary past, genes that once had a purpose but now do not. But this is mostly conjecture since the absence of an identifiable function is not the same as definitive knowledge that it has no function. More recent research suggests that junk DNA may be involved in the regulation of the protein-coding genes or some other activity whose mechanism isn't exactly obvious. This is an area of active research.

In addition to junk DNA, it turns out that scientists actually have little understanding of how specific phenotypic traits are produced from DNA. For instance, where are the genes that determine that you will have two eyes in front of your face instead of one eye on each side of your head, or four eyes instead of two? What specific genes create an elephant's trunk? In the few cases where scientists have discovered a link between a particular gene and a particular phenotypic trait, they still can't explain how it works. The exact chain of chemical events that causes a phenotype to develop as the result of the expression of specific genes remains elusive. Just as for junk DNA, there is lots of ongoing research into how genotypes produce phenotypes.

To give you an idea of the complexity of the genotype-phenotype connection, consider this: the number of genes in human DNA is only about ten times higher than the number of genes in bacteria. Does this mean that humans are only ten times more complex than bacteria? I think anyone would answer that with a clear no. So what gives?

When it first became known that the human genome only contained about 23,000 genes, many scientists were astonished. It seemed to be far too few to code for all our phenotypic traits. But the problem was simply that scientists had been thinking that there was a one-to-one correspondence between genes and traits: one gene produced one trait. But what if each trait is the result of the combined effect of multiple genes? Then the issue of only 23,000 genes in the human genome ceases to be a problem. A little math will make it clearer:

- If one gene codes for one trait, then 23,000 genes can generate 23,000 traits

- If two genes code for one trait, then 23,000 genes can generate 264 million traits

- If three genes code for one trait, then 23,000 genes can generate over 2 trillion traits

Because of the additional complexity that this creates, scientists have only made modest gains in deciphering the connection between particular genes and particular phenotypic traits.

There is new research going on all the time, and our knowledge of how a genotype produces a phenotype and what this might say about evolution continues to expand. But we are by no means in command of some detailed, molecular-level description of how this works. The fact that our knowledge in this area isn't as robust as it is sometimes portrayed means that the theory of evolution cannot provide a specific, biochemical explanation for every phenotype we see in nature.

The connection between genetics and evolution

Evolution requires phenotypic variability within a species, meaning that the individuals in a group must be slightly different from one another. If there's no variability - if every individual is exactly the same as every other - natural selection has nothing to choose from. Or rather, natural selection is just as likely to choose one individual from a group as another. The primary source of this phenotypic variability among individuals in a group is small errors that occur during the process of transferring DNA from a parent to an offspring. This is a key component to the evolutionary process, so you need to understand exactly how it happens.

In order to reproduce, the first step that every organism must take is to create a copy if its DNA. This copy will then form the starting point from which the new individual will develop. For sexually-reproducing organisms (pretty much everything that's not a single-cell microorganism), the DNA copy becomes part of gametes, the egg and sperm from mother and father. For microorganisms, the single cell simply divides into two new cells, with the original DNA going into one cell and the DNA copy going into the other cell. It is in the process of copying DNA that errors arise, and any error in the DNA of a gamete ends up being an error in the DNA of every single cell of the offspring.

The process of copying DNA is similar in some ways to the production of proteins:

- Just as in the production of proteins, the first step is for an enzyme called helicase to "unzip" the DNA stand by breaking each rung of the ladder (which is composed of a pair of nucleotides) into two separate nucleotides

- Another enzyme called DNA polymerase attaches to one of the separated strands of DNA

- The DNA polymerase identifies the first nucleotide on its strand, and then grabs the corresponding nucleotide from the soup of chemicals floating around it. For instance, if the DNA polymerase identifies the first nucleotide on the stand as thymine, it grabs adenine, since adenine is the only nucleotide that connects to thymine.

- The DNA polymerase attaches the adenine to the thymine, forming the beginning of a new double helix.

- The DNA polymerase then moves on to the next nucleotide on the separated strand, identifies it, and again grabs the corresponding nucleotide from the soup of chemicals floating around it.

- This process continues until each of the separated strands from the original DNA molecule is itself a new double helix.

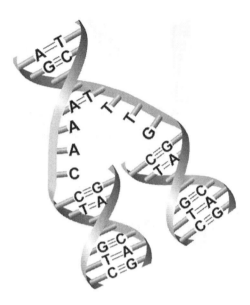

Unfortunately, this process of copying DNA isn't perfect, and sometimes there are errors. When this happens, it might affect the production of proteins from the new DNA chain, which might affect the phenotype of the offspring organism. There are three primary ways that these errors can be made during the DNA copying process:

1. A wrong nucleotide can be substituted for the correct nucleotide.

2. A nucleotide can be deleted.

3. A nucleotide can be inserted.

To see how these types of errors affect the DNA, imagine that the DNA is composed of a series of three-letter words that make up a sentence instead of a series of three-letter nucleotides that code for a protein. Here's an example:

The cat and dog ate pie

By way of analogy, each letter corresponds to one nucleotide, and each three-letter word represents a codon, which codes for a specific amino acid. This string of words conveys a particular idea, just as a string of amino acids produces a protein having a specific purpose.

In a substitution error, one of the letters is wrong, so you might end up with something like this:

The cat apd dog ate pie

Clearly there is something wrong, but you can still more or less understand the sentence. In the same way, a substitution error in DNA may affect one small part of a protein, leaving the protein still able to do its job.

Deletion and insertion errors, however, can totally mess up the protein. Imagine that the first letter of the sentence has been deleted. The sentence must still be composed of three-letter words, just like a protein is always coded by three-letter groups of nucleotides (codons). So, if you delete the first letter of our sentence, you get this:

hec ata ndd oga tep ie

All the letters are still there except for the first letter, and they are still in the proper order. But since the three-letter grouping is now off, the whole thing is meaningless. The same problem arises if you insert a letter instead of deleting one. So, if a nucleotide gets deleted or inserted during the DNA copying process, the gene may become totally useless as a template for creating a protein.

Errors that occur during the DNA copying process are called mutations. Scientists know for a fact that mutations occur because they can be observed so easily. This is no disagreement between Theistic Paradigm and Organic Paradigm folks on the fact that mutations can and do occur during the DNA copying process. The disagreements arise in the context of determining whether and how such mutations could lead to new phenotypes.

It should not surprise you that the majority of mutations are bad. If a deletion or insertion error occurs in a protein-coding gene, the protein may still be produced but it may be totally unable to do its job. For particularly important proteins, this could be lethal for the offspring organism.

The second-most frequent mutations are those that are neutral, having essentially no impact on the function of a gene or the protein that it codes for. There are several reasons that a mutation might be neutral. First, a substitution error will only affect one amino acid, and even the simplest proteins have hundreds of amino acids, so it's possible that a single amino acid that's wrong might not affect the protein's function. Second, the 64 possible codons (all possible sequences of four different nucleotides in groups of three) actually code for only 20 different amino acids used to make proteins. This means that several codons can code for the same amino acid, and this further reduces problems that might occur when a substitution error changes one codon into another. Finally, in many cases the third nucleotide in a codon doesn't actually contribute to the type of amino acid that the codon codes for. So, if an error occurs in the third nucleotide of a codon, odds are good that there won't be any effect on the protein at all. With some simple math it is possible to determine that the odds of a mutation in a single nucleotide having no impact at all on the protein are about 24%.

When it comes to evolution, the mutations that matter are the least frequent kind: those that actually do something good. For a genetic mutation to be beneficial, it must result in a modified protein that can still perform a function, but the function must be beneficial to the organism in some way. Understandably, this is difficult to imagine since proteins are very complex molecules whose function is very specific and depends heavily on how the molecule is folded around itself. For the protein molecule to exhibit some new, beneficial function, it must be folded in a slightly different way to perform the original function more efficiently, or to perform an entirely new function. It would seem much more likely that a new folding would simply render a protein non-functional rather than having some new, beneficial function. Moreover, even if a protein has a new function that's beneficial, it would seem that the loss of the original function could be a problem for the organism (similar to the way that an insertion or deletion error results in a non-functional protein).

Despite these legitimate objections, there is some evidence that beneficial mutations do occur. The vast majority of this evidence comes from experiments on microorganisms. In addition to being the simplest forms of life, they also reproduce quickly, making them ideal subjects.

If you start with a single bacterium and let it reproduce over and over, all of the daughter bacteria should have exactly the same genotype as the first bacterium you started with. They should also all have exactly the same phenotype, meaning that they should all process the same nutrients in the same way, produce the same types of waste products, reproduce at the same rate, and so on. But scientists have found that if they place this batch of identical bacteria under some kind of stress over the course of many generations (high temperatures, different nutrients, etc), bacteria will arise that appear to have different phenotypic traits, and some of the bacteria will be better suited than others to handle the stress that the scientists have subjected them to. In other words, some bacteria have gained an advantage. Since all the bacteria is this experiment started out being genetically identical, the only way that some could have gained any sort of phenotypic advantage over others is if something changed in their DNA. The conclusion is that mutations in the DNA conferred some sort of advantage to some of the individual microorganisms under the induced stress, and so they were better able to survive and reproduce.

Such experiments, which strongly suggest that beneficial genetic mutations are occurring, are nevertheless not definitive unless DNA sequencing (mapping the detailed sequence of nucleotides in a gene) was done both on the original parent microorganism as well as on the daughter (or great-great-granddaughter) microorganism that appeared to have gained an advantage. A comparison of the two DNA sequences would then show if mutations occurred that could have been responsible for the change in phenotype. Genetic sequencing has only recently become widely available and at least within reach in terms of cost, so some researchers have actually done this. In most cases, researchers have only been able to make a "black box" connection between the mutation(s) and the change in phenotype. By black box I mean that the researchers can identify the specific mutations that have occurred, and these mutations are presumed to have caused the change in phenotype. However, the biochemical connection between the mutations and the changed phenotype are typically not known. It is only in very rare cases that scientists doing such experiments have been able to map out the biochemical connection between the mutations and the fitness advantage gained.

There is also evidence for beneficial mutations leading in multicellular organisms. For instance, it is possible to induce mutations in fruit flies with chemicals, radiation, or some type of environmental stress, and then measure the relative fitness of the offspring. While the vast majority of the offspring in such cases will have developed some type of disability, including lethal ones, a very small fraction of the offspring will have gained some small advantage and will be better than their parents at surviving under whatever environmental stress the scientist subjected them to. Again, the specific biochemical link between a mutation in DNA and the observed phenotypic advantage may not be known, but there are almost no other explanations for how the phenotypic advantage would have come about.[14]

The evidence that beneficial mutations can occur is reasonably clear, at least for microorganisms and other organisms that can be easily studied in a laboratory. It may be logical to assume that the appearance of beneficial genetic mutations in microorganisms also occurs in plants and animals, but it is important to keep in mind

---

[14] One alternative theory is that changes in phenotype can occur without genetic mutations through chemical triggers that determine which genes are expressed and which ones lie dormant. In other words, the phenotypic advantage was always there, but wasn't expressed until some environmental trigger caused the appropriate genes to start working. This area is called epigenetics and is a relatively new area of research. As yet it is too early to say whether and to what degree epigenetics plays a role in phenotypic changes and evolution in general.

that such extrapolations are not the same as direct evidence in more complex organisms. It's also worth noting that all direct experimental evidence of beneficial genetic mutations has been observed under very controlled conditions. Real life is much more complicated, and there are an enormous number of factors that influence whether a beneficial genetic mutation actually survives and comes to predominate a group of organisms.

Fossil DNA

One of the fascinating areas of new research that has been made possible by the recent availability of gene sequencing is comparisons of DNA between different organisms. When combined with an understanding of how mutations occur, these studies have provided a whole new category of data that scientists can use to test the theory of evolution.

The ideal would be to have DNA from organisms that went extinct long ago to compare to DNA from organisms that still exist today. This would allow scientists to see what mutations have occurred between a past organism and a current organism that is thought to have evolved from it. However, except in rare cases, this isn't possible. After an organism dies, its DNA begins to degrade. Depending on the conditions, the DNA might be completely unrecognizable after only a few decades. On the other hand, if the conditions are optimal (i.e. environments which are very cold, dry, and chemically inert), it is possible that DNA could last for hundreds of thousands of years. Few studies have succeeded in finding intact DNA from remains that are this old, however. The oldest known DNA samples were from ice that was buried 2 km below the surface of Greenland and is estimated to be about 800,000 years old. Even though this sounds old, it's not old enough to provide much insight into evolution. The bottom line is that the odds of finding even pieces of dinosaur DNA is extremely low. You won't be seeing any Jurassic Park dinosaurs anytime soon.

Since DNA from extinct organisms is largely unavailable, the next best thing is to examine the DNA of living organisms to see if it can offer any clues about how those organisms might have evolved. The best way to do this is to compare the DNA from two different species. As I said earlier, we would expect the DNA from similar species to be similar, and the DNA from dissimilar species to be dissimilar, regardless of whether the theory of evolution is true or not. Surprise surprise, this is exactly what scientists have found. However, sometimes DNA taken from two very different species is found to be very similar, contrary to what one might expect. Scientists have started calling these strange DNA strands "fossil DNA" under the assumption that they contain a sort of record of the evolutionary history of an organism.

For example, as described earlier, the process of making proteins requires that a structure in the cell called a ribosome read the string of codons from messenger RNA, and then use this information to determine the proper sequence of amino acids in the protein that the ribosome is building. It should not surprise you that the actual process is a bit more complicated than I described earlier. For example, another chemical called an "elongation factor" must also be present to facilitate the connection of one amino acid to another. The elongation factor is itself a protein, and thus there is a gene that codes for its production.

Since all living things have DNA which must be translated into proteins, we would expect elongation factors to also be present in all living things. More importantly, we would expect the amino acid sequence of elongation factor proteins to look more or less the same in all living things, since they perform almost exactly the same function in all living things. Indeed, this is what scientists have found. You have a gene in your DNA that codes for the production of elongation factors, and bacteria have the same gene. Your gene and the bacterial gene are (almost) exactly the same.

The fact that the simplest organism on earth has the same gene as the most complex organism is taken by those in the Organic Paradigm as evidence that all life has evolved from some sort of bacteria-like life form. The reasoning goes like this: without elongation factors, cells cannot produce proteins, and without manufacturing proteins, a cell can't survive. Since the production of proteins is essential to all life, genes that are responsible for directing the protein-making process - including genes for elongation factors - must be passed from generation to generation without experiencing any detrimental mutations. So how does nature ensure that genes coding for elongation factors stay the same over very long periods of time? The answer is natural selection. As soon as a bad mutation arises in the gene coding for elongation factors, the organism either has a difficult time making proteins, or can't make them at all. Either way, the organism is less fit than others in its group, less likely to reproduce, and thus over time that particular genetic mutation is weeded out of the population entirely. This is the essence of natural selection at work. It would appear logical, then, that genes coding for elongation factors would remain the same even as new species arise from old species.

While this particular argument in support of evolution is reasonably compelling, there are a few things that prevent it from being airtight:

First, it presumes that humans have a gene coding for elongation factors because humans evolved from an ape-like creature which had the same gene, and the ape-like creature evolved from a rodent-like mammal that had the same gene, and so on all the way back to the bacterium that had the elongation factor gene. Someone in the Theistic Paradigm could point to the obvious alternative: all organisms came from one Source who decided to use the same basic biochemical processes in all of them. While this alternative view fits logically with the data, it can also sound a bit evasive to those in the Organic Paradigm. It's akin to saying, "organisms have the genes they do because that's how God made them." Regardless of whether it's true or not, it's more of a statement of belief because it does not include any sort of step-by-step mechanism through which elongation factors are proposed to have arisen.

Second, the use of elongation factors as support for the theory of evolution actually turns the traditional arguments in favor of evolution on their head. In the traditional arguments, the environment is constantly changing (not just climate, but predators, food sources, etc), and this requires a constant readjustment on the part of organisms in those environments to adapt or go extinct; the combination of random genetic mutations and natural selection causes life to evolve from one phenotype to another. But in the case of elongation factors, there was essentially no evolution, no changes, no improvements on the original design. This despite the fact that the environment of earth has changed repeatedly and in dramatic ways over 3 billion years (chemical composition, temperatures, availability of raw materials, etc). We are left with a paradox: natural selection worked to ensure that elongation factor genes did not change while also simultaneously allowing many other genes to change. How do we explain this?

Within the Organic Paradigm, the simple answer is that elongation factors must have been perfectly adapted to all possible environments from the start and needed no improvements, whereas there was room for improvement in all other proteins and biochemical processes. Indeed, since all known life has essentially the same genes for elongation factors, it would seem that there is no alternative explanation. Natural selection preserved elongation factor genes, continuously weeding out the smallest mutations that dampened their effectiveness, and (apparently) no mutations arose that increased their effectiveness. But genes that guide other biochemical processes, or are connected to other phenotypic traits, were not perfectly adapted to all possible environments. So, as environments changed, natural selection allowed other genetic mutations to produce organisms who could adapt to new environments.

This type of argument is perfectly sound, but it does rest on the assumption that evolution is true. If instead you take a broader view in which evolution is not assumed a priori to be true, then you might be led to ask other questions in an effort to really understand what might be going on. For instance:

- Since genes for elongation factors were preserved over 3 billion years, and no alternatives ever developed, does this mean that nature had no choice but to use them?

- How is it that elongation factors appear to have been perfectly adapted to all possible environments from the very start, whereas the vast majority of other proteins have changed repeatedly and dramatically over time?

Currently, scientists don't have enough information to answer these types of questions. For those in the Theistic Paradigm, the lack of answers leave open the possibility that God was somehow involved in the process. As I said in Chapter 5, however, the current lack of understanding is no guarantee that answers might not become available somewhere down the road.

One more example of fossil DNA.

In addition to genes that have been preserved over long periods of time and through many transitions from one species to another, there are also genes that have not been preserved but which nevertheless have left traces of themselves. These fossil genes may be completely non-functional - they don't produce proteins - but they contain so many similarities to functional genes that it's hard not to believe that they weren't functional at some point in the past.

For example, all dolphins and whales have a fossil gene for something called short-wavelength sensitive (SWS) opsin. It's there, but it doesn't do anything. The gene is easy to identify in dolphin and whale DNA because 99% of it is exactly the same as the functional SWS opsin gene in other mammals, where it codes for a particular type of pigment in eyes that is tuned to the color blue. Out of the 350 nucleotides that make up a functional SWS opsin gene, four are missing in this gene in dolphins and whales. The absence of these four nucleotides means that the three-at-a-time sequence of codons is off, rendering the gene useless.

So what is it doing there? The theory of evolution provides a logical answer.

Genetic mutations can occur in any gene at any time. But under the theory of evolution, some of these mutations will be weeded out of the population through natural selection, and others won't. The determining factor for whether a mutation stays or goes is the importance of the gene to the fitness of the organism. Natural selection will work to preserve genes that are very important to the organism. If a mutation occurs in an important gene, and as a result the organism becomes less fit than others in its group, the organism will be less likely to reproduce. Over multiple generations, then, organisms having the mutated gene with a resulting reduction in overall fitness will tend to die out. The important gene is preserved.

But what happens if a mutation occurs in a gene that is not particularly important to the organism? In this case, even if the mutation renders the gene unable to produce a protein, the organism is essentially unaffected. Mutations can continue to build up in genes that are not important to the organism's fitness because natural selection won't weed out the individuals with the mutated gene.

Given this conceptual framework, it's not difficult to construct a plausible narrative for what may have happened to the SWS opsin gene in dolphins and whales. The prevailing theory of the evolution of dolphins and whales is that they descended from creatures that once dwelt on land, and that those ancestors had full color vision (see Chapter 15 for a more complete story). But as the creatures became more aquatic and began to spend more and more time under water where light levels are low, their need for full color vision was reduced. Over time, SWS opsin simply didn't factor into the creature's fitness anymore. In other words, whether the creature could see the color blue or not didn't matter - under water, everything is bluish. So, as deletion errors occurred in the SWS opsin gene, there was no natural selection mechanism to get rid of the individuals who had those genetic mutations. In fact, since SWS opsin was no longer necessary, individuals that did not waste metabolic resources to make SWS opsin might have actually had a slight advantage over those individuals that still produced SWS opsin. Thus there could have been a sort of reverse natural selection going on, where individuals with a non-functional SWS opsin gene had a slight fitness advantage other those with functional SWS opsin genes.

There's no way to prove that this explanation is true since we don't have DNA from a land-dwelling ancestor to dolphins and whales. However, it's logical and fits the known facts. Within the

Organic Paradigm, it is a plausible narrative that is commonly treated as the best[15] explanation for why dolphins and whales have an inactive SWS opsin gene.

However, it turns out that there is an alternative explanation that has been proposed by some in the Theistic Paradigm. It is that so-called fossil genes are not remnants of active genes that have fallen into disuse, but rather are genes that are lying dormant, waiting to be activated. In essence, the genes in question have always been there but have never been used, not in the current organism nor in any supposed ancestor. They will become active only if the organism needs them to cope with some change in its environment. The catch is that it's not clear how this would occur. In order to activate a dormant gene, certain specific nucleotides would need to change in very specific ways. The random genetic mutations that are fundamental to the theory of evolution don't seem to be a good way for this to happen. Instead, the changes in nucleotides for dormant fossil genes would need to be almost deliberate. It is for this reason that many folks in the Organic Paradigm reject this idea.

There are lots of other examples of organisms that contain non-functional genes that look similar to functional genes in other organisms. In some cases the non-functional and functional genes look very similar, as in the case of the SWS opsin gene in whales and dolphins. In other cases the non-functional gene has so many mutations that matching it with a known functional gene is more difficult. Within the Organic Paradigm, the degree of similarity between a functional and non-functional gene is assumed to be proportional to the amount of time that has passed since the functional gene became non-functional, because genetic mutations would be expected to accumulate over time if something (like natural selection) doesn't stop them from doing so.

---

[15] Or more accurately, most current.

Chapter 10

Natural Selection

If genetic mutations are one side of the evolution coin, natural selection is the other side. The basic concept of natural selection is something like a filter: some things get through, and others don't. Here's a simple analogy:

Imagine a box that contains some machinery. You can't see into the box, so you don't know what the machinery is or how it works. What you do know is that what comes out of the box is a series of small plastic spheres. Being the intelligent person that you are, and drawing on all of your experience and deductive skills, you conclude that what's in the box is a sphere generating machine.

Then you are told that while the box does in fact contain a sphere-generating machine, that same machine also generates small plastic cubes. Moreover, you are told that the objects are randomly generated, but without any bias towards either spheres or cubes. Thus there is no way to predict which object - a sphere or a cube - will be produced next from the machine inside the box, but in general you would expect the same number of cubes and spheres to be produced.

This would strike any reasonable person as ludicrous. After all, what's coming out of the box is only spheres. If cubes are also being generated, why aren't they coming out of the box as well?

You open the box and peer inside. You do in fact see a random object-producing machine which is spitting out both spheres and cubes, but you also see a plate that is full of spherical holes. The spheres can pass through the plate, but the cubes can't.

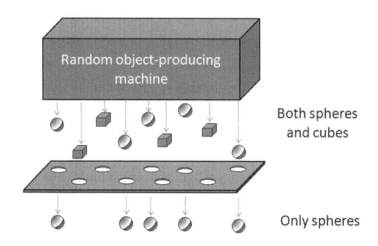

So in fact it is true that both spheres and cubes are being produced, but the plate is filtering the objects so that only the spheres get through and exit the box. The combination of the random object-producing machine and the plate with spherical holes makes it appear from the outside as though the machine is producing only spheres when in fact it is producing both spheres and cubes.

In this analogy, the random object-producing machine corresponds to the generation of random mutations in DNA as described in Chapter 9, and the plate with the spherical holes corresponds to natural selection. Just as the machine produces both spheres and cubes, an organism's DNA produces both beneficial mutations and detrimental mutations. And just as the plate in the box allows only spheres to pass through, natural selection allows only beneficial mutations to continue in a species.

Natural selection doesn't actually choose between beneficial and detrimental genetic mutations per se. Instead, it acts on the expression of those mutations in an organism's phenotype. To put it another way, genetic mutations are not beneficial or detrimental by themselves. Instead, a mutation is beneficial if it results in some sort of change to the organism's structure, form, function, or activity (it's phenotype) that gives the organism some slight advantage over its brothers and sisters. Likewise a genetic mutation is detrimental if it results in some sort of change to the organism's structure, form, function, or activity that leaves the organism at some slight disadvantage in comparison to its brothers and sisters.

Natural selection is the process through which variations in phenotypic traits, which are created by random genetic mutations, are filtered. The organism's environment does the filtering automatically: the phenotypic traits that are most likely to continue from generation to generation are those that best help the organism to survive and thrive. Due to random mutations in DNA, there will always be variation in the phenotypic traits of a group of organisms, and thus some organisms will naturally fit better into their environment than others. Those that fit best are more likely to survive and more likely to find a mate, and thus are more likely to pass their DNA onto the next generation.

It sounds simple, and in concept it is. It is also extremely logical. But it turns out that in practice natural selection is incredibly complicated, in fact far more complicated than genetic mutations, and more difficult to study as well. In genetics there are only four nucleotides, and thus only three possible ways that one of those nucleotides can mutate into another nucleotide. While there are many thousands of possible proteins that can be generated by DNA, and innumerable biochemical connections between DNA and specific phenotypes, scientists have made tremendous strides in learning how it all works. Moreover, the chemistry of life follows some well-established principles concerning how molecules interact that give scientists a leg up on understanding how the biology of life works.

But the connection between an organism's phenotype and its environment is considerably more complicated, particularly when the environment changes. Experiments that have definitively made a connection between changes in the environment and changes in an organism's phenotype over time are typically very simple, involving microorganisms subjected to one very specific and controlled change. More realistic experiments involving complex organisms and multiple changes in their environments are considerably more difficult (and expensive, and time-consuming) to conduct.

To appreciate this complexity, consider what an organism's "environment" includes:

- Climate, including:
  - Amount and type of precipitation
  - Humidity
  - Temperature
  - Wind
  - Air pressure and oxygen concentration
  - Amount of sunshine and cloudiness
  - Daily and seasonal fluctuations in all these factors
- Type and number of predators
- Food and water sources
- Types and numbers of other organisms
- Terrain
- Forms of shelter and living space
- Social environment: The number of individuals of the same species in the same area

For organisms living in bodies of water, other factors could include:

- Visibility and availability of sunlight
- Water pressure/depth
- Salinity
- Currents

Moreover, every one of the factors listed above can exist in a multitude of degrees and forms. The number of different environments that exists today, or are possible on earth, is simply too large to count.

Every organism that exists today does so in the context of a particular environment to which it is adapted. This shouldn't surprise anyone. If an organism is not adapted to a particular environment, it won't be there. Some Organic Paradigm folks have suggested that the perfect adaptation of organisms to their local environments is evidence that evolution occurred. However, at most you could say that this observation is consistent with the theory of evolution rather than evidence for it, because it simply can't be any other way. The biochemistry of an octopus is tuned to life in salt water, not to life in fresh water, so you won't find an octopus in fresh water. Is this evidence that the octopus has evolved to live in salt water? Not really. You get exactly the same result if God created the octopus to live in salt water as you do if evolution produced an octopus that lives in salt water. It lives where it lives because that's the environment to which it is adapted.

The theory of evolution posits that a given environment filters the organisms within it in such a way that those individuals that are best adapted to it will be most likely to reproduce and thus pass their DNA on to the next generation, while individuals who are not as well adapted to their environment are less likely to reproduce. While other aspects of natural selection as a driving force for evolution may be problematic (as discussed in more detail in Chapter 12), this basic idea of natural selection as a filter is largely unassailable for two reasons:

1. In every environment there are limited resources and many dangers, and the combination of these two things means that every individual within a group is in competition with all others to survive and reproduce. If it were otherwise - if organisms lived in utopias where there was no need for competition - populations would quickly soar out of control.

2. The individuals in a group of organisms are never 100% identical.[16] There will always be small variations in

---

[16] Even identical twins are not 100% identical. Errors in DNA duplication that occur during the process of a single fertilized egg splitting into two separate individuals can result in changes to only of of them.

phenotype, meaning that individuals will have slightly differing abilities to acquire and use the available resources and to escape the dangers.

Within every species, and within every group within a species, some individuals are better able than others to survive and reproduce. This process plays out all the time in every local environment with every kind of organism. There is a significant amount of agreement between the Theistic and Organic Paradigms about this aspect of natural selection, at least as it occurs over relatively short timeframes (hundreds to thousands of years).

One of the most common sources that Organic Paradigm folks use as evidence that natural selection has the potential to create new species is to look to examples of artificial selection. In artificial selection, it is the conscious effort of human beings rather than nature that is choosing which individuals within a group will reproduce. Artificial selection has been used by farmers for many hundreds of years in the domestication of livestock and in the process of increasing grain yields in agriculture. One of the best examples is the process of creating dog breeds.

Genetic studies of different dog breeds have confirmed what had long been suspected: all dogs are closely related to the grey wolf. The current belief is that gray wolves were domesticated somewhere between 8,500 and 15,000 years ago. For most of that time, a dog was just a dog: a companion, a hunting buddy, something to eat scraps off the floor. But within the last several hundred years, interest in artificially selecting dogs for particular traits and behaviors for specific functional roles grew dramatically. By choosing the dogs from a litter with desirable traits and ensuring that only they mated, and repeating the process over many generations, humans were able create very different breeds. A Pekingese weighs only a couple of pounds, while a St. Bernard can weigh over 180 pounds. Some dogs make excellent guard dogs or hunters, while others are better at snuggling. Some do little more than look pretty. The American Kennel Club currently recognizes about 155 breeds of dog.

There is no denying that selection worked in the case of dog breeds. Given more time and continued efforts in selective breeding, the theory of evolution posits that individual dog breeds could become so genetically different from one another that they could no longer interbreed. At that point they would be considered separate species. But as of today this hasn't happened as technically all breeds of dog are the same species. Moreover, the creation of separate dog species isn't likely to happen any time soon - even the fastest rates of speciation require thousands of years.

When pointing to examples of artificial selection, Organic Paradigm folks generally make the argument that natural selection would work in essentially the same way that artificial selection works with dog breeding. Indeed the parallels between artificial selection and natural selection are pretty clear: both involve a filtering process that chooses among a group of individuals with varying phenotypes. The fact that artificial selection involves an intelligent being making intentional choices, while natural selection is both mindless and unintentional, is generally regarded by those in the Organic Paradigm as having little if any relevance. However, this difference between artificial and natural selection is gaining new scrutiny among scientists as they work to dive down deeper into the mechanisms proposed to be at work in evolution. Even some in the Organic Paradigm will admit that it appears (though, they will be quick to add, only appears) that natural selection is making an intentional choice.

In addition to artificial selection, there are a number of examples of natural selection at work. Classic examples include the case of the peppered moth and antibiotic resistance as described in Chapter 11. There are also other, less well-known examples. For instance, a severe drought on one of the Galapagos Islands in 1977 had the effect of filtering different varieties of finches such that only those with the largest, strongest beaks survived. On further examination, it was determined that the reason was a simple matter of access to food: the drought had eliminated all but the hardest nuts, and it was only the finches with the strongest beaks who could break them open.

Chapter 11

Degrees Of Evolution

One of the basic tenets of the theory of evolution is that individual organisms don't evolve. Mortimer the pig will never evolve into Mortimer the pig version 2.0. It is only groups of individuals that evolve, and then only as one generation gives way to the next.

But while the common understanding of evolution is that it is something that occurs over millions of years, this isn't always the case. In some organisms changes that can be categorized as evolution can be observed in as little as a single generation. This is because the theory of evolution as it is typically defined today is actually quite broad: evolution is simply the change in gene frequencies in a population over time. This is a technical way of saying that if the mix of genes as measured across a group of organisms is different than the mix of genes in a previous generation, evolution has occurred. Sometimes you can detect this difference in only a single generation, and other times (indeed most of the time) it takes many, many generations for the difference across generations to be noticeable.

When Charles Darwin wrote *Origin of Species*, his entire focus was on the outward characteristics of organisms, their functions and activities, form and structure. In short, their phenotype. The reason for this is simple: nobody at that time had any understanding whatsoever of genetics. Today we understand that every aspect of an organism's phenotype is a function of its DNA. It should be no surprise, then, that evolutionary scientists have shifted their focus from studying phenotypes to studying genotypes in the 150 years since *Origin of Species* was published. So, you might say that my shorthand equation for evolution in Chapter 6 should be revised slightly. Instead of this:

Genetic variation + natural selection = evolution

the shorthand description of evolution should really be this:

Genetic mutations produce changes in an
organism's phenotype
↓
Within a group of organisms, genetic mutations
create variations in phenotypes among the
individuals in that group
↓
Variations in phenotype within a group + natural
selection = evolution

Since changes in genotype occur in tiny steps, it's perfectly logical to expect that changes in phenotype as a result of changes in genotype won't be obvious in the short term. When it comes to one species evolving into another species, this is certainly true. But there are cases of evolution in which the changes don't actually result in a new species. To show how this can be the case, here's an example:

Only about 1% of people have green eyes. What would happen if green eyes became the very definition of true beauty? What if every magazine and talk show and blog espoused the benefits of green eyes to your health and happiness? Under such (ridiculous) circumstances, it's easy to imagine that having green eyes could become a consideration in who you chose to date and eventually marry. Since a larger fraction of couples would include at least one person with green eyes, the next generation would likely have a larger fraction of green-eyed people, say 2% instead of 1%. In this case, the frequency of "green eye genes" would be greater in the children's generation than in the parent's generation, and thus evolution would be said to have occurred.

You might protest that my green-eye example doesn't include any changes in DNA, so it can't really be an example of evolution. You would be half right. My example is certainly focused on the natural selection side of the equation and pre-existing variations in eye color. But according to the theory of evolution, the green eye gene formed at some point in the past for reasons that may never be clear, and those genes would only come to dominate human populations if some mechanism arose to select for it (for example, a mate with green eyes is considered more desirable than a mate whose eyes are any other color). So, in this example, both the genetic process that led to the creation of green eyes and natural selection were at work. Evolution has occurred because the frequency of green eye genes is greater in the next generation than it was in the previous generation.

This is not how most people think of evolution, which is why this chapter exists. Evolution actually occurs to varying degrees in different circumstances. In the simplest form, natural selection acts on variations in phenotype that already exist within a species. In this case you have something akin to my green-eye example, and changes within a group of organisms may be noticeable over short time periods. This is particularly true when the variations within a group are already obvious to the casual observer, as they are with different color eyes. However, the process of creating new variations that didn't exist before (for instance, purple eyes) can take considerably longer because the genetic mutations that are responsible are infrequent and are more likely to be detrimental rather than beneficial. As natural selection acts on each new variation in phenotype, successive generations of organisms will change to greater and greater degrees over longer and longer time periods.

To visualize the various degrees of evolution, I've broken it into four successive steps. In reality evolution is not a series of discrete steps, but rather a continuum. Someone else might break it into three or five steps. The point is merely to show how evolution is believed to play out.

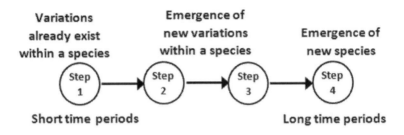

Step 1

In the first step, natural selection is acting on variations that already exist within a group of organisms. We're not talking about genetic mutations in this step. For Step 1, various genetic mutations have already occurred in the past to create variations in phenotype within a group of organisms, all of whom are nevertheless still the same species, and natural selection is simply acting to choose between those phenotypes. In Step 2 and beyond, genetic mutations come into play in an active way.

If there is a wide range of variations within a group of organisms (very different colors, running speed, beak shape, whatever), then the effects of natural selection may be easy to observe, particularly if there is some sudden change in an environment that favors one phenotype over another. If, on the other hand, the variations between individuals in a group are so subtle that they would hardly be noticed by a casual observer (for instance, spots that are very slightly smaller), the effects of natural selection will likewise also be difficult to observe.

This step can occur in as little as a single generation, and there are several well-known examples that have been directly observed. One example cited in biology textbooks is the case of the European peppered moth. This moth has two common variants, a light-winged version and a dark-winged version. They are the same species, but like humans with different eye colors, this species has different wing colors.

Up until the 19th century, the dark-winged version was much less common than the light-winged version. But in the 1850's, this trend reversed itself: there were suddenly many more dark-winged versions that light-winged versions. It soon became apparent that the rise of new industries was resulting in large amounts of soot in the air, which settled on trees and made many of the lighter trees darker in color. The lighter moths, normally camouflaged on white bark, became more obvious to birds when they rested on the soot-covered bark. Birds could see the lighter moths more easily, and therefore targeted them for dinner. The darker moths, on the other hand, blended in more readily with the darkened trees, and were not eaten by birds. To confirm this hypothesis, experiments were done wherein an equal number of each color of moth was released in different areas. Some time later, they were collected to see how many of each color had survived. True to the theory, moths with darker wings did better in areas with significant soot production, while moths with lighter wings did better in areas far from the soot-producing industries.

Another common example of this step in evolution is the case of the use of antibiotics to kill bacteria that may cause sickness. It has been well-established within the medical community that many forms of bacteria have developed resistance to antibiotics. For a few years, antibiotic A may do a very good job of killing a particular type of bacteria. But then people start noticing that antibiotic A isn't working so well, so they switch to a new antibiotic B. This new antibiotic works extremely well in killing bacteria X, but over time this antibiotic B also loses its potency. Researchers are constantly trying to develop new antibiotics that will kill the same bacteria that used to be so easy to kill way back when.

It may seem like the bacteria are consciously aware of the fact that people are trying to kill them and are intentionally developing new chemistries to fend off the attackers. It might make a decent B movie, but the reality is much less interesting. Within any given batch of bacteria, there are variations in their individual abilities to resist antibiotics. If your antibiotic soap kills 99% of the bacteria on your hands, the 1% that remains is likely to be those bacterial cells that just happen to have a stronger-than-average resistance to antibiotics. Since bacteria multiply quickly, sometimes as fast as once every 15 minutes, in no time at all you have a whole new batch of bacteria. This new batch has descended from the 1% that had the strongest resistance to your antibiotic soap. Your antibiotic soap won't work quite so well on this new generation of bacteria.

The bacterial cells with the strongest resistance to antibiotics arose without planning or intention through the process of random genetic mutations. But even if we had no understanding of how genetic works, it would still be obvious that natural selection is at work in this process to cause the most "fit" bacterial cells (those which were most resistant to antibiotics) to survive and reproduce while the "less fit" die out.

One more example. Every year there is a new strain of influenza virus because the previous strain has gone through the process of random genetic mutations and natural selection. Even though your body developed antibodies against the previous strain of the flu virus and you are therefore immune to it, you can get sick again if you happen to be exposed to a new variant of the virus that is sufficiently different than the previous version.

There are other examples as well, but the story is more or less the same with all of them: Some organisms fared better than others when faced with some sort of selection pressure, and the net result is that the population changed over several generations. There is little disagreement among Theistic Paradigm and Organic Paradigm folks about this level of evolution because the evidence is so strong.

Step 2

For this and subsequent steps, natural selection isn't simply acting on variations in phenotypes that already exist within a group of organisms. Instead, new variations are appearing within a group through random genetic mutations, and natural selection is acting on those new variations as they arise. During this process it would be easier than it is in Step 1 to see that something fundamental is changing in a group of organisms because some trait that didn't exist before now appears in at least some members of the group. Instead of peppered moths having only two varieties (light and dark-winged), maybe now there is a third variety: speckled.

It is easiest to think of this step as one in which a group of organisms is differentiating into subgroups. The subgroups are all still the same species, but they are also distinctly different from one another. They all have nearly the same phenotype, but not exactly the same phenotype. Depending on the type of organism, these subgroups have different names:

Domesticated animals	Breed, landrace
Plants	Cultivar, variety
Microorganisms	Strain
People	Race, tribe, ethnic group

Other less formal terms are also used in some cases. These include variant, variety, form, kind, and class. But when it comes to scientific classifications, the only formal term that is used is subspecies. This is probably the easiest term to remember anyway, since it suggests a level below species.

Subspecies within the same species are different only in their form and/or structure, not in their functions and activities. They may look different, but they don't act different. Moreover, they can freely interbreed. For instance, a Chihuahua and a great Dane can mate and produce healthy and fertile offspring.[17]

Evolutionary scientists have theorized that a process called geographic isolation is often responsible for creating subspecies. Imagine that a group of foxes are all the same species and that there are no subspecies (they all look more or less alike). If they are spread out over a very large area, it is possible that some type of geologic feature could arise over time that separates the single group of foxes into two groups. Maybe some low hills push up to

---

[17] Theoretically.

become mountains, a new river forms, etc. In this case, the two different groups can't interact with one another because they can't get around the new mountain or cross the river.

Now let's imagine that fox clan #1 is living in a different climate than fox clan #2. The different climates could produce different "selection pressures" on their respective fox clans. In northern areas, for instance, larger foxes might have an advantage over smaller foxes, since larger animals conserve heat better and thus can handle colder temperatures. The northern area might also have more snow, such that natural selection might favor the lighter-colored foxes over the darker colored ones. Given enough time (in other words, over multiple generations), the foxes on the north side of the mountain range or river might, as a group, begin to look different than those on the south side of the mountain range - they might be bigger and lighter-colored. At the point when there are clear, discrete differences in appearance between the two groups, we would say that two subspecies have formed out of the original, single species.

Geographic isolation isn't absolutely necessary for two (or more) subspecies to develop out of a single species, but it's much less likely to occur otherwise. If, for instance, the two groups of foxes weren't separated from each other by mountains or a river, they might still be subject to different selection pressures due to being in different climates. As a result, the two groups might still begin developing into separate subspecies. If the two groups can still interact, then they can freely interbreed as well, and any distinctions between the two groups might quickly be washed out. In this case, no new subspecies develop. On the other hand, if any phenotypic differences between two subspecies make it less likely that they interbreed (for instance, if the northern group of foxes aren't attracted to the skinnier, darker-colored foxes from the south), then they might no longer interbreed even though biologically they could. This is the notion behind "reproductive isolation", which is broader than geographic isolation and does not necessarily involve a physical barrier keeping the two subspecies apart.

This step in evolution is considerably more difficult to directly observe than Step 1 for the simple reason that it occurs over much longer time periods. From the breeding of dogs, we know that subspecies for mammals can form in as little as a few hundred years. Of course, in dog breeding you had humans who were forcing it to happen, and with specific goals in mind for the different breeds (artificial selection). In nature, the selection pressures are believed to work much more slowly. Moreover, there is a great deal of variability in how long it might take for one species to develop into two or more different subspecies. The time it takes will be a function of three main things:

1. The rate at which new traits (phenotypes) are formed (i.e. how many genetic mutations occur per generation)

2. The strength of the selection pressure (i.e. how much the environment is changing)

3. The rate at which an organism reproduces

A new subspecies can form in a relatively short period of time if the organisms mature and reproduce quickly, if the selection pressure is strong, and if the rate of genetic mutations is high. However, there is a balancing act in this process. If the selection pressure is too strong - for instance, if the climate suddenly becomes much drier - all the organisms in a group may simply die out before random mutations that are beneficial have a chance to permit the group to adapt to the new conditions. That's extinction. So the mutation rate needs to be high when the selection pressure is strong. Unfortunately, a high rate of genetic mutations also increases the chances of bad changes in traits. Since most random genetic mutations are actually bad, a high mutation rate can cause bad phenotypic traits to build up faster than good phenotypic traits, with the result being that the overall fitness of the group decreases. This can also result in extinction.

So, a species can go extinct if the mutation rate is not high enough to keep up with the selection pressure, and it can also go extinct if the mutation rate is too high. In short, you've got extinction to the left and extinction to the right, and a narrow path down the middle where the genetic mutation rate and the environmental selection pressure are balanced. This balancing act is a theoretical description of what scientists believe must occur in order for evolution to work. By and large it hasn't been quantified, largely because there is currently no way to quantify selection pressure (how do you measure the stress on a group of foxes resulting from slightly greater than average rainfall?). I describe this issue a bit more in Chapter 12.

As I said before, there are very few cases where the evolution of two or more subspecies out of a single species has been directly observed. Most cases that are cited by scientists as directly observed examples of evolution are actually examples of Step 1, not Step 2. The reason for this is that in Step 2, new phenotypic traits are being created, and the rate of genetic mutations that underlies these new traits is rather slow. A typical rate of mutation for mammals would be about 1 mutation for every 30 million nucleotides per generation. At this rate, mutations would need to occur over hundreds, and more likely thousands, of generations in order to produce a change in phenotype on which natural selection can act.

Step 3

In this step, the phenotypes of two subspecies within the same species continue to diverge. The process is the same as described in Step 2: the two groups experience different types of selection pressures. Assuming neither group goes extinct (which, according to the fossil record, appears to be very common in the history of life on earth), the two subspecies eventually become two separate species, though still closely related.

This begs the question: How do you know when two subspecies are now separate species? It turns out that there are no clear criteria for this. The word species is sometimes used simply as a name for a morphologically distinguishable form, meaning it looks different than any other organism. A more common criterion is interbreeding:

If two different organisms cannot interbreed (they cannot produce healthy and fertile offspring), then they are not the same species.

This statement is clear-cut and applies to any organism that reproduces sexually. You would think that the inverse would also be true: If two different organisms can interbreed, then they are always the same species. Unfortunately, this isn't the case. For instance, donkeys and horses are different species, but they can interbreed - the result is a mule. But in this and most other cases, while the two different species can produce healthy offspring, those offspring are usually infertile. Mules can't reproduce.

Other examples of different species that can interbreed and actually produce fertile offspring include:

• Lions and tigers
• Wolves and dogs
• Canadian lynx and bobcat
• Polar bear and grizzly bear

So if two species can interbreed and yet are clearly different in size, coloration, or whatever, why not just call them subspecies? The answer is that scientists who classify organisms into different groupings base their decisions on lots of different factors, only one of which concerns whether two groups can interbreed. Another, more important criterion is whether the two groups will interbreed. For instance, the natural habitats of lions and tigers don't overlap. Thus, there aren't any ligers in the wild because tigers and lions never see each other. Ligers do exist, but only in zoos where tigers and lions are forced into the same environment. In other cases, two different species may interact, but may not find one another particularly attractive (or whatever counts for "attractive" in the wild). They could technically interbreed, but they choose not to.

The only cases in which two species can interbreed are when they are both part of the same genus. Genus is a taxonomic classification that is one step broader than species, but one step narrower than family. A genus can contain multiple species, and a family can contain multiple genera. Below is an example of the full classification for tigers and lions:

	Lion	Tiger
Kingdom	Animalia	Animalia
Phylum	Chordata	Chordata
Class	Mammalia	Mammalia
Order	Carnivora	Carnivora
Family	Felidae	Felidae
Genus	Panthera	Panthera
Species	Leo	Tigris

The fact that both lions and tigers are classified in the genus Panthera is an indication that scientists believe that they are closely related. From a strictly phenotypical view, this means that lions and tigers are very similar in terms of biological structure, appearance, physiology, function, etc. Many folks in the Theistic Paradigm are content with this descriptive use of the modern classification system. However, from an evolutionary view, the fact that lions and tigers are part of the same genus means that they are believed by those in the Organic Paradigm to have descended from a common ancestor at some point in the (relatively) recent past. Given that the habitats of lions and tigers don't overlap, it should be no surprise to you that geographic isolation is assumed to have been at work in the evolutionary process of turning a single group of cat-like creatures into two subspecies, and then into the two separate species Leo and Tigris.

The time required for one species to split into two separate species is a matter of some contention among evolutionary biologists. Broadly, there are two ideas: gradualism and punctuated equilibrium. In gradualism, the changes occur gradually[18], with every group of organisms being in a constant state of phenotypic change. A new species would be the result of the continuous accumulation of tiny change upon tiny change over very long periods. Under gradualism, it would typically take a few million years for one species to develop into two species, though scientists have estimated that for some organisms it might be possible in only a few hundred thousand years.

In punctuated equilibrium, there are long periods of time when a species changes very little, and then short periods of time when the changes are dramatic and result in the formation of new species. These "sudden" changes would occur on much shorter timescales than expected under gradualism, with some estimates as short as tens of thousands of years. I talk a bit more about punctuated equilibrium in Chapter 13 in the context of the fossil record.

Step 4

The last step needs very little explanation. Once two groups of organisms can no longer produce fertile offspring, then they are going to respond independently to whatever additional selection pressures may exist, and they will adapt in different ways (again, assuming one or both doesn't go extinct). In short, they can continue to evolve away from one another. Organisms that are in the same genus, and thus are considered to be very closely related, may become less closely related over time. They may in fact evolve into completely distinct families of organisms. Give them even more time, and they may further diverge into separate orders and classes.

The relationships between species are often shown pictorially using a "tree of life" (though "bush of life" would probably be more descriptive). Even before Darwin's time, biologists had been mapping the relationships between organisms in this way. The first such drawings were meant only to show how organisms seemed to change from one stratigraphic layer (fancy geological term for a layer of rock that is estimated to be of a particular age)

---

[18] Duh.

to another. But over the last 150 years, trees of life have become a basic tool of evolutionary biologists to show how various species are believed to be related and to have descended from common ancestors. These trees can take on several different forms. For instance, some trees merely show how various species that exist today are related in terms of their taxonomic classifications (species, genus, family, etc). Other trees are designed to identify when a given species first appeared in the fossil record, and when extinctions occurred. Still other trees include blank spaces to mark the existence of an unidentified species (so-called "missing links") that are theorized to have existed.

A complete tree of life would be unwieldy if you tried to include every one of the known 1.6 million species that exist today or are known from the fossil record. So, biologists either look at only one very small part of the tree at a time (such as the family Felidae, which includes all 41 species of cats that exist today as well as numerous extinct cats), or they use a tree that leaves out a lot of the detail. Below is an example of the latter type of tree.

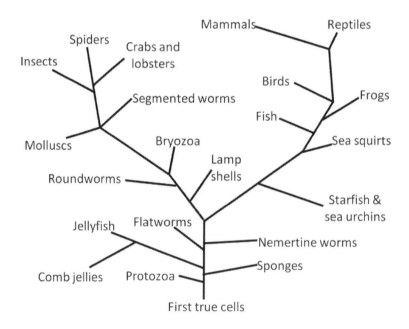

Chapter 12

Limitations In The Theory Of Evolution

The theory of evolution has a lot going for it. In addition to having a certain logic, scientists have a reasonably good (though not always detailed and precise) understanding of the three basic components of the theory of evolution:

- How genetic mutations occur, and how often

- How DNA produces different phenotypes

- How environments automatically sort the individuals in a group so that the most fit (i.e. those best adapted to their environment) are most likely to survive and thus reproduce

There is good experimental evidence that evolution occurs in microorganisms. For more complex organisms, the available evidence is at least broadly consistent with what one would expect from natural selection acting on phenotypic variations produced by random genetic mutations. For many in the Organic Paradigm, evolution is an open and shut case.

But in reality it's not quite as straightforward as that. Nearly every demonstrated example of natural selection acting on variations in phenotype within a group of organisms is simple and straightforward: a single trait X is favored over others due to the influence of a single environmental factor Y. By their very nature it is these examples that are the easiest to find, study, and understand. Unfortunately, the real world is filled with complex systems, and the whole of the debate over whether and to what degree evolution is true depends on whether the proposed mechanism behind evolution can be said to be true for the complex systems of which the real world is made. To further compound the problem, there are almost no cases in which someone has observed a genetic mutation occurring, then observed that genetic mutation producing a benefit to the organism, and finally observed natural selection choosing the organism with the beneficial mutation over organisms that do not have that same genetic mutation.

How well do we understand how particular phenotypes in the real world came to be so well adapted to their environments? In short, not very well. It's one thing to point to a specific phenotypic trait and describe how it benefits the organism vis-a-vis a particular environmental factor (an eagle's keen eyesight helps it to spot prey very far away, etc). But while there are lots of such examples, there are substantially more examples of phenotypic traits that we can't actually explain in terms of fitness or adaptability - we don't know why it is the way it is.

For instance, consider the robin's orange breast feathers. What is it about the robin's environment that makes an orange breasted robin more fit - better adapted - than, say, a green-breasted robin? You might guess that robins prefer orange breasts over green ones when it comes to choosing a mate, but that just begs the question of what the fitness advantage might be of such a preference. Or you might guess that orange is an indicator of the overall health of a robin, such that females choose males on the basis of how healthy they look. But of course any coloration could serve this purpose: bright colors mean healthy, dull colors mean not healthy. So we're back to the original question: why is the robin's breast orange? At this point no one knows.

The extrapolation of conclusions drawn from simple cases to more complex cases that are more difficult or even impossible to study directly is a common approach to understanding the world in all scientific disciplines. But in the case of evolution, there are a number of things that make such extrapolations more challenging. Before describing some of these challenges, let me first summarize how this issue of extrapolation from the simple to the complex might be viewed from the Organic and Theistic Paradigms.

Organic Paradigm

Complex systems are composed of all the same fundamental pieces that simple systems are composed of. There are simply more of them in complex systems. So, for instance, while a mouse has thousands of phenotypic traits, every single one is the product of genes that can be affected by random genetic mutations. Moreover, while that mouse lives in a particular environment that is defined by thousands of individual factors, each environmental factor exerts some sort of selection pressure on each trait. The number of ways that thousands of phenotypic traits can interact with thousands of environmental factors may be immense and the nature of all those interactions may not currently be quantifiable or even identifiable, but there is nothing fundamentally different between those complex interactions and the simple interactions demonstrated by much simpler systems (for instance, a microorganism affected by one change in its environment). Since we have a very good understanding of these simpler systems, it is perfectly legitimate to extrapolate the conclusions drawn from simple systems to the more complex systems that exist in the real world.

Theistic Paradigm

Science has yet to uncover how complex biological systems really work. If it were otherwise, there would be no reason to extrapolate from the study of simple interactions between one phenotypic trait and one environmental factor to the complex systems that make up real life. Complex structures by their very nature cannot be understood merely as the summation of many simple parts. In complex biological systems, the whole is greater than the sum of the parts. We know this to be true of complex molecules, whose properties and functions cannot be defined merely as the sum of the properties and functions of the individual atoms of which those molecules are composed. It is no different in biological systems, which after all are comprised of a multitude of complex molecules. While we understand the basic biochemistry of life, we do not understand how all the individual interactions between phenotypic traits and environmental factors operate together and at the same time. Therefore, it is premature at best and illegitimate at worst to extrapolate the conclusions drawn from simple systems to the more complex systems that exist in the real world.

These two viewpoints can be summarized in the following question: is the complexity inherent in the real world truly just a matter of degree, or instead is it a matter of kind? Those in the Organic Paradigm would say it is merely a matter of degree; the fundamental principles at work in evolution are the same in both simple and complex systems. Those in the Theistic Paradigm would say that it is both a matter of degree and of kind; whatever the mechanism may be for simple systems, there is something additional, or something different, going on in complex systems.

To get at the issue of whether and to what degree it is legitimate to extrapolate from simple cases to complex, real-world cases, it's important to know more about some of the quirks of the relationships between genotypes, phenotypes, and environments.

Consider the single phenotypic trait of organism size. While there are a number of ways that an organism's size might interact with its environment, one that is commonly discussed is the connection between size and climate, particularly temperature. The reason for this is that the relationship between size and temperature might be expected to follow some well-known heat transfer mechanisms:

- The rate at which heat is lost from a hot object to a cold environment is proportional to the surface area of the object

- The rate at which heat is generated in an object (through chemical reactions, for instance) is proportional to the volume of the object

Basic geometry tells us that the larger an object is, the smaller the ratio of its surface area to its volume. Putting this together with the above heat-transfer facts, you can conclude that a large object will retain heat longer than a small object. For organisms in the real world, then, you might expect that those living in colder environments will in general be larger than those living in warmer environments, since being large helps an organism to endure the cold.

In an excellent example of physics predicting biology, this trend between temperature and size occurs frequently in nature. A well-known example is the observation that polar bears living in the arctic are considerably larger than black bears living in Canada and the U.S. Study after study has confirmed that this trend occurs more often than not among animals.

But what are we to make of the cases in which it does not occur? For instance, while turtles seem to follow the expected trend, snakes actually seem to follow the opposite trend (smaller sizes in colder temperatures). The largest land mammal on earth, the African elephant, lives in one of the hottest places on earth. If there is such a strong correlation between size and temperature that can be supported by simple physics, how do we explain the environmental factors that lead to the opposite result? Certainly we can make logical guesses: being larger make keep you warm, but it may also make it more difficult to run from predators, or to climb trees, or to fly. But the net result is still that we aren't in a position to explain how, in any particular case, an organism's size was determined through a natural selection process.

My point is that, even with the simplest cases, it may be next to impossible to sort out why a particular phenotypic trait was selected by its environment. Moreover, real life isn't about a single phenotypic trait (e.g. size) being selected for by a single environmental factor (e.g. temperature). The real world is thousands of phenotypic traits interacting with thousands of environmental factors. It's complex, but not merely complex. It's complex in ways we can't yet define. It's inarticulately complex.

Recall in Chapter 5 how I presented the basic ideas behind science, and how theories develop. Theories are testable, in that you should be able to make a prediction about something, do some kind of research or investigation or experiment, and determine if your theory has been upheld or not. The theory of evolution certainly lends itself to this process, but not in the way that you might expect.

In the hard sciences (e.g. physics or chemistry), theories are typically based on precise numerical data and are used to make specific predictions about experiments that are highly repeatable. They typically involve only a few, easily identified variables, making it easier to infer specific causative effects (this caused that). For theories in the hard sciences, you should be able to predict the outcome of an experiment with a high degree of accuracy.

The theory of evolution, in contrast, involves an uncountable number of variables, and is rarely used to make predictions about the outcome of a particular organism subjected to an array of selection pressures within a realistic environment. Instead, most predictions based on the theory of evolution involve what sorts of fossils one might find based on expectations from the tree of life, or what sorts of genes might be expected within the genome of a particular organism given its relationship to other organisms.[19] While there are certainly laboratory experiments that have been used to test the theory of evolution, they always involve variations in a single environmental factor, and most often involve microorganisms.

In some ways, the theory of evolution is similar to economic theory. Economists know an awful lot about the mechanisms that are theorized to be at work in economies, and may be able to provide plausible explanations for why something in particular has occurred in the past. But predicting the future of the economy is something else entirely. There have been many attempts to create complex mathematical models designed to process massive amounts of data and make predictions. But if such models really worked, the economists would be a whole lot richer than they are. The fact that they can't predict the future with any reasonable precision makes all of us non-economists wonder if they really understand the mechanisms behind economies after all. Isn't the proof in the pudding? If they can't predict the future of the economy, how can we be sure that explanations that they offer for past events in the economy are really the correct ones? In short, there's no way to know. The explanations economists give for past events are plausible narratives, and they seem reasonable to the rest of us non-economists who have no alternative but to trust the experts.

A similar situation exists for the theory of evolution. For all the understanding of genetics and biology and natural selection, the theory of evolution is almost entirely explanatory, not predictive. That is, it provides an explanation for why something happened in the past, a plausible narrative that appears to fit the facts, but it can say almost nothing about what will happen in the future. Apart

---

[19] Some folks in the Theistic Paradigm view this as circular reasoning: Fossils are used to develop the theory, and then fossils are used to verify that the theory is correct. While this is true to some degree, the original concept developed by Charles Darwin was based less on fossils and more on observations of living organisms in natural habitats, and artificial selection.

from rare situations like the physics-based correlation between organism size and temperature, which may or may not actually apply in any particular situation, there are no algorithms which indicate what kinds of selection pressures might be placed on a particular phenotype by a specified set of environmental factors, nor what the outcome of those selection pressures might be.

The primary reason for this is that what the theory of evolution offers is not specific mechanisms, but rather general processes. A specific mechanism is something that provides a direct link between a set variables such as one might find in physical or chemical laws. They always work the same way all the time. When two billiard balls strike at such-and-such an angle, conservation of momentum dictates that ball A will go this way and ball B will go that way. General processes, in contrast, provide trends, probabilities, generalizations. The basic description of evolution - natural selection acting on phenotypic variation brought about through random genetic mutations - is quite general in nature.

Textbooks are full of very clear, documented examples of environmental selection processes that have chosen particular phenotypic traits, and this makes it seem as though scientists understand exactly how it works. However, these are all historical explanations that, while they may reasonably fit the facts, are not as strong as they might seem. For any one of those textbooks examples, one could reasonably ask "Why did things turn out the way that they did instead of some other way?" In nearly every single case, the theory of evolution is simply not robust enough to answer this question. The construction of plausible evolution narratives based on the available evidence is illustrated more in Chapter 15 for birds, whales, and horses.

The lack of specificity in the theory of evolution opens the door to yet another issue.

One of the hallmarks of the theory of evolution is that all phenotypic traits are the result of adaptations to an environment. However, there is increasing evidence that this may not be true. Consider the machine-in-a-box example from Chapter 10. As before, a box contains a random object-producing machine and some sort of filter that determines which objects come out of the box. But as a twist, this time imagine that all the spheres being generated by the random object-producing machine are white, and that all the cubes that it produces are black.

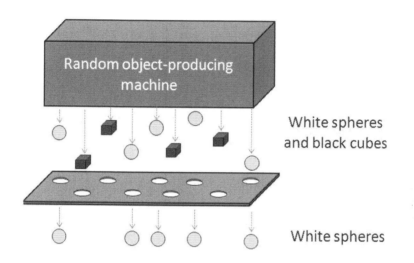

Before opening the box and peering inside, all you know is that white spheres are exiting the box. If you were told that the machine is actually producing both white spheres and black cubes, you could reasonably conclude that the box contains some sort of filter that only allows white spheres to exit. However, you would be left with a conundrum: Is the filter sorting for color or shape? If the filter is allowing only sphere-shaped objects to pass through, then the color white is coming along for the ride. If, however, the filter is allowing only white objects to pass through, then the sphere shape is coming along for the ride. One of the traits is being chosen (analogous to adaptation through natural selection) while the other is a free-rider. The free-rider isn't an adaptation at all.

In this particular example, you can peer into the box and determine which of the two types of filters you have: the filter is choosing for object shape, which means that color is a free-rider trait. But in real life, this is almost never the case. We don't know which traits are being chosen by natural selection and which traits are free-riders. Worse, we don't know the relative frequency of traits that are chosen by natural selection versus traits that are free-riders. Are the majority of an organism's phenotypic traits chosen by natural selection, with only a minority being free-riders? Or is it the other way around? Just how much of an organism's phenotype is really the direct the result of natural selection?

Scientists have known for a long time that phenotypic traits can be linked together. It's called pleiotropy, and occurs when one gene has a connection to multiple traits. In the case of a gene that codes for a single protein, that protein may play multiple roles in different tissues or organs. Other parts of DNA operate as control centers or switches that determine how the organism develops from the beginning of its existence as a fertilized egg, and these switches can affect multiple traits at once.

While it is likely that every gene is pleiotropic to some extent, pleiotropy is difficult to measure, and the networks of interconnected traits that it produces are currently only poorly understood. Nevertheless, there are a number of documented examples. For instance, in sheep, animal weight and the amount of fleece they produce are linked. Similarly, in some flowers size and color are linked. In fruit flies, wing development and egg development are linked.

In the arena of artificial selection, pleiotropy can sometimes be directly observed. About 50 years ago, researchers in Siberia attempted to selectively breed silver foxes to be more domestic. With each new litter, they specifically selected those foxes that seemed to connect best with humans, and ensured that only those foxes bred. After only nine generations, they achieved their goal of developing a completely domesticated fox, as friendly as any dog. But this selective breeding process came with a surprise: they had floppy ears, tails that curled up, and darker fur. The wild foxes had no such traits. The domesticated foxes also whined and wagged their tails in response to a human presence, behaviors never seen in wild foxes. In short, selective breeding for one particular trait brought with it a number of other free-rider traits that had in fact not been selected for at all. It's not clear where those free rider traits came from, since they aren't exhibited among wild foxes. Presumably the potential for those traits was hidden away in the fox's original DNA, and only manifested when they were drawn out through the artificial selection process. This despite the fact that the artificial selection was not aimed at producing fixes with floppy ears and curled tails.

This example with artificial selection in foxes raises the possibility that something similar might occur in natural selection. Traits that lie dormant in an organism's DNA might manifest themselves under the appropriate selection pressure, even though natural selection is not actually choosing those traits. The robin's orange breast, for instance, might have nothing to do with the robin's fitness at all, but may instead have been a dormant trait whose manifestation is inexplicable. Currently, scientists are unable to say how much of any given organism's phenotype is an adaptation produced through natural selection, and how much is the result of the activation of dormant genes through the free-rider process. In short, there are good reasons to think that the current form of the theory of evolution - natural selection acting on phenotypic variations produced by random genetic mutations - is at a minimum incomplete, and at the extreme might be in need of an overhaul.

With that diversion into some oddities in the relationship between genotypes, phenotypes, and environments, let me return to the issue of extrapolating from simple cases to more complex ones.

Extrapolations are always risky. By definition they require that we make assumptions about things that we understand poorly, based on the things that we understand well. The legitimacy of extrapolations is a function of how strong the data is and how far into the unknown you want to stretch that data. You can visualize it mathematically like this:

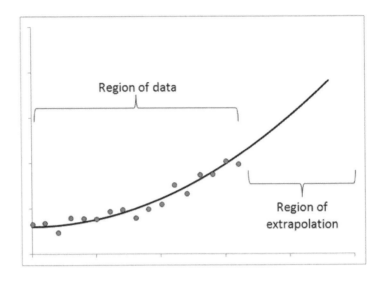

In general, if you have nothing else to go on, an extrapolation can be a reasonable way to guesstimate[20] how things might behave in regions where you have little or no data. But extrapolations can be called into question if new data doesn't fall where you think it should, like this:

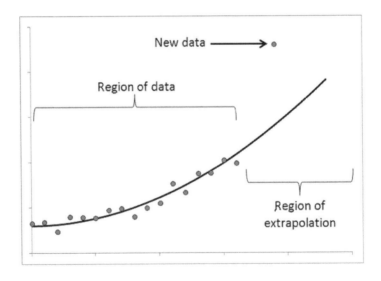

---

[20] It's a real word. I looked it up.

In such cases, it may not be clear if the extrapolation has been invalidated or not. Maybe the new data isn't accurate. Or maybe the new data is accurate, but represents a special case. Maybe the extrapolation is still valid, but the confidence placed in its accuracy has been diminished. And maybe the original extrapolation is just plain wrong.

In the context of the theory of evolution, the proposed mechanism of natural selection acting on phenotypic variation generated by random genetic mutations has been extrapolated from simple cases we can understand and observe to much more complex cases that are, currently, out of reach of modern science. In the absence of an alternative mechanism, this is a reasonable application of scientific principles. But since the complexity of the real world makes it nearly impossible to determine whether those mechanisms actually operate as one might expect, this sort of extrapolation must be taken with a grain of salt. Add to this the fact that some phenotypic traits are merely free-riders and are not actually the result of natural selection, and a reasonable person could legitimately question how thoroughly the proposed mechanism explains the evolution of life on earth.

Chapter 13

The Fossil Record

You can't talk about evolution without talking about fossils. It was fossils that spurred the idea of evolution decades before Darwin's *Origin of Species*, and the hunt for and study of fossils has been the primary tool of scientists studying evolution in the 150 years since. Without the fossil record, the theory of evolution would be much, much weaker.

Both Theistic and Organic Paradigms generally agree that fossils represent real organisms that lived in the distant past. While there remain some parties in the Theistic Paradigm who argue that fossils were never live organisms, but instead are merely rocks created by God or manipulated by Satan to test our faith, this view is in the minority.

But while there is widespread agreement about what fossil are, the Theistic and Organic Paradigms generally disagree about most other things related to fossils. These disagreements generally fall into two areas:

1. How well phenotypes of extinct organisms can be reconstructed from fossil evidence

2. What fossils can tell us about how organisms are related to one another

With regard to #1, folks in the Theistic Paradigm are generally less comfortable than those in the Organic Paradigm with hypothesizing about the phenotypes of fossil organisms. This is understandable, since most fossilized organisms are fragmentary - maybe just a few bones. Though some fossils preserve soft tissues, feathers, scales, and the like, most only preserve the hardest parts of an organism: bones, teeth, shells, etc. In some cases a fossil organism may be conveniently arranged to make all parts visible, but in many other cases fossil remains are jumbled and indistinct. Finally, while in some cases there are thousands of fossils of the same organism, in other cases there may be only one.

Folks in the Organic Paradigm take an "educated guess" approach to phenotypes of extinct organisms in which all the information collected from a given fossil is used to construct a best guess as to what the original organism looked like, how it moved, what environment it likely lived in, etc. These descriptions invariably include some conjecture and maybe outright speculation as well, but this generally does not concern those in the Organic Paradigm since the general understanding is that all conclusions are provisional. That is, if more information is discovered, the description of the phenotype of the organism will simply be adjusted. For this reason, folks in the Organic Paradigm typically see no harm in making guesses about the phenotypes of extinct organisms.

For those in the Theistic Paradigm, however, there is indeed harm in making guesses because the phenotype of an extinct organism has implications beyond just biology. This is why it is not uncommon for someone in the Theistic Paradigm to pose an alternative view about the phenotype of a fossil organism that challenges the prevailing view. Even if only a minority of scientists agree with the alternative view, it can be a legitimate scientific contribution to the debate since the prevailing view is only one of the possibilities and is typically based on incomplete data.

With regard to #2 above (what fossils can tell us about how organisms are related to one another), the disagreement between the Theistic and Organic Paradigms often comes down to what the word "related" means. In the Theistic Paradigm, two organisms are more closely related if they have a similar phenotype, and are less closely related if their phenotypes are different. Such distinctions have nothing to do with whether one organism evolved from another - they are merely a result of comparing and contrasting phenotypes. For this reason, many in the Theistic Paradigm are comfortable with placing a given fossil organism in a phylogenetic tree of life as a way of describing and categorizing it.

For those in the Organic Paradigm, however, describing a fossil organism is more than just how similar or different it is from other organisms, living or extinct. The primary goal of the Organic Paradigm is to develop explicitly evolutionary connections - which organism evolved from which. These evolutionary relationships are established on the basis of not only the reconstructed phenotypes, but also the relative age of the two organisms, where they were found, and the type of environment in which they lived. Since the fossil record is notoriously incomplete, it is rare that a paleontologist is able to identify two fossil organisms that he can confidently say represent a parent and daughter (i.e. one evolved directly from the other). Much more frequently he is forced to place the two organisms in different genera within the same family, or even different families within the same order.

Despite the many gaps in the fossil record, there are many broad trends. This was true even in the decades before Darwin published *Origin of Species* when geology and paleontology were just picking up steam and new discoveries were being made on a regular basis. In 1841, about 20 years before Darwin's Origins, John Phillips developed the first systematic categorization of layers of rock that had formed in different time periods.[21] He identified and named three "eras" that were based on how deep the rock was and what sorts of fossils were found there:

Deepest layers: Paleozoic era, "The age of fish"

Not-so-deep layers: Mesozoic era, "The age of reptiles"

Shallowest layers: Cenozoic era, "The age of mammals"

---

[21] This is one of the only history lessons in this book, I promise.

This was the beginning of stratigraphy, the geologic science of distinguishing between different layers of rock based on certain characteristics that are unique to each layer. The labels associated with the different layers of rock have become synonymous with specific time periods in earth's history. In the 170+ years since John Phillips published his description of the three eras, geologists have continued to expand the stratigraphic descriptions. In addition to adding one more time period to Phillips' original three, the Precambrian which represents the oldest known rocks, geologists have subdivided Phillips' three eras into a dozen periods, thirty-eight epochs, and about 100 ages based on techniques that have grown progressively more precise.

Fun fact to impress your friends: The Michael Crichton book *Jurassic Park* was supposedly based on the dinosaurs that existed in the Jurassic period of the Mesozoic era. However, both of the star carnivores of the movie, tyrannosaurus rex and velociraptor, are actually from the more recent Cretaceous period, not the Jurassic. Maybe Cretaceous Park didn't have the same ring to it.

At the time that John Phillips proposed his three eras, geologists had a basic understanding about how sedimentary rocks formed, and had theorized about how long it would have taken. The general consensus was that it would have taken a long time, certainly longer than thousands of years. But most attempts to actually date the layers were little more than educated guesswork, and radioisotope dating was a long way off. So, all that John Phillips really knew was that the deepest layers were the oldest, and the shallowest layers were the youngest.

But even without knowing the age of the rock layers, early paleontologists made important observations about the fossils that were found in those layers, and these observations persist today:

1. Most species of plants and animals that exist as fossils do not exist as living plants and animals today.

2. Species of plants and animals that are alive today are less and less likely to show up in the fossil record the deeper you dig.

3. Different types of fossils are found in different rock layers.

4. The oldest fossils of plants and animals, found in the deepest layers of rock, are simpler in form and structure than more recent fossils of plants and animals which are found in shallower layers of rock.

These four observations have been very consistent since the science of paleontology began, and there is little disagreement among Theistic Paradigm and Organic Paradigm folks about them.

To get a better picture of points 3 and 4 above, below is a chart showing the sorts of organisms that can be found in different layers of rock.

Era	Period	Million years ago	Invertebrates	Jawless fish	Bony fish	Amphibians	Reptiles	Dinosaurs	Mammals	Birds	Primates
	Pre-Cambrian	2500	•								
Paleozoic	Cambrian	543	•	•							
Paleozoic	Ordovician	490	•	•	•						
Paleozoic	Silurian	443	•	•	•						
Paleozoic	Devonian	417	•	•	•	•					
Paleozoic	Carboniferous	354	•	•	•	•	•				
Paleozoic	Permian	290	•	•	•	•	•	•			
Mesozoic	Triassic	248	•	•	•	•	•	•	•		
Mesozoic	Jurassic	206	•	•	•	•	•	•	•	•	
Mesozoic	Cretaceous	144	•	•	•	•	•	•	•	•	
Cenozoic	Tertiary	65	•	•	•	•	•		•	•	•
Cenozoic	Quaternary	1.8	•	•	•	•	•		•	•	•

It's difficult not to see the expansion of the types of organisms over time, from the simplest water-bound organisms in the oldest fossils to the appearance of primates in the most recent fossils. It's worth spending some time looking more closely at this trend.

The oldest fossils are of invertebrates that all lived in water. There were no fish, no whales, no sharks, not even in miniature form. Nor was there anything that could have lived on land. Everything was either entirely soft-bodied - think jellyfish, starfish, worms - or had a hard shell - think crabs and lobsters. The oldest known vertebrate having an internal skeleton like ours is

Haikouichthys[22], a 2-inch fish without fins or a jaw that appears in the Cambrian period. Prior to Haikouichthys, the fossil record shows many different types of organisms, but nothing with a backbone.

After the more complex "bony" fish that had jaws appear in the fossil record in the Ordovician period, amphibians show up. Today amphibians are represented by frogs and salamanders. Amphibians can move about on land, but they must always be near water because their skin is delicate and can dry out quickly. In a broad sense, amphibians are somewhere between fish and reptiles, somewhere between organisms that live in the water and organisms that live on land.

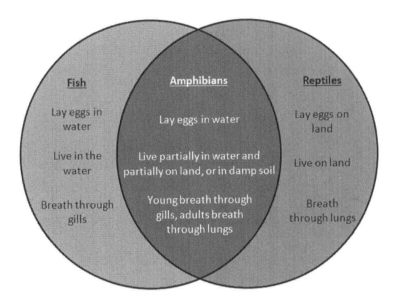

The next group of organisms to appear in the fossil record are reptiles in the Carboniferous period. Many reptiles have a similar body design to amphibians, but their skin is tough and waterproof, allowing them to live entirely on land. There are telltale differences in the vertebral columns of amphibians and reptiles that

---

[22] Challenge: Say that three times fast.

make them relatively easy to tell apart based only on their bones. Reptiles lay eggs like amphibians, but those eggs have hard shells that can survive in dry conditions. Thus while amphibian eggs must be laid in water, reptile eggs can be laid on land.

After reptiles come every 3rd-grade boy's fascination: dinosaurs. The primary difference between dinosaurs and reptiles is that dinosaurs stand erect with their legs under their body, whereas the legs of reptiles stick out to either side of the body. Without this body form, dinosaurs could not have supported the enormous weights that some of them achieved. For instance, the largest land animal that lives today, the African elephant, can weigh up to 7 tons. Compare that to Argentinosaurus, which lived in the Cretaceous period and which is estimated to have reached 90 tons. That's like thirteen elephants glued together.

Mammals do not appear in the fossil record before the Triassic period, long after dinosaurs first appear. While the most obvious difference between mammals and reptiles/dinosaurs is fur versus smooth or scaly skin, there are two other differences that are actually more significant. The first is that mammals don't lay eggs but instead carry their young with them until birth.[23] The young are more protected as a result. Second, mammals have several different kinds of teeth, whereas each species of dinosaur had just one kind. Dinosaur teeth were only good for one thing: either tearing so that they could swallow chunks of meat and bone whole, or grinding so that they could eat plants. Mammals, with their multiple kinds of teeth, were able to both tear and grind their food, making it easier to eat a variety of different types of food and to digest that food more efficiently.

Birds and primates appear most recently in the fossil record. Since these two groups have been the focus of many disagreements between the Theistic and Organic Paradigms, I discuss them in more depth in Chapters 15 and 16, respectively.

While the overall trend in the fossil record seems clear enough, there is one big problem that has plagued paleontologists since the

---

[23] Yes, I'm ignoring the platypus and spiny anteater, both of which are mammals that lay eggs. I talk about these exceptions a bit more in Chapter 14.

first fossils were discovered: the gradual change from one species to another that one would expect based on the theory of evolution doesn't actually show up in the fossil record. While there are a few examples of a series of fossil organisms that seem to show one species changing into another over time, in the vast majority of cases there is no such gradual change. Instead, individual species seem to appear suddenly in the fossil record, persist for a few million years, and then disappear suddenly. This persistence of a single species over long periods without notable changes in phenotype has been termed "stasis."

Organic and Theistic Paradigms interpret stasis differently. The Organic Paradigm points to the relative rarity of fossils in general and the narrow conditions under which they form, and concludes that the fossil record is simply incomplete. The transitional forms (sometimes loosely called "missing links") between species really do exist, but it is understandable that so few have been found. Some paleontologists within the Organic Paradigm have also suggested that species may appear suddenly in the fossil record not because the species came into existence suddenly, but because the species migrated from some unknown environment to the one in which the fossils were found.

The Theistic Paradigm, on the other hand, interprets the lack of transitional forms in the fossil record as evidence that no such forms exist. This approach takes the evidence (or in this case, the lack of evidence) at face value and makes no effort to construct an argument for why stasis appears to be inconsistent with the theory of evolution. Instead, stasis in the fossil record is taken as evidence that evolution does not occur.

While it is true that the fossil record overwhelming demonstrates stasis, transitional forms continue to be discovered on a regular basis, and they have helped to fill in the many gaps between species in the tree of life. Some of these transitional forms are discussed in Chapter 14. Nevertheless, it is extremely unlikely that the fossil record will ever produce enough direct evidence to make the tree of life complete, assuming that all the transitional forms that are posited to have existed did in fact exist. For the vast majority of organisms, even Organic Paradigm folks admit that step-by-step examples of gradual evolutionary changes will never be found.

But what if there was a biological mechanism that actually supported stasis in the context of the theory of evolution? What if the gradual changes presumed in the theory of evolution were the exception, and stasis in the fossil record is exactly what you would expect to find?

Enter punctuated equilibrium.

Based on the study of trilobites, invertebrates that are extremely common in the fossil record and which persisted from the Cambrian period all the way through the Permian period, scientists in the 1970's concluded that evolution did not in fact continue at the same rate all the time. Instead, it was "punctuated" - long periods of relative stability in phenotypes followed by short bursts of phenotypic change. The short bursts seemed to occur over very short time periods (in geologic terms) of thousands to tens of thousands of years. These bursts would be too short to be captured in the fossil record.

Punctuated equilibrium fits the fossil record very well. The trick, of course, is developing a biological mechanism to explain why punctuated equilibrium makes sense. Without such an explanation, punctuated equilibrium is little more than a statement that the stasis observed in the fossil record is what one would expect, which could amount to circular reasoning (stasis in the fossil record is due to punctuated equilibrium, and the proof that punctuated equilibrium is true is the stasis observed in the fossil record).

The details of the proposed mechanism behind punctuated equilibrium are messy, but here is the short version:

Organisms always have some limited ability to adapt to their environments without a change in their phenotype. For instance, an animal may sweat or pant when it enters a hotter environment, which helps it to stay cool. The animal's phenotype may not be optimized for the hotter environment, but it can survive and reproduce. This limited adaptability means that many organisms may be able to maintain the same phenotype over long periods of time even if their environment changes, so long as those environmental changes are not too severe. If the environment does change in a dramatic way, some threshold may be crossed wherein a species either goes through a rapid period of phenotypic change, or simply cannot adapt and goes extinct.

Closely related to this limited adaptability that is inherent in all organisms is the notion of reproductive isolation that was discussed in Chapter 11. Under punctuated equilibrium, reproductive isolation is not merely a footnote to the evolutionary process, but instead takes center stage.

A given group of organisms of the same species is continually splitting into subgroups, which then tend to drift apart geographically. As a result, each of of these subgroups experiences different environments and thus different selection pressures. These subgroups can use their limited adaptability to persist in their new environments, and if they stay in those new environments long enough, the limited adaptability can become "fixed" into more optimized phenotypes. At that point the different subgroups becomes subspecies, distinct from one another in some ways but still able to interbreed. However, if some form of reproductive isolation interferes, the different subspecies may cease to have contact with one another, eliminating any chances to interbreed. Given enough time, the different subspecies will continue to diverge from each other phenotypically until they are different species.

In short, punctuated equilibrium posits that one species does not slowly turn into another species in a gradual fashion. Instead, every species is continually splitting into subspecies, and these subspecies persist in different environments until and unless the environmental pressures cross some threshold. At that point, some of the subspecies simply die out while others undergo rapid change and survive.

Yes, that was the short version of punctuated equilibrium. Be thankful I didn't give you the long version.

Punctuated equilibrium certainly helps to explain stasis in the fossil record, but there are also some problems with it. For instance, while it posits that long periods of stasis followed by short periods of phenotypic change are to be expected, the random generation of genetic variation does not work this way. Recall that random genetic mutations are the source of phenotypic variation on which natural selection acts. But genetic mutations occur at a steady rate that do not vary dramatically over time - no long periods of genetic stability followed by short periods of dramatic mutation. There have been attempts to explain this mismatch between the steady rate of genetic mutations and the decidedly non-steady rate of species change in the fossil record, but they are by and large theoretical.

Another problem with punctuated equilibrium is that it relies entirely on observations of the fossil record. There is little about the idea that can actually be tested in a laboratory. In particular, the idea that a species may retain the same phenotype over long periods, and then suddenly and rapidly evolve, is not something that anyone has any idea how to test. In fact, all the cases that are typically cited as evidence for evolution but which don't rely on the fossil record (such as the studies involving micro-organisms cited in Chapter 9) never demonstrate stasis. Instead, they demonstrate natural selection working to actually change phenotypes of an organism. There has been little progress in explaining why stasis appears in the fossil record but not in any real-life examples.

Finally, the idea of a threshold presents its own problems. If organisms can adapt to some environmental changes without phenotypic change until some sort of threshold is reached, what defines that threshold? In other words, what forms the dividing line between stasis and sudden (in geologic terms) evolution? No one is really sure. Moreover, it's not clear from the fossil record that this threshold, whatever it may be, is even definable - it seems to be very different for different organisms in different circumstances. There is evidence in the fossil record that some organisms endured for long periods without phenotypic change despite dramatic environmental changes that seem to exceed any reasonable threshold.

When it comes to evidence for or against evolution, stasis in the fossil record and the attempt to explain it through the idea of punctuated equilibrium typically put Theistic Paradigm folks on the offensive and Organic Paradigm folks on the defensive. However, the fossil record does in fact provide some examples of transitions from one type of organism to another as described in Chapter 14.

Chapter 14

Transitions Between Different Species

Any reasonable and objective person[24] scrutinizing the theory of evolution should expect to see evidence of transitions from one species to another. The two most common types of evidence for these transitions are:

1. A series of fossils of progressively more recent age that demonstrates how one species evolved into another.

2. Remnants of the phenotype of an ancestral species in a living organism, commonly called vestigial structures.

While both kinds of evidence do exist and lend credence to the theory of evolution, they are also incomplete and, in some cases, ambiguous.

Transitions in the fossil record

The most famous of all transitions in the fossil record is probably the evolution of the horse, which I discuss in detail in Chapter 15. There are also examples of transitions from one species to another for mollusks, trilobites, and other organisms that thrived over very long spans of time and for which the fossil record

---

[24] If there is such a thing.

is particularly complete. Nevertheless, as compelling as these examples may be, they are the exception rather than the rule. If you were to pick any organism at random, one that is living today or is extinct, and ask to see the ancestral species that immediately preceded it, you would most likely be disappointed. In some ways, the fossil record is both the greatest source of evidence to support the theory of evolution, and the most compelling reason to doubt it.

While a series of fossils depicting the evolution of one species into another is rare, there are many examples of fossils demonstrating transitions between classes of organisms. As described in Chapter 13, the general trend displayed in the fossil record in terms of the first appearance of organism types is roughly as follows:

Invertebrates → Fish → Amphibians → Reptiles → Mammals

The first transition, that of invertebrates to fish, would have required the development of a backbone to which muscles could attach, and a skull. A number of fossil organisms have been found that appear to contain transitional versions of these structures:

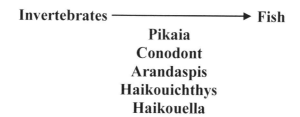

Invertebrates ⎯⎯⎯⎯⎯⎯⎯→ Fish
Pikaia
Conodont
Arandaspis
Haikouichthys
Haikouella

Interestingly, there are some organisms living today that also appear to have characteristics of both invertebrates and fish. These include hagfish which have a skull but no backbone, and lampreys which have a skeleton made of cartilage rather than bone, and no jaw at all.

The next transition that appears in the fossil record is that of fish to amphibians. This transition would have required the development of lungs for breathing air and limbs for moving about on land. Some of the fossil organisms that appear to have some of the characteristics of both fish and amphibians are shown below:

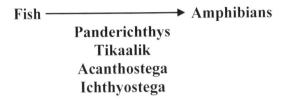

Organisms that live today which also appear somewhere between fish and amphibians include salamanders that can only live under water such as mudpuppies and sirens, and lungfish which are fish that can breath air in addition to being able to obtain oxygen from the water through gills. Lungfish can even use stiffened fins to push themselves along the ground for short distances.

The transition from amphibians to reptiles would have required the development of waterproof skin and eggs with tough shells that do not need to be laid in the water. There are also characteristics of reptile skeletons that differ from the skeletons of amphibians, particularly with regards to the backbone. Some of the fossil organisms that seem to bridge the gap between these two classes are shown below.

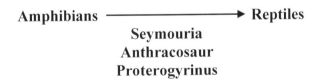

The next transition in the fossil record is from reptiles to mammals. Most mammals give birth to live young while reptiles lay eggs. Mammals are also typically covered with hair and have several different types of teeth that permit them to eat a wide variety of foods. Some of the fossil organisms that appear to fall somewhere between reptiles and mammals are shown below:

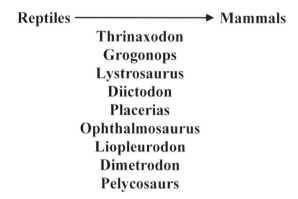

There are also some mammals living today that seem to have some reptilian characteristics, such as the spiny anteater and platypus which lay eggs, and hairless mammals such as elephants.

Vestigial structures

In addition to these transitional organisms, there are structures in some living organisms that appear to be remnants of past transitions from one species to another.   These "vestigial" structures either have no function, or limited functionality, or they function in ways that seem inconsistent with the type of structure. The case for a structure being vestigial typically involves a comparison to a similar structure in other organisms that do have a function.   This comparison of useless vestigial structures to similar, useful structures is often regarded as evidence that the vestigial structures lost their adaptive value at some point in the past, and over many generations simply degenerated, but have not yet disappeared altogether.

The most commonly cited vestigial structure is the human appendix. Many believe that the human appendix has no function since there is no evidence that its removal has any adverse affect on the body. If it truly has no function, then why is it there? From the Organic Paradigm, the answer is that the appendix is the useless remnant of an organ that once had a function. For instance, in plant-eating animals, the appendix is considerably larger and helps in digestion. However, there is some (as yet inconclusive) evidence that the human appendix may help to maintain the balance of bacteria in the intestine or is somehow associated with the immune system. Some in the Theistic Paradigm point to such functions as evidence that the human appendix is not a vestigial organ at all.

Another example is the eyes of certain animals that still exist but are nearly or completely useless. For instance, the blind mole rat does have eyes, but they are completely covered by skin - there are no eyelids that can open. The mole rat lives almost entirely underground where eyes are more or less useless. Another example is cavefish which live in complete darkness and which are blind. A particularly interesting example of these cavefish is the species astyanax mexicanus which has eyes while it is developing in the egg, but by the time it hatches the eyes have degenerated to a collapsed remnant of an eye covered by flap of skin - the eye of the hatchling is completely useless. Moreover, fish of the same species living outside of the cave where there is light have fully functioning eyes.[25]

One of the more profound examples of vestigial structures are the pelvic bones of whales. These bones are not connected to the vertebral column nor to any other bones as they are in other mammals, but instead float within the body cavity in approximately the position that a pelvis would be in a land mammal. From the Organic Paradigm perspective, these bones are taken to be all that is left of the pelvic bones of the whale's ancestor which is believed to have had rear legs and walked on land (see more on the evolution of the whale in Chapter 15).

While vestigial structures would seem to be straightforward evidence of a transition from one phenotype to another, the fact that many of them still have some sort of function means that their classification as "vestigial" is not obvious. The pelvic bones of the whale, for instance, provide an anchor for certain other organs, and they actually play a role in both copulation and defecation. The

---

[25] Both the blind and seeing versions are considered the same species because they are otherwise morphologically the same in all respects. Of course, the ability to see is a pretty big difference in morphology, so maybe they ought to be considered different species.

bones themselves don't look exactly like a pelvic girdle either - they appear to lack the ilium and pubis, two of three main parts of a typical mammalian pelvis - and they actually include an odd extra piece of bone that would not normally be seen in a mammalian pelvis. This extra piece of bone makes the overall structure appear even less like a pelvis. Some have interpreted it as a small femur (upper leg bone) that has fused with the pelvis. The question, then, is whether whale pelvic bones should be interpreted as vestigial structures, or instead as just another functional aspect of whale morphology, no different than any other aspect of its musculoskeleton.

Or take the blind mole rat. Its eyes may be small and hidden under skin, but the rat isn't totally blind - its eyes can detect light and dark. Its eyes might be useful in those rare instances when the rat needs to repair parts of its tunnels that have opened to the air and made it possible for predators to enter.

Other structures commonly identified as vestigial have similar issues. The wings of flightless birds such as ostriches and emus might be useless for flight, but they can be used for balance, mating displays, and cooling. The tiny legs of some skinks may be far to small to carry the creature's weight, but they can be used in copulation. Same goes for the tiny stubs on the rear underbelly of some python snakes. While they might look to some like the atrophied remnants of rear legs, maybe the python's ancestor never had rear legs. It's impossible to know whether those stubs always had the singular purpose of aiding in copulation.

All in all, very few "vestigial" structures have no function whatsoever. This does not rule out the possibility that vestigial structures are in fact remnants of some past transition from one species to another, but the case is more difficult to make if the structure still has some function. For folks in the Theistic Paradigm, a structure is only truly vestigial if it serves no function whatsoever. For folks in the Organic Paradigm, a structure is vestigial if its functions appear to be minor and/or different from a similar structure in a related or ancestral organism, and a plausible narrative can be constructed to explain how the structure degenerated from something more purposeful.

Speaking of plausible narratives, all examples of transitions from one species to another are accompanied by them. As described in Chapter 12, plausible narratives aren't themselves proof that the transition occurred, but without them the transitions are more difficult to fit into the theory of evolution.

For some of the transitions described above, it is not difficult to create plausible narratives that align with the theory of evolution. For example:

- Some of the tissues of soft invertebrates could progressively become more firm, providing greater stability to an organism in the face of strong currents. If such tissues continued to become more rigid and turn into cartilage, they could provide an anchor for muscles which in turn would give the organism greater maneuverability and strength.

- The skin of an amphibian could get progressively tougher, thicker, and more waterproof, providing a means for straying away from water for longer periods. Eventually the descendants might develop the skin of a reptile. A similar gradual process could have occurred with amphibian eggs: the outmost covering could have become gradually tougher until eventually the eggs no longer needed to be kept wet. Eggs laid on dry land might be safer from water-bound predators.

- Most fish have an organ called an air bladder which is used to adjust its buoyancy in the water. It is not difficult to imagine some fish co-opting this organ as a primitive lung to allow it to take short forays onto land, for instance to escape predators. Eventually the adaptive benefits of using the air bladder in this way could lead to the development of true lungs.

Despite the fact that such narratives do have a certain logic about them, there are many other transitions between classes of organisms for which a plausible narrative has yet to be developed.

For instance the transition from cartilage to bone would require the development of bone cells (osteocytes) from cartilage cells (chondrocytes). While there is ongoing research in this area and some promising leads involving proteins that are critical in mineralizing tissue, there don't appear to be any examples of skeletons made of something that is partway between cartilage and bone.

The transition from laying eggs to giving birth to live young is another area where there are some intriguing clues, but as yet there is no clear mechanism for how this transition could have occurred. For instance, monotremes such as the platypus and spiny anteater produce eggs, but those eggs stay in the mother's bodies for 28 days. Once the eggs are laid, they remain only about 10 days outside before hatching. Compare this to a chicken egg which is held in the mother's body for only one day, and then spends an additional 21 days outside the body before hatching. Thus, a story for the transition between laying eggs and giving birth to live young might involve a process wherein the eggs are held in the mother's body for essentially the entire gestation period, and then the egg hatches within the mother's body and the offspring is born. However, the plausible narrative would also need to include some gradual mechanism whereby the egg develops into a uterus and the fetus receives nutrition directly from the mother instead of from a separate yolk sac. To date no one has been able to propose how this part of the transition might have occurred.

The development of additional vertebrae is another area where it has been difficult to develop a transition story. The number of vertebrae in a given organism is controlled by what are called Hox genes, which are like master control genes that determine the form, number, and evolution of repeating body parts. One specific type of Hox gene determines whether an organism has 20 vertebrae as in chickens, 10 as in frogs, or to 300 as in snakes. It might be reasonable to assume that some slight variation in one of the Hox genes could add one more vertebrae to an organism instantly instead of gradually over many generations. While rare, such mutations have been known to occur, even in humans. But in order for the additional vertebrae to be passed along to future generations, it would need to offer an adaptive benefit. Otherwise, it simply wouldn't persist. Unfortunately, known cases of additional vertebrae are typically detrimental - the organism does not gain an advantage over others in its group, but generally loses some advantage. So, while in theory the appearance of additional vertebrae seems like it might be straightforward, in practical terms it's not clear how it would play out.

Transitions between species, or between classes of organisms, are the outer manifestations of the otherwise invisible machine of natural selection acting on phenotypic variations. Although many transitions are difficult to reconstruct, there are some cases in which the transitions seem relatively clear. The next chapter focuses on three such examples.

Chapter 15

Three Evolution Stories

Your average high school textbook description of evolution contains one or more of the three evolution stories described in this chapter: the evolution of birds, whales, and horses. In comparison to many other organisms, the fossil record for these organisms appears to be particularly complete, and plausible narratives for how various structures appeared and disappeared have been constructed that are simple enough for children to understand. At the same time, each of these stories includes some aspects that are problematic, and your average high school textbook tends to gloss over the complexity of the data.

Birds

The idea that birds evolved from dinosaurs is nearly as old as the idea of evolution itself. While a direct line of descent from dinosaurs to birds has never been found, the idea has persisted based both on a comparison of the anatomy of modern birds and dinosaurs as well as fossil evidence of organisms that appear to have characteristics of both birds and dinosaurs.

One of the controversial aspects of the idea that birds descended from dinosaurs is how to categorize an organism that seems to share the characteristics of both. Is it a dinosaur with bird-like characteristics, or a bird with dinosaur-like characteristics? In the Organic Paradigm, there is general agreement that there is no clear dividing line between dinosaurs and birds, and as a result your choice of whether to call it a bird or a dinosaur is really just a matter of convenience for taxonomic purposes. But to Theistic Paradigm folks it is not merely a matter of choosing a convenient label, but instead gets at the heart of whether evolution has really occurred or not.

From the Theistic Paradigm perspective, if every organism that is even remotely similar to modern birds is called a bird, then the family of all birds that have ever existed simply includes some (admittedly strange) species that have become extinct. Moreover, dinosaurs would then be comprised of a group of organisms that are clearly distinct from and unrelated to birds. If, on the other hand, some organisms that are rather bird-like are called dinosaurs, then it would indeed appear that there once existed organisms that were transitional between dinosaurs and birds. So, to understand the argument that birds evolved from dinosaurs, it is very important to define what is meant by a "bird."

The most obvious characteristics of modern birds are wings and feathers. Most have the ability to fly, though some do not, so flight is not a necessary defining feature of birds. Other notable characteristics include a beak without teeth and reproduction through laying eggs. There are also other characteristics associated with their skeletons that are less obvious, such as hollow bones that reduce weight, a wishbone that supports the skeleton during flight, and a breastbone with a projecting keel (a bone that sticks straight out the front of the chest) to which flight muscles attach. It should be no surprise that flightless birds such as the ostrich have no such keel.

The dinosaurs that are thought to be the progenitors of birds are called theropods. Theropods are the dinosaurs that stood on their hind legs and were good runners. In addition to the familiar Tyrannosaurus Rex, theropods also included much smaller dinosaurs such as Raptorex and Compsognathus which would have been no taller than your knee. The defining characteristics of theropod dinosaurs include sharp teeth for eating flesh, scaly skin, claws on the ends of all fingers and toes, and a long, bony tail used as a counterbalance to the head and upper torso.

Except in the most superficial way, theropod dinosaurs would not appear to have much in common with birds. The leg of an ostrich might look like the leg of a theropod, but no one would confuse an ostrich with a dinosaur. Nevertheless, there are a few characteristics that, it turns out, are strangely similar between the two. For instance, theropods appear to have had hollow bones and a wishbone, features they share with birds but which do not appear in any other organisms including other types of dinosaurs. And like theropods, birds also have scales on their legs and feet that is reptilian in nature and they lay eggs just like reptiles. Other similarities between theropods and birds have been found in ankle joints, the pelvis, and hips.

These are interesting similarities, but they are little more than suggestive. With all the variety of animal life on the earth, both living and extinct, it should not be a surprise that one groups of animals would share some features with another group. So, the theory that birds evolved from dinosaurs depends mostly on the existence of transitional organisms in the fossil record.

The most famous fossil, the one that makes it into all the high school textbooks, is that of Archaeopteryx, for which about ten different fossils have been found. Archeopteryx had classic bird-like features such as a wishbone and feathers that were of the type needed to fly. Certain features of its upper arm and shoulder bones suggested that it could not raise its wings as high as modern birds, making it a poor flyer. But it also had teeth, a long bony tail, and claws on its wings, none of which appears on any modern bird.

Archaeopteryx is one of many species of what might be categorized as extinct birds. Many of these fossil birds had teeth and claws on their wings, but were otherwise very much like modern birds. Some birds were enormous, like Phorusrhacos, whose head and beak looked similar to an eagle's, but which stood over 8 feet tall. Others had strange features, such as Ichthyornis which had teeth in the back of its mouth and a toothless beak in front, but otherwise was structured very much like modern birds.

Then there are the fossils of what are typically categorized as dinosaurs, but which had feathers or some other bird-like characteristics. For instance, Coelophysis was not very bird-like, but it did have a wishbone just like modern birds. Epidexipteryx appeared to have feathers on its tail but nowhere else. Pedopenna had bird-like leg structures and feathers only on its feet. Psittacosaurus had a toothless beak and some sort of quills on its back that bore a weak resemblance to feathers.

In all there are over a hundred different species of organisms in the fossil record that appear to show characteristics of both theropod dinosaurs and birds. Below is a summary diagram showing some of the species and how they form a continuum of phenotypes. While there is no obvious dividing line between dinosaurs and birds based on their phenotypes, I've added a line that seems to represent the views of most paleontologists.

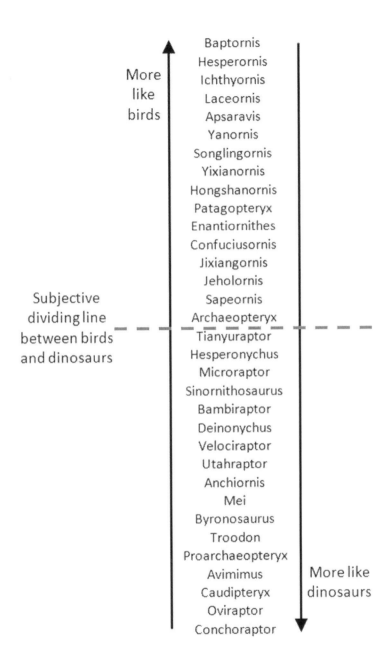

There are two main areas of disagreement between the Theistic Paradigm and Organic Paradigm when it comes to interpreting the evidence for birds evolving from theropod dinosaurs. The first involves the order in which the organisms appear in the fossil record. It would be reasonable to expect the evidence to demonstrate a progression over time from dinosaurs to birds something like this:

In reality, the evidence shows that the fossils that are most bird-like tend to be older than the fossils that are more like dinosaurs, like this:

Since this is not what one would expect if birds evolved from dinosaurs, one could either conclude that birds evolved from some organism other than theropod dinosaurs, or did not evolve at all.

While paleontologists generally agree that this "backward" trend in the fossil evidence is real, they have devised an explanation that, while it may never be proven true or false, is at least logical and consistent with other aspects of evolutionary theory.[26] It is based on the idea that new species appear as branchings from existing species, and then the two (the original species and the newer species) continue to exist in parallel over some period of time.

---

[26] Some folks in the Theistic Paradigm aren't fond of such creative explanations, and see them as an attempt to weasel out of the prima facie evidence that birds did not evolve from dinosaurs.

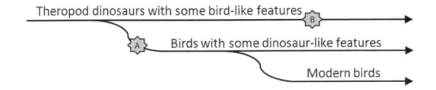

In this diagram, "A" represents Archaeopteryx, the oldest known bird at about 150 million years old, and "B" represents Shuvuuia, a small dinosaur that had feathers but which was incapable of flight, and which lived about 75 million years ago. Based strictly on the ages of the fossils, it would seem that the more bird-like Archaeopteryx appears before the dinosaur-like Shuvuuia from which it supposedly evolved. But if it is true that theropod dinosaurs continued to exist in parallel with the first birds as shown above, then it is possible that theropod dinosaurs could have continued with fewer bird-like features than the birds that had evolved from them. Under this explanation, the fossil record appears as it does simply because too few fossils have been found to fill out the true picture. Thus only the discovery of many more fossils will determine the truth or falsity of this idea.

The second significant area of disagreement between the Theistic and Organic Paradigms is in regards to the evolution of feathers.

Being rather delicate to begin with, one might not expect to find evidence of feathers in the fossil record at all. But there are in fact some unambiguous examples of fossilized impressions of feathers, such as from Microraptor, Archaeopteryx, Confuciusornis, and Jinfengopteryx. These feather impressions look very similar to feathers on modern birds, and in many cases enough detail has been preserved to allow paleontologists to determine whether the fossilized feathers were of the sort that would be required for flight. There is also some indirect evidence for feathers. For instance, both Velociraptor and Rahonavis have "quill knobs" on their forearm bones, telltale signs of the presence of long quills of the type that modern birds have on their forearms.

Most organisms with obvious feather impressions are structurally very similar to modern birds, and so might reasonably be categorized as birds. The problem is that many other fossil impressions of what are often labeled as feathers aren't obviously feathers, and they tend to appear on organisms best categorized as dinosaurs rather than birds. These structures are sometimes referred to as proto-feathers since they are thought to be precursors to true feathers. Proto-feathers can include barbs, bristles, filaments, or "dino-fuzz" similar to the hair-like feathers on such birds as the kiwi. Dinosaurs as small as Shuvuuia (at 2 feet long) and as large as Yutyrannus (at 30 feet long) have been found with evidence of structures frequently called proto-feathers. In some cases chemical tests of the fossilized proto-feathers have confirmed the presence of beta-keratins, providing strong evidence that the structures are in fact feathers. But in other cases the chemical tests either weren't possible or were inconclusive. There is also some evidence that what appear to be hair-like feathers in fossils were instead collagen fibers from the organism's skin.

Whether proto-feathers are truly evidence of evolutionary steps in the development of feathers, or were instead merely structures that bore a resemblance to feathers is unclear. Since most of the dinosaur fossils having evidence of proto-feathers are not ancestral to birds, the most that paleontologists can now say is that the evolution of feathers from proto-feathers is a working hypothesis.

Another aspect of the controversy over the evolution of feathers is how the ability to fly could have evolved from proto-feathers which were clearly not designed for flight. There is no direct evidence for the adaptive advantage of proto-feathers on theropod dinosaurs, so paleontologists have only been able to provide educated guesses based on examples of non-flight-related uses of feathers in modern birds. Such uses include warmth, protection of eggs during brooding, and ornamental uses and sexual display (think peacocks). Once proto-feathers were present, gradual modifications might have provided some additional adaptive advantages, such as a flapping stabilizer when catching prey or a sort of "scoop" to gather flying insects. Eventually, the proto-feathers might have become large and strong enough to provide a small amount of lift when running or jumping, and there is evidence that prior to flapping flight, feathers may have provided a means for gliding flight. However, all of this is conjecture based on the idea that feathers evolved from proto-feathers.

Whales

As described in Chapter 14, the vestigial pelvic bones in whales (including dolphins and porpoises) have long been thought to be remnants of a full pelvis connected to the spinal column, including functional legs, that existed in a land-dwelling ancestor to whales. This idea is further bolstered by the fact that whales are the only fully aquatic mammals other than manatees.[27] Like land-dwelling mammals, whales breathe air, give birth to live young, and suckle their young with mammary glands. Based on DNA sequencing, whales are more genetically similar to hippopotami than to any other living animal, which is strangely coincidental given that hippos are land animals that spend a great deal of time in the water.

But whales are also very different than land mammals. The most obvious differences include a lack of hair, flippers instead of front legs, a dorsal fin, a fluke (flattened tail) for propulsion, and a blowhole on the top of their heads. There are also other, less obvious features that are different from land mammals, such as an enormous lung capacity with highly efficient oxygen exchange (some species can go for several hours on a single breath), eyes and ears designed for high pressures, fatty blubber and an internal heat exchange system to minimize heat loss, kidneys that can handle the high salt content of the ocean, and the use of echolocation to locate objects. While the fossil record does provide examples of organisms that appear to be transitional between land mammals and whales, the exact mechanism through which each of these specialized features might have evolved is unclear.

The families of fossil organisms that have been proposed to tell the evolutionary story of whales can be roughly lined up as follows:

---

[27] Coincidentally, manatees also have reduced pelvic bones disconnected from the spinal column and no rear limbs.

Pakicetids
↓
Ambulocetids
↓
Remingtonocetids
↓
Protocetids
↓
Dorudontids
↓
Modern whales

The first step in the proposed evolutionary chain were the Pakicetids which were about the size of a wolf, and superficially looked like wolves as well. But they also had some features that have led paleontologists to believe that they were at least partially aquatic as well, such as eyes close together at the top of their heads (like a crocodile's) and dense bones. Other features provided the critical links to whales: The ear region of Pakicetids is shared by both modern and fossils whales but no other organism, and their teeth were very similar to those of fully aquatic fossil whales such as the Dorudontids. Folks in the Organic Paradigm take these similarities between Pakicetids and whales to be telltale signs of an evolutionary link, while folks in the Theistic Paradigm emphasize that the differences between Pakicetids and whales far outnumber the similarities.

Appearing a few million years after the Pakicetids were the Ambulocetids, which similarly had eyes close together at the top of their head, teeth that were similar to those of fossil whales, and ear bones that had a structure like those of whales. But they were also different from the Pakicetids in several ways. Their legs were shorter, their feet were bigger, and their tails were stronger. Their back legs were better adapted for swimming than for walking on land, though they clearly did both.

The skeleton of the Remingtonocetids had hind limbs, but they were even shorter than those of the Ambulocetids. Based on the fact that all fossils have been found along the coasts of marine environments, Remingtonocetids are believed to have been even

184

more aquatic than the Ambulocetids. However, the structure of the backbone suggests that it was not flexible enough to allow a Remingtonocetid to undulate its whole body for propulsion as whales do, but instead must have kicked with its back legs. Compared to the Ambulocetids, the Remingtonocetids had smaller eyes and a longer snout, and were smaller overall, like that of an otter.

With the appearance of the Protocetids, there are more obvious similarities to whales. For instance, the nostrils were higher up on the skull rather than at the front tip of the snout, and the eyes were on the sides of the head rather than at the top. The structure of the ears suggests that the Protocetids were able to hear properly underwater, and by contrast would have been unable to hear well in open air. The vertebrae of the sacrum (where the backbone connects to the pelvis) were not fused together as in earlier species, allowing greater flexibility. While this would have allowed the Protocetids to undulate their bodies as whales do, it is not clear how much of their propulsion was due to paddling from the large hind legs versus the use of their tail. Tail flukes (the broad fan at the end of a whale's tail) do not contain bones, and there is no direct evidence in the fossil record of the existence of tail flukes on Protocetids or any fossil whales. However, there are some telltale structures in tail vertebrae suggesting that they were built for significant up-and-down movements. Protocetid tail vertebrae also appear to have attachment points for the muscles that would have been needed to make a tail fluke the primary source of propulsion. Based on the evidence at least some Protocetids likely had tail flukes while still retaining hind limbs, though it is also certain that other Protocetids did not have tail flukes.

Protocetids had two other features that make them appear to be transitional between land mammals and modern whales. First, the structure of Protocetid ankle bones were very similar to the ankle bones of cows, deer, and hippos, but not to any other mammal, aquatic or otherwise. Second, one particular species of Protocetid called Georgiacetus had a spine disconnected from its pelvis, but nevertheless had legs connected to that pelvis. With a disconnected pelvis, Georgiacetus would not have been able to support its weight on its hind legs. The hind feet of Georgiacetus were large but it is not clear if they were used in propulsion.

The fossil organisms closest to whales are the Dorudontids and their close cousins the Basilosaurids. They were fully aquatic and enormous, on the order of 60 feet long. The nostrils were further towards the top of the head than were those in Protocetids. The structure of their tail vertebrae strongly suggests that they had tail flukes. Even so, they had complete hind limbs that included a mobile knee and several toes. These limbs were so small that they would not have been useful for propulsion, though it is possible they played a role during copulation. Moreover, the pelvic bones to which the limbs were attached were not connected to the backbone.

When these fossil organisms are described in this fashion and in this order, it is not difficult to see why paleontologists believe that the small pelvic bones of modern whales are the remnants of fully functional legs in the ancestors to whales, and that fully aquatic whales evolved from largely terrestrial mammals. Even so, the story of the evolution of whales, like most evolutionary stories, depends heavily on the idea that a succession of species can be established based on fossils of different organisms found in different places and of different ages. It's worth taking a short digression to see how this works in the Organic Paradigm.

In the world of paleontology, two organisms that are very similar in overall phenotype are presumed to be closely related: either one evolved from the other, or both evolved from a recent common ancestor. While the theory of evolution allows for some phenotypic traits to be developed independently in completely unrelated organisms (for example, flight among bats and birds), such instances of "convergence" are generally thought to occur for only one or two traits at a time. In the Organic Paradigm, it would be unthinkable for two organisms to have evolved nearly identical overall phenotypes and yet be completely unrelated in an evolutionary scheme.

In addition, rare traits are often used as key links between otherwise dissimilar species. It is the ear bones of Pakicetus that provide the key link to whales, since the particular ear structure in question is found only in these two organisms (and the presumed links in between). Otherwise the evidence linking Pakicetids and whales is rather weak. Again, it would be unthinkable to most paleontologists that such a unique trait would be shared by Pakicetus and modern whales without the former being a distant ancestor to the latter.

That said, most paleontologists recognize that the fossil evidence is typically too thin to permit them to propose a direct line of descent through a series of transitional organisms. This is true in most cases, whales included. In other words, the diagram I showed above in which Pakicetids evolve into Ambulocetids, Ambulocetids evolve into Remingtonocetids, etc. is an oversimplification designed to make the proposed evolutionary links easy to understand. In reality, the fossil evidence is much too weak to support such a direct line of descent. A diagram that is more faithful to the available evidence would show links based on something like cousin relationships rather than parent-offspring relationships:

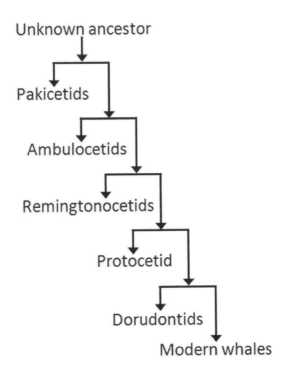

This "cousin" approach to drawing trees of life is a common way to describe proposed evolutionary links while simultaneously admitting that the fossil record has not offered up all the transitional forms that paleontologists in the Organic Paradigm believe existed.

There are two other issues with whale evolution that are worth noting. First, the timeframe over which the evolution is estimated to have occurred (about 12 million years) is very short given the dramatic changes required to turn a terrestrial mammal into a whale. In comparison, the evolution of the horse, described in more detail below, is estimated to have occurred over 50 million years and involved significantly fewer changes.

Second, the development of the tail fluke is somewhat of a mystery. Between the Pakicetids and Protocetids, the hind limbs actually appeared to get bigger rather than smaller, and there is no obvious indication in these organisms that the tail was becoming a means of propulsion. Moreover, otters and seals use their hind limbs for propulsion and are adept at catching aquatic prey, so it's not clear what advantage the shift from limb propulsion to tail propulsion would have. Why didn't the hind just legs keep getting bigger and bigger until they were gigantic?

The lumbar region of the spine (just forward of the pelvis) also presents a puzzle with respect to propulsion. In the Protocetids and Dorudontids, the lumbar region gained additional flexibility to allow the spine to undulate up and down and thus make the budding tail flukes more efficient. But in modern whales, the lumbar region is actually less flexible than it was in the Dorudontids.

Horses

Historically, the evolution of the horse has been presented as one of the clearest and simplest examples of evolution at work. Even in many museums, a series of four or five horse-like skeletons, each a little larger than the last, provided what appeared to be a straightforward example of one type of creature slowly evolving into another over 50 million years. In reality the story is considerably more complicated.

Fossils of horse-like creatures have been found in abundance all over the world. In fact, there may be more fossils of horse-like creatures than for any other large animal. Moreover, it is clear that there were many different species. The most commonly cited distinctions between species involve the number of toes, the form of teeth, and their overall size, but there were many other more subtle differences that would only be obvious to experts in comparative anatomy.

While having so many fossils of horse-like creatures is certainly better than having too few, it has also presented a problem for those trying to create an evolutionary story for the horse. Many of the species existed at the same time, or at overlapping times. Below is a diagram showing most of the horse-like creatures that have been identified, arranged from the oldest to the most recent. At any given point in time, there could be anywhere from three to fourteen different types of horse-like creatures coexisting.

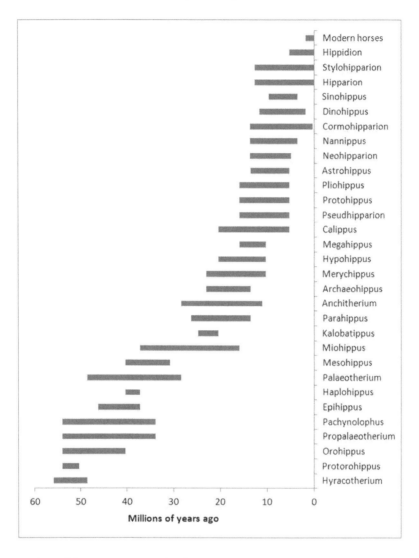

The oldest creature cited as an ancestor to modern horses is Hyracotherium, a dog-sized animal with four toes instead of a single hoof. It only resembled a horse in the most superficial sense, in the same way that the Pudú (the world's smallest deer which lives in the rain forests of South America) resembles a horse. Hyracotherium's neck and legs were proportionally shorter than a horse's, its tail was longer, and its ribcage was smaller. Its teeth were design to eat leaves and twigs rather than grass.

While there are many phenotypic variations between Hyracotherium and modern horses, there are also broad trends. The average size of horse-like creatures does generally increase over time between Hyracotherium and modern horses, though it decreases in some cases. The teeth of all creatures older than Miohippus were designed for eating a wide variety of plants, but after Miohippus there are more creatures whose teeth were designed to eat grass like modern horses do.

And then there is the story of their toes, probably the most oft-cited characteristic in horse evolution stories. Only a few horse-like creatures had four toes like those of Hyracotherium. Beginning with the appearance of Mesohippus, nearly all horse-like creatures had three toes. The jump from four to three toes is sudden and there is little to indicate any obvious transition. However, the transition from three toes to one toe is a different story.

Orohippus had three toes, which were all about the same size and all touched the ground at all times. But with the appearance of Miohippus and Mesohippus, the middle toe was obviously larger and the two side toes didn't always touch the ground. It's likely that they supported very little of the animal's weight. Some creatures that appeared more recently than Miohippus and Mesohippus, such as Parahippus and Merychippus, had side toes that never touched the ground. Finally, creatures such as Pliohippus and Calippus had only small nubs on the sides of the single hoofed middle toe. These nubs are typically interpreted by those in the Organic Paradigm as the vestiges of the side toes that shrank down to nearly nothing.

As convincing as the case for horse toe evolution seems, it's complicated by the fact that the trend is not consistent between Hyracotherium and modern horses. For instance, the side toes of Kalobatippus actually seem to be longer that Miohippus, its presumed predecessor. This would require that the toes grew longer in this case, not shorter. Moreover, Hipparion had four small toes even though it is one of the most recent horse-like creatures and is presumed to have evolved from Merychippus which had only three toes.

Despite these and other differences between the various horse-like creatures that existed over the past 55 million years, paleontologists have been able to construct a phylogenetic tree of life that incorporates them all. This process is essentially a statistical affair. Since there are many more phenotypic characteristics than just size, teeth, and toes, all the characteristics for every horse-like creature are entered into a database, and a probability analysis choose the links between those creatures that seem most likely. In essence, the analysis presumes that every horse-like creature evolved from some other horse-like creature, with the only outstanding question being which one. So, for instance, Archaeohippus is believed to have evolved from Miohippus for the simple reason that Miohippus is the best candidate to be the direct ancestor to Archaeohippus among all horse-like creatures that are currently known.

Based on the currently available data, the picture of horse evolution looks more like a bush than a tree, and many of the creatures would more appropriately be labeled as cousins to modern horses rather than ancestors.

Millions of years ago

I've marked the direct ancestral line from Hyracotherium to modern horse in darker bars to make it more obvious. If a new species of horse-like creature is discovered, its phenotypic traits will also be fed into the database. The probability analysis might then change some of the links in the diagram above.

Horse evolution provides a good example of the disagreement between the Theistic and Organic Paradigms on the issue of evolution versus devolution and the expression of latent genes. Under the Organic Paradigm, all changes over time would properly be called evolution, even if the change means the loss of a function or the shrinking of a particular body part like the two outside toes in horse-like creatures. The vestigial structures discussed in Chapter 14 would be examples of this form of evolution. However, many holding a Theistic Paradigm would argue that loss of function should more properly be called devolution. While it may seem like it's just semantics, in fact there's a deeper issue at play in this disagreement. One of the primary views of the Theistic Paradigm is that the evolutionary model is insufficient to explain increases in genetic information and complexity ("evolution"), but that the evolutionary model works just fine if an organism is losing genetic information or complexity ("devolution"). Thus to some people, it is only evolution in the more restrictive sense that is the subject of debate, not devolution.

This view is bolstered by the fact that even modern horses are occasionally born with extra toes on the sides of their hoofs. There is general agreement between the Theistic and Organic Paradigms that this occurs when a "latent" gene that controls the number of toes is activated. While this gene exists in all horses, normally it is dormant. But due to some sort of mutation or poorly understood chemical signaling, it gets activated when it shouldn't be.

Since latent horse toe genes are still functional even though they may not be activated, it's possible that modern horses could all develop three toes again under the appropriate environmental conditions. In this case, it might appear that modern single-hoof horses had evolved into a new genus of three-toed horse-like creatures, but in fact nothing of the sort would have happened. The new three-toed horse-like creatures would still be horses. Nothing in their genes would have changed, except for how those genes are expressed.

The existence of latent genes raises an important question about the presumed evolutionary predecessors to the modern horse. Might they all be truly horses, no different genetically than modern horses? Is it possible that the phenotypic variability seen among all the horse-like creatures over the past 55 million years is not due to changes in their genotype (wherein natural selection acts on phenotypic variation caused by random genetic mutations), but instead is simply a function of which genes are activated at any given time?

The implication of this idea is that all horse-like creatures shown in the diagrams above would have the same genotype, and the variability in phenotypes seen in the fossil record would only be a function of which genes were expressed. This idea is plausible when you consider that all dog breeds are still the same species even though they can appear very different. In the Organic Paradigm, however, the phenotypic differences among horse-like creatures is typically viewed as being greater than the variability that could be expected within a single genotype, the number of toes notwithstanding. Regardless, there is no way to test this idea since DNA is not available from most extinct horse-like creatures.

Chapter 16

Human Evolution

Many people much smarter than I have made attempts to find common ground between the Bible and evolution, and in these attempts the biggest sticking point inevitably comes down to human evolution, the story of Adam and Eve, and the origin of sin and death. Even some in the Theistic Paradigm who might be sympathetic to evolution sometimes view humans as a special case in which evolution either did not apply at all, or it worked in some way different than it did for all other organisms. Of course for those in the Organic Paradigm, human evolution is no different than the evolution of plants and fish and birds. Because of these strong differences between the Theistic and Organic Paradigms on human evolution, there's no avoiding at least some discussion of how human evolution might or might not fit with the Biblical story. I'll get to that at the end of this Chapter.

Under the Organic Paradigm, all organisms are related to one another through evolutionary descent from common ancestors, and this is just as true for humans as it is for any other organism. If you are going to add humans to the tree of life, it helps to know which other creatures we most closely resemble at the genetic level. Based on studies of DNA, it turns out that of all the primates on earth today, humans are most similar to chimpanzees (the next closest are gorillas, followed by orangutans, followed by gibbons and lemurs and all the rest). Within the Organic Paradigm, this suggests that a common ancestor to humans and chimps existed at some point in the past, and that this common ancestor had already diverged from the lineage of organisms that led to other monkeys and apes. From the Theistic Paradigm, the fact that chimpanzees have DNA that is the most similar to human DNA among all primates is not an indication that humans and chimpanzees have a common ancestor, but only that our overall physical structure and biochemistry are very similar.

Molecular clocks

Scientists have made estimates for how long ago the common ancestor of humans and chimps lived by using a "molecular clock." Molecular clocks rely on the idea that genetic mutations occur at a relatively constant rate for specific genes in a specific species. So, if you can count the number of mutations that have occurred in a particular gene, you can estimate how long it took for those mutations to build up.

To use this tool to identify the age of the common ancestor of humans and chimps, first you need to come up with a list of proteins that are identical in both species. Given how similar the biochemistry of humans and chimps is, this isn't difficult. You then examine the genes that code for those proteins. You might expect that those genes are the same in humans and chimps, but it turns out that they aren't. There are clear differences, but those differences don't affect the production of proteins because they all occur in the third nucleotide in each codon. As described in more detail in Chapter 9, each codon is composed of three nucleotides that together correspond to one amino acid. A chain of codons corresponds to a chain of amino acids, which forms a protein. But it turns out that, due to an inexplicable quirk of genetics, the third nucleotide in codons usually doesn't matter. In other words, it can usually be any one of the four types of nucleotides (A, T, G, or C) and the codon will still code for the proper amino acid. So, if a mutation occurs at the third nucleotide in a codon, natural selection won't "notice" it and it will remain there forever.

Now you have a list of genes that code for the same proteins in humans and chimps, but those genes have some differences in the third nucleotides of the codons. If there are very few such differences, it would suggest that the common ancestor of humans and chimps is very recent. If there are lots of differences, then the common ancestor of humans and chimps must be very old. To quantify the age of the common ancestor, you need to come up with a mutation rate in the form of X mutations per year. For the purposes of identifying the age of the common ancestor of humans and chimps, this mutation rate was based on the common ancestor of primates and rodents which has been estimated to have occurred 90 million years ago through radiometric dating of fossils. The end result, after applying this mutation rate to the number of mutations measured in the analogous genes in humans and chimps, is that their common ancestor is estimated to have lived 6-7 million years ago.

Molecular clocks are now common tools to measure the divergence of groups of organisms from common ancestors, but because they rely on a number of assumptions they are sometimes criticized. For instance, the mutation rate is often based on fossils that have been dated using radiometric dating methods. Insofar as one might distrust these dating methods, the calibrations used in molecular clocks would likewise be suspect. Moreover, molecular clocks rely on the assumption that mutation rates are constant when in fact this is not really true. They can differ significantly between species, between different parts of DNA within the same species, and can even vary over time. Thus there is no way to be sure that the mutation rate based on the divergence of primates and rodents is a good representation of the mutation rate between humans and chimpanzees. There is also no way to know for sure if the mutation rate has sped up or slowed down for either the lineage leading to humans or the lineage leading to chimps.

Scientists who use molecular clocks try to estimate the potential error that these uncertainties might introduce into their calculations, and thus often provide ranges for the ages they calculate. They also try to repeat the same calculation using multiple proteins shared between humans and chimps. This provides multiple estimates of the age of the common ancestor that can be used to generate both an average and an estimate of the error associated with that average.

Fossil evidence of human evolution

No fossils have ever been found that unequivocally represent the human-chimp common ancestor. However, there are several candidates that some scientists think come close:

- Sahelanthropus tchadensis
- Orrorin tugenensis
- Ardipithecus kadabba

In all cases the fossils found were very fragmentary, but by and large they appeared to be more similar to chimps than humans. This finding suggests that the lineage of humans underwent significant change over the last 7 million years while the chimp lineage underwent very little change during that same time. There is no obvious explanation for why this might be, but the prevailing theory is that the common ancestor split into two groups, one of which remained in the forests and the other of which ventured out into neighboring areas. Those in the forests more or less stayed in the forests over the last 7 million years, and thus experienced little pressure to evolve. Those that did not remain in the forests, however, experienced repeated and dramatic changes in environment which drove their evolution towards bipedalism (walking on two legs) and larger brains. What drove the initial separation of the common ancestor into two groups, and why the first members of the human lineage didn't just head back to the forest when things got tough, is largely a matter of speculation.

Paleontologists have identified about twenty-five different species of ape-like creatures in the fossil record that have some human characteristics, and these species have been grouped into two genera based on those fossils having similar characteristics: genus Australopithecus and genus Homo. Any species within either of these two genera is called a hominin. While there is some overlap in the time at which these two genera existed, in general the Australopithecines are older.

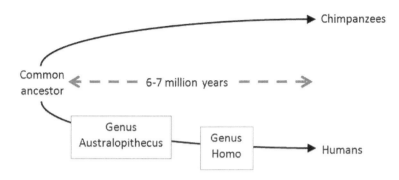

Modern humans are also considered to be within the genus Homo (full taxonomic name: homo sapiens sapiens), though I have shown them as a distinct group above.

The Australopithecines were very chimp-like in size and overall shape of heads and bodies, but they had adaptations that made it much easier for bipedal walking than modern chimps. In some cases this is evident by the shape of the pelvis and ankles, while in others it is suggested only by how the spine attached to the skull. The proportions of arm and leg lengths are somewhere between humans and chimps. But even within the genus Australopithecus there are differences between individual species, from the type of teeth and jawbones to the overall structure of the face which varied between chimp-like and gorilla-like.

All fossils of Australopithecines have been found in the central, western, and southern parts of Africa. The most famous of the Australopithecines is "Lucy" which had one of the most complete skeletons of an Australopithecine ever found, although by "complete" I mean that 40% of it was found. In most other cases, individuals were found with far fewer bones, sometimes amounting to only a skullcap or a piece of leg bone. Many in the Theistic Paradigm point to the scarcity of fossil finds as a reason to doubt any firm conclusions about the body structure of the Australopithecines.

The genus Homo is characterized primarily by having a larger brain size than that of the Australopithecines. Unlike the Australopithecines, none of the species within genus Homo have any obvious adaptations for tree-climbing, such as toes that can grip branches, an upward-facing shoulder joint, and a high arm-to-leg length ratio. From the neck down, they were extremely similar to modern humans. But many of the Homo species were more robustly built than modern humans, and their skulls in particular had a number of distinctive features such as a bony ridge above their eyes and the lack of a clear chin. The hands of genus Homo are much more dexterous than those of the Australopithecines, and some species are extremely similar to modern humans in this respect.

While species of genus Australopithecus have only been found in Africa, species of genus Homo have been found in Africa, Europe, and Asia. There are also more specimens of genus Homo fossils than there are of Australopithecus fossils. Nevertheless, there still aren't a lot. If you put all the Homo and Australopithecus fossils together they would just about fill up the back of a pickup truck.

Differences between the Theistic and Organic Paradigms on the 25 or so different species of hominin often start with the question of whether they really are different species or not. This is actually a question that is relevant for both sides, though for different reasons. The problem is compounded by the scarcity of fossils which increases the likelihood that a particular specimen will not have features typical of its species. The one specimen you find might be shorter or taller than the average, for instance. More importantly, the same species can exhibit different physical features in different environments. For example, among modern humans, native Inuit from the Arctic typically have shorter arms and legs, and are in general more stoutly built, than natives of Africa. This could also be true of hominins.

From the Organic Paradigm, which fossils belong to which species is a matter of continual debate. Some species, like Homo erectus, include many individual specimens, and thus the species can be fairly well defined. In other cases, such as Australopithecus bahrelghazali, there is only a single specimen consisting of only a piece of lower jaw. Thus it's not clear if bahrelghazali is a distinct species or, for instance, simply a variation of Australopithecus afarensis. Other species that might actually be the same species include:

- Australopithecus africanus and Australopithecus garhi
- Homo erectus, Homo ergaster, and Homo cepranensis
- Homo antecessor, Homo heidelbergensis, and Homo rhodesiensis

For the Theistic Paradigm, the concern is less about how each species is defined and more about whether a particular specimen should be considered to be human or not. This is similar to the treatment of the evolution of birds, where the question facing many in the Theistic Paradigm is the dividing line between dinosaurs and birds. Similarly, many in the Theistic Paradigm believe that there is a dividing line between human and not-human somewhere within all the specimens of hominin that have been found.

As described in Chapter 11, the primary (though not the only) criterion that separates one species from another is the ability to interbreed. For the most part, there is no direct way to determine whether modern humans and any of the extinct species of hominin could have interbred. The one exception is for Homo neanderthalensis, for which DNA has been extracted from 38,000 year old bones and compared to the DNA of modern Europeans. It turns out that there is strong evidence that our own species Homo sapiens and Homo neanderthalensis did interbreed somewhere between 50 and 80 thousand years ago. Even so, neanderthalensis and sapiens continue to be treated as separate species by most paleontologists based on physical attributes, similarly to the way that lions and tigers are treated as separate species even though they can interbreed.

All other Homo species fossils are too old to permit the extraction of DNA, so the only alternative is to compare body structures. One of the primary features that is used to compare extinct hominins to modern humans is brain size. Brain size is not a perfect indicator of intelligence - an elephant's brain is three times bigger than a human's but elephants aren't exactly chess masters. Nevertheless, people in both the Theistic and Organic Paradigms generally agree that brain size is a strong indicator of intelligence, and is a particularly accurate measure of relative intelligence for two species that are very similar in other respects.

A chimp's brain size typically falls in the range 330 - 500 cm3, while modern humans have a brain size that typically falls in the range 1000 - 1550 cm3. Most hominins fall in between these two ranges as shown below.

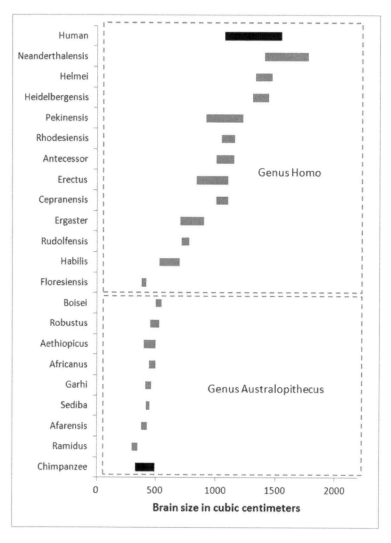

Clearly, all the Australopithecines are much closer to chimps than humans with regard to brain size. Among the Homo species, however, the range is broad and several species have brain sizes that at least come close to that for modern humans. In rare cases a normal human brain can be as small as 900 cm, so any hominin whose brain size is estimated to reach this value is a potential candidate for being the same species as modern humans. On this basis, nine of the twelve Homo species shown in the diagram above might arguably be called human.

But of course brain size is not the only relevant factor. Despite the scarcity of hominin fossils, paleontologists know a fair amount about the overall structure of their bodies. We know, for instance, that all Homo species were fully bipedal and had no obvious adaptations for tree climbing. Below the neck, there were variations in height, ratio of arm and leg lengths to whole body height, and how slender or robust they were. Unfortunately, none of this tells you much about how "human" a hominin might be.

The primary difference between modern humans and other species within the genus Homo is in the skull. Here too there are variations among different Homo species, but by and large they share these common characteristics:

- Boney ridge above the eyes
- Protruding midface
- Large jaw and mouth
- Absence of a chin

If you saw one of these Homo species on the street[28], you might do a double-take. But then again, you might not. They would look different, but not obviously non-human. But even if they do look oddly brusk from our viewpoint, how important are looks when it comes to whether we should call them human?

Beyond their physical structure, there are also other clues that have been unearthed that give some indication of what sorts of lives species within the genus Homo lived. These include stone tools, artwork, the use of fire, and burying their dead, among other things. In many cases it isn't possible to determine which Homo species is associated with which of these other finds, so paleontologists often use diagrams that simply line up the relevant

---

[28] Presumably wearing a suit rather than bear skins.

time periods, like this:

Use of Stone Tools by Genus Homo

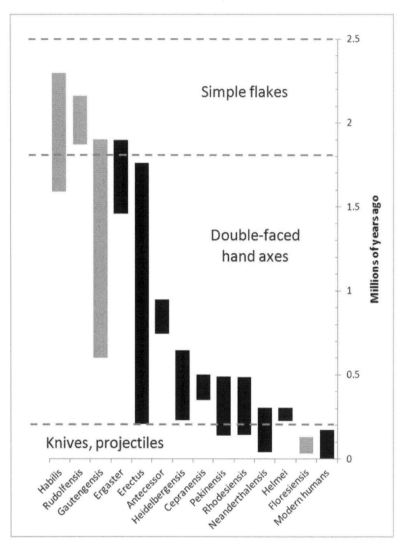

In this diagram, I've shown the age ranges for each of the Homo species, as well as the types of stone tools used in different time periods. Darker bars represents species with a brain size similar to Homo sapiens. The simplest stone tools, consisting of a single sharp-edged flake knocked of a rock, were common all the way back to the earliest species Homo habilis. More sophisticated tools such as the hand axe appeared around 1.8 million years ago, and predominated for the next 1.5 million years. These all-purpose hand axes were chipped on two sides and consisted of a rounded end for holding and a pointed, two-edged end for chopping or digging. The majority of Homo species existed during the time that hand axes were common. More sophisticated tools, such as stone knives and projectiles, only appear after about 200 thousand years ago. The most sophisticated tools of all, including long, thin blades, barbed projectiles, and other specialized tools requiring great skill to produce, only appear in the last 50,000 years or so. At this point in time, the only species that would have been around to produce such tools would have been Homo sapiens and to a lesser extent neanderthalensis and floresiensis.

What does the use of tools tell us about how human a given Homo species might have been? It's largely conjecture, and complicated by the fact that even chimps have been known to use tools occasionally (though they generally just use what's handy rather than fashioning a tool for a specific purpose). But any species that produced stone tools would have had to have been able to imagine the finished product before starting, and would have had a particular purpose in mind for the tool being made. Even for the simplest tools, purposeful imagination such as this is far beyond what chimps can accomplish.

Fire provides another clue about what Homo species were capable of. The oldest known example of the intentional use of fire was about 1 million years ago, though most verified cases of the use of fire are less than half as old. These dates mean that most Homo species probably used fire to cook food, harden bone tools, keep warm, etc. Unfortunately, there is no way to tell when hominins learned to make fire (as opposed to just using fire started by a lightening strike or lava flow).

Other indicators of how Homo lived are much more recent. The oldest evidence of an intentional burial is about 100,000 years old and is associated with our own species Homo sapiens, but more recent burials have also been identified with neanderthalensis. The oldest form of art, small shells strung together to make some type of necklace and a small stone with intentional criss-cross markings, is about 75,000 years old and was most likely produced by Homo sapiens. The cave art that is more commonly known does not appear until about 40,000 years ago and is definitely produced by Homo sapiens.

So where do you draw the line between human and non-human? How smart is smart enough to be human? How creative is creative enough to be human? It's not clear that we know enough to answer such questions, and moreover what we do know implies a spectrum of physical forms and abilities rather than two distinct and unique groups of hominins.

How do humans differ from chimps?

This leads to a wholly different approach that is sometimes used to define what makes us human: compare all the traits of humans with those of chimps and divide those traits into two groups: those which are a matter of degree and those which are a matter of kind. A trait that is a matter of degree is something that is shared by both humans and chimps, but humans have more of it, or are better at it, than chimps. Traits in this category imply that humans are simply more sophisticated versions of apes. A trait that is a matter of kind, on the other hand, is something that only humans have. Traits in this category imply that humans are something altogether different than apes. By separating human and chimp traits into these two groups it might be easier to define what makes humans unique, and this in turn might enable us to better determine where the dividing line is between human and non-human hominins.

Traits that are exhibited by both chimps and humans and which are clearly a matter of degree include the ability to learn, social hierarchies, and culture. There are also a whole set of emotions that are shared by chimps and humans, such as grief, curiosity, jealousy, anxiety, and others. Many of these traits are also exhibited by some non-primates as well, so they aren't really very good indicators of what makes us human.

There is another set of traits that might arguably straddle the fence between matters of degree and matters of kind. For instance, chimps use simple tools and weapons, but only humans make tools and weapons from raw materials. Likewise chimps exhibit hostility and are capable of killing one another, but racism and genocide appear to be uniquely human.

One of the most commonly cited examples of a trait that could conceivably be a matter of degree or a matter of kind is language. Some chimps and gorillas have been taught a basic vocabulary in sign language and have been able to communicate simple concepts with it. Of course they do not have the ability to use vocal speech - they lack the necessary anatomical features of the larynx, jaw, and mouth. Evidence for vocal speech among extinct Homo species is thin, with the exception of neanderthalensis for which fossils have been unearthed that include portions of the hyoid bone, a structure that is critical for vocal speech.

Aside from the fact that the use of sign language by gorillas and chimps had to be taught by humans and was not something that is part of their native culture, there is ongoing debate about what these primates really understand when they use sign language. Human language is intensely symbolic, and it requires the ability to manipulate mental symbols of things, actions, and conditions with a nearly infinite range of nuances. It's not clear if chimps even come close to having such mental abilities, so it's possible that language - or at least language as we humans experience it - is a matter of kind. In other words, language might arguably be one defining characteristic of true humanity.

There are also other human traits that appear to be matters of kind. Some of these are listed below.

- Clothing
- Technology, medicine, agriculture
- Music, art
- Hairless body

Aside from these, a common description of the uniqueness of humankind is found in our being generalists and in being able to adapt to a much greater variety of environments than chimps or any other organism. Our bodies are not perfectly adapted to any particular climate, terrain, or food source, but we can work with just about anything. We aren't the best tree climbers, but we can climb if we need to. We aren't the best runners, but we can run. We aren't the best swimmers, but we can swim. We would freeze in the polar bear's world, but we can build fires and wear clothing to compensate. We build shelters to protect ourselves from the elements, we carry food to where there is none. In a very real sense, long before civilization as we know it began, we were already masters of the biological world, in versatility if not in numbers.

All of the potential indicators of true humanness discussed so far could take on a variety of forms, so they may or may not provide a way to clearly distinguish human from nonhuman among extinct hominins. Ideally we would have some other, more concrete way to identify the dividing line.

Human chromosome number 2

One of the more fascinating and unique traits of humans is that we have 23 pairs of chromosomes, whereas all other primates including chimps have 24. Since we have been able to extract DNA from fossils of Homo neanderthalensis, we know that it too had 23 pairs of chromosomes just like humans. At first this would seem to provide a clear way to distinguish between human and non-human.[29] However, the picture is actually not so simple.

Scientists have carefully compared the chromosomes of humans and chimps and have discovered that they are very similar. Human chromosome number 5 is very similar to chimp chromosome number 5, human chromosome number 13 is very similar to chimp chromosome number 13, and so on.[30] But human chromosome number 2 is different. This chromosome actually looks like the

---

[29] If we could measure the chromosome number in extinct hominins, this could provide a test of "humanness". Alas, there are no viable DNA samples from hominins other than neanderthalensis.

[30] The numbering isn't arbitrary. The longest chromosome is always number 1, the second longest is number 2, etc.

combination of chimp chromosomes 2A and 2B. That is, human chromosome number 2 looks as if it was created by the fusion of two separate chromosomes, one of which was very similar to chimp chromosome number 2A and the other of which was very similar to chimp chromosome number 2B.

The evidence for such a fusion is relatively strong, and is based on our understanding of the locations and functions of what are called telomeres and centromeres in normal chromosomes. Here is the basic structure of a chromosome:

Typical chromosome

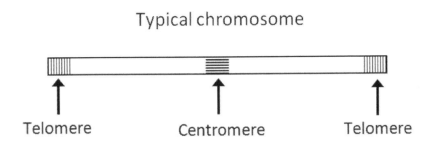

Telomere   Centromere   Telomere

A telomere is a string of nucleotides that mark the end of the chromosome. They may be 2,000 - 30,000 nucleotides long, but they are always composed of repeats of the sequence TTAGGG. A centromere, on the other hand, is somewhere in the middle of a normal chromosome. Its function is to be the point where pairs of identical chromosomes connect to one another. During cell division, fibers from opposite ends of the cell attach to the centromeres like handholds to pull apart the two sides of the chromosomes and deposit each into the two new daughter cells.

Human chromosome number 2 has a structure that is different than all other chromosomes, as shown below.

Human chromosome 2

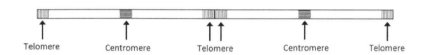

Telomere   Centromere   Telomere   Centromere   Telomere

This clearly looks like two chromosomes have fused together end-to-end. In addition, the center of chromosome 2 has a typical telomeric sequence followed by a reversed telomeric sequence, exactly what one would expect to find if two chromosomes fused end-to-end. If this type of fusion did occur, it is reasonable to expect that it would have had no overall effect on phenotype because none of the genes were changed or destroyed by the fusion.

While the evidence that a chromosome fusion occurred in the hominin lineage at some point in the last 6-7 million years is reasonably strong, how it could have occurred and come to dominate Homo sapiens is more difficult to establish. One of the functions of telomeres is to prevent chromosomes from fusing with each other. While a variety of different types of genetic translocations that cause chromosome fusions are known to occur in humans today, a telomere-telomere fusion is extremely rare. So rare, in fact, that the only other place it has been observed is in tumors and cancers.

Chromosome fusions have been studied in other animals, and in general they tend to reduce the reproductive potential of offspring. If this was also true for the fusion that took place in the hominin lineage, it seems likely that hominins with this fusion would have disappeared rather quickly and humans would still have 24 chromosomes just like chimps. Since this did not happen, the only alternative explanation is that the fusion in the hominin lineage generated some sort of adaptive advantage such that all hominins without the fusion were at a fitness disadvantage and thus eventually disappeared. However, there is no evidence that the number of chromosomes has any impact on fitness. If there is no fitness advantage to having a single, fused chromosome rather than two separate chromosomes, then half of all humans alive today should have 24 chromosomes and the other half should have 23. Since there is no documented case of a human without a fusion of chromosomes 2A and 2B, there is no clear explanation for how 23 chromosomes came to be the norm in modern humans.

The fact that chromosome number 2 has two centromeres creates another problem. In modern humans, one of these two centromeres on chromosome number 2 is inactive. That is, enough of the nucleotide sequence has become scrambled to make it nonfunctional while still leaving it identifiable as a (former) centromere. But when the fusion first occurred, both centromeres would certainly have been functional. A chromosome with two functional centromeres, particularly if they are far apart as they are on chromosome number 2, runs the risk of being torn apart during cell division since two fibers could attached to it rather than just one, and those two fibers might pull in opposite directions. It is possible that one of the two centromeres could have become inactive immediately after the original fusion, but this would have been quite a coincidence. Alternatively, it may be that one of the centromeres was better able than the other to connect to the fibers during cell division, and the less able centromere simply fell into disuse. But even in this case it would have needed to occur consistently in every single cell division in order to produce a viable organism. This too seems unlikely. So as yet there is no clear explanation for how the fusion in human chromosome number 2 came about.

What makes us human?

For many in the Theistic Paradigm, all of the distinctly human traits discussed above miss the point. It's true that humans differ from chimps in certain elements of physiology, genetics, and intelligence. But more important is the fact that we are who we are because God created us in his image, as described in Genesis 1:26-27. This, more than anything else, is what makes us unique.

Few Christians today believe that being created in God's image means we look like him. When it comes to the Son of God, there's good reason to think that we do, but it's unlikely that this is what the author of Genesis had in mind. Instead, being created in the image of God is more about having certain characteristics that set us apart from all other creatures.

There are several different ways of describing these characteristics. Here I have broken them into three groups, though there are probably other ways of describing them.

1. Morality: The ability to know right from wrong
2. Abstract thinking: The ability to be conscious of God
3. Spirituality: The ability to know God

To begin with, there is no concept in the chimp world of morality. It is true that chimps make decisions whose outcomes may prove to be good or bad, helpful or hurtful. In doing so they learn what they can and can't do if they want to stay part of the group and for the group to function well. In this sense, chimps do develop and operate within a rudimentary code of conduct. But this is nothing like morality as humans know it. There is no evidence that chimps weigh issues or actions on the basis of principles of goodness or badness that are separate from the anticipated good or bad outcomes. If a chimp is inclined to do something, he will do it if he can get away with it given whatever social norms might exist in his group that limit self-serving behavior. Morality in the principle-driven sense that humans know it seems to be absent from the chimp world.

As best we can tell, this is because morality is a strongly abstract concept. Unlike simple mental images of things in the physical world or actions that involve those things, abstract concepts are generalized ideas less likely to be tied to a tangible object. It is abstract thinking that permits humans to guess others' motives, to philosophize, to make predictions, and to be creative. Abstract thought is closely tied to symbolic thought, where one thing is used to represent something else. This is why abstract thinking is closely tied to language, as words are verbal or written symbols that represent things, ideas, actions, and the like. There is no evidence that chimps have anything close to the abstract and symbolic thought world that we do.

From an evolutionary perspective, it isn't clear what the adaptive advantage of abstract thinking might be for Homo sapiens and possibly other hominins. Because no other creature has evolved this ability, we can safely assume that it was generally not critical for survival. After all, chimps seem to have managed just fine without the ability to think abstractly over the last 7 million years during which the human lineage was changing so dramatically. From the Theistic Paradigm perspective, the uniqueness of humans in this regard is evidence of divine intervention. Further, the ability to think abstractly allows humans to believe in God, angels and demons, and the spiritual realm without being able to experience them with our five senses. Even atheists are capable of thinking about such things, at least as concepts. One verse in the Bible suggests that this ability to think abstractly, to draw inferences about the unseen through what can be seen, is part of what it means to be human:

For his invisible attributes, namely, his eternal power and divine nature, have been clearly perceived, ever since the creation of the world, in the things that have been made. So they are without excuse. (Romans 1:20)

No other creature is charged with a transgression for not believing in the unseen God. From this we can infer that only humans have this capability.

Beyond merely knowing that God exists, humans have the ability to have a relationship with him because we have a spiritual component in addition to our bodies and minds. This spiritual component can relate to God because God is spirit. In traditional Christian theology, no other creature has a spirit, and thus no other creature can relate directly to God in the way that humans can.

The Organic Paradigm has little to say about the spiritual component of humans. If it is not dismissed altogether, it is treated as just another aspect of our minds and/or emotions, something closer to intuition or imagination. The Organic Paradigm likewise may treat religious experiences as the outworkings of our subconscious in the same way that dreams are driven by our subconscious, and yet dreams can sometimes seem otherworldly, as if they are being influenced or even imposed by something outside of ourselves. There is some evidence to support this idea. Research on brain activity suggests that there are predictable patterns to the parts of the brain that are most active during times of worship, prayer, or meditation, leading some scientists to believe that spirituality is nothing more than one particular manifestation of human mental capacities. There is, of course, no way to prove that the human spirit, created by God, is something more than biology. As I said in Chapter 5, spirit doesn't lend itself to measurement and analysis. Science, for all its worth, can't tell us much about spiritual things, so it's no surprise that the notion of a human spirit is viewed by many scientists with suspicion.

Adam and Eve

And now to the heart of the matter, and probably the most important topic in this whole book: If humans evolved from something that was not human, what is a Christian to think about Adam and Eve and their fall into sin? How does the Biblical story of Adam and Eve fit with the evidence we have about hominins and their apparent ancestral link to ourselves?

This is where the rubber hits the road, where all the debates over evolution converge. And this is where many Christians find themselves drawing a firm line no matter how flexible they might be with the concept of evolution generally. After all, if humans evolved, doesn't that mean that there was no Adam and Eve? And if there was no Adam and Eve, there was no point when humans disobeyed God and sin entered the world. And if there was no fall from grace, there is no need for a savior. The entire tapestry of Christianity unwinds.

As I said in Chapter 2, Christians have a range of views on evolution, and for convenience I grouped them all into the Theistic Paradigm to highlight the common theme that God was somehow at work in bringing all life to earth, whatever the specifics.

Likewise, there are a range of views among sincere Christians on the more narrow issue of the interplay between human evolution and the Biblical story of Adam and Eve. Below I discuss four approaches to reconciling these seemingly incompatible stories. But rather than present each of them in terms of how the Theistic and Organic Paradigms might view them, instead I've discussed them primarily from the viewpoint of a Christian. That is, I've made an attempt to describe whether and to what degree each of the four approaches succeeds in maintaining the foundational tradition of Adam and Eve's fall into sin while also accounting for human evolution.

One more thing before I get into these ideas. I'm not a theologian[31], and I don't know Hebrew or Greek. My primary intention in this book has been to discuss science as it relates to evolution and to avoid to the extent possible discussions of the meaning of relevant Bible verses. That's for others much smarter than I. So, in what follows I don't try to determine how the Bible might be interpreted or re-interpreted to accommodate human evolution. I make no bones about the fact that the four approaches described below deviate progressively from a literal reading of the Bible, and very likely generate more questions than answers. Nevertheless, they represent the range of ideas that sincere, well-meaning Christians have considered.

Approach #1:   Adam and Eve were real individuals, created directly by God, and were the very first humans. There were other hominins on earth before Adam and Eve, but those other hominins were not human.

This approach comes closest to preserving a literal reading of the Bible while recognizing the reality of the many different forms of hominin that have existed. Further, it allows for the other hominins either to have been created instantly along with all other creatures as Genesis suggests, or to have evolved. In either case, Adam and Even did not evolve.

---

[31] But I play one on TV. Raise your hand if you get that joke.

This approach requires that there be a clear dividing line between human and non-human hominins. Many in the Organic Paradigm would say that there is no such line, rather there is a continuum of features across the different hominin species, up to and including modern humans (Homo sapiens). Those in the Theistic Paradigm might counter that there is a dividing line even if it cannot be clearly identified based on the fossil evidence available to us today.

There is some flexibility for which species Adam and Eve might have been under this approach. If they were not Homo sapiens but instead some very closely related species such as Homo neanderthalensis, we would be forced to conclude that all Homo neanderthalensis were as fully human as you and I despite the obvious physical differences. In other words, Homo sapiens and Homo neanderthalensis are really the same species. Indeed there is evidence that the DNA of modern humans includes some DNA from neanderthalensis, which suggests that the two species commingled and interbred at some point in the past. As I said in Chapter 11, the ability to interbreed is one strong indicator that two species should be treated as a single species.

There are several possibilities for what happened to the other non-human hominins under this approach. One is that they simply died during the Noachian flood. Noah and his family happened to be of the species Homo sapiens, and they were the only ones that survived. All Homo neanderthalensis and all other hominin species drowned and went extinct.

Another possibility is that modern humans outcompeted all the other non-human hominins. In other words, natural selection chose Homo sapiens over all other hominin species. A third possibility is that modern humans intentionally wiped out other non-human hominins. In Genesis 1:26 and 28, God says that the humans he created were to rule over all other creatures on earth. If there were other non-human hominins on earth at the time, then Adam and Eve would have ruled over them as well. It isn't too difficult to believe that humans could have subjugated non-human hominins considering the ways in which different hominin species differed as described above. Following the entrance of sin into the world, "ruling over" might have evolved into "fighting with", with the end result being that non-human hominins were exterminated. This is also not too difficult to believe given that in just one generation, murder was introduced into the human story when Cain killed his brother Abel. Killing a non-human hominin would have been easier in comparison, more like killing an animal.

In this approach, as well as in Approach #2 below, there remains a problem with the timing of Adam and Eve's arrival on earth. According to the Organic Paradigm, Homo sapiens first appeared around 170,000 years ago. In Genesis 5 we are told that there are only ten generations between Adam and Noah, and another 10 generations between Noah and Abraham. Since Abraham's story is generally placed at about 2,000 b.c., this means that about 166,000 years must have separated Adam and Abraham. With only 20 generations between Adam and Abraham, that works out to more than 8,000 years per generation, which of course makes no sense. The only alternative to bring the number of years per generation down to a more reasonable level would be if the lineage between Adam and Abraham given in the Bible is incomplete, i.e. there are many hundreds of generations rather than only 20. Given that the Bible's list of 20 generations is name-specific, however, this solution seems untenable unless you are willing to treat those names as only the most noteworthy people among many other unnamed individuals.

If there were indeed only 20 generations between Adam and Abraham, then it seems more reasonable that Adam would have lived about 6,000 years ago, which fits nicely into the view that some in the Theistic Paradigm have about the age of the earth. This could be the case if the radiometric dating methods that give us a Homo sapiens age of 170,000 years are wrong. As discussed in Chapter 8, there is good reason to believe that radiometric dating methods are reasonably accurate. However, those methods cannot account for isotopic half-lives that may have been different in the past than they are today due to, for instance, God's miraculous work to create the earth in only six days. This is an untestable hypothesis, however, and so represents a sort of plausible narrative on the Theistic Paradigm side, not unlike the many plausible narratives that those in the Organic Paradigm have generated.

If radiometric dating methods are accurate and Homo sapiens have been around for 170,000 years, Adam could still have lived only 6,000 years ago if all Homo sapiens that lived prior to Adam were not truly human. This possibility is difficult to establish based on fossil and historical evidence which strongly suggests that Homo sapiens older than 6,000 years were every bit as human as we are, including the ability to think abstractly and a belief in the spiritual realm (or at least the afterlife). Nevertheless, Homo sapiens prior to Adam may have been missing some crucial element that makes modern humans unique as special creations of God. What that element might be, however, is not something we can currently identify.

Finally, studies of genetic variability present a problem with the idea that all modern humans descended from two individuals who lived 6,000 years ago. By estimating the rate at which genetic mutations occur, scientists have determined that the variability in DNA that exists in the human population today would have required many tens of thousands of years to accumulate. In order for all humans alive today to have descended from Adam and Eve 6,000 years ago, there would have needed to have been an incredibly high genetic mutation rate ever since. While this is theoretically possible and it could have occurred with divine intervention, there is no direct evidence for it.

Approach #2: Adam and Eve were real individuals, and were the very first humans. But they were not created directly by God. Instead, Adam and Eve were humans born of non-human hominin parents.

This approach is similar to Approach #1, but places the appearance of Adam and Eve within the evolution story. However, it does so in a decidedly discontinuous way that is based on something called "saltation."

Saltation was the predominant idea behind evolution prior to Darwin, and it continued as a plausible alternative to Darwinian evolution for several decades afterwards Darwin's *Origin of Species* was published. Under saltation, a large number of mutations were believed to occur all at once, resulting in sudden jumps in an organism's phenotype. In the extreme, an organism's offspring would actually be a different species from its parent. While some scientists in the Theistic Paradigm still view some form of saltation as a potentially viable evolution mechanism, most scientists in the Organic Paradigm do not because it requires many mutations all occurring at the same time, in a coordinated fashion, and with an overall effect on the organism's fitness. Based on our current understanding of mutation rates and their effect on fitness, the odds against this happening are so low as to be negligible, but of course it is possible that God could have intervened to make it happen.

If Adam and Eve were indeed humans born of non-human hominin parents, they would both had to have been born at approximately the same time, in approximately the same location, but in separate families (to avoid the possibility that they were brother and sister). These requirements further reduce the likelihood that this approach could have occurred without some kind of divine intervention.

When they reached adulthood, Adam and Eve would have needed to find their way to the garden of Eden where they would begin their new, unique relationship with God. In this approach, Eden is a sort of oasis in the midst of a planet that is otherwise hostile. Eden provides everything that Adam and Eve need. They still have work to do in tending the garden, but apparently it was relatively easy work and the plants yielded all the food they needed. There was no need to hunt animals for food. This would be consistent with the Bible's depiction of Adam and Even as being vegetarians. If God was in Eden in a special way, there may have been no need to fear any animals in Eden either.

Outside of Eden, things were different. There were carnivorous animals, harsh weather, and rough terrain. Shelter is more difficult to find. And gardening wasn't so easy. The soil wasn't the same fertile stuff that was in Eden. It would take hard work to get things to grow, and plants grown for food would compete with weeds. Life outside the garden of Eden would have been rough.

Under this approach, life outside of Eden would also have

included death. Hominins might have hunted animals for food, and animals would have hunted each other. Certainly many organisms would have died of disease, injury, or old age. Adam and Even would thus have been familiar with the concept of death when they entered Eden. If so, this would solve a minor dilemma in the Genesis story when God tells Adam that if he eats of the tree of the knowledge of good and evil, he will die. If there was no such thing as death in Eden, and Adam had been created by God in Eden, how would Adam have known what death was? And if he didn't know what death was, how could he have understood God's statement that he would die?

This approach also presents an alternative to the idea that Adam and Eve would never have died if they had not sinned by eating the fruit from the tree of the knowledge of good and evil. Since they had been born outside of Eden, presumably they would have been subject to all the natural laws that applied to all life outside of Eden, including death. In other words, Adam and Eve were always going to die someday. But while they were in the garden of Eden, they had access to the tree of life. Genesis 3:22 suggests that the purpose of the tree of life was to provide eternal life to anyone who eats of its fruit. So long as Adam and Eve lived in Eden, they could eat freely of the tree of life and escape death indefinitely. Once they had been banned from Eden, they no longer had access to the tree of life and were once again subject to the natural laws that applied outside of Eden, including death.

> *Approach #3:* *Adam and Eve were real individuals, but they were not the first humans nor the only humans at that time. Adam and Eve were specially called by God out of an existing population of humans to live in Eden, a place prepared by God for them. Here they enjoyed special favor with God until they disobeyed and were sent back out into the world outside Eden.*

This approach is similar to approach #2, but Adam and Eve were merely two humans out of the many that existed on earth at that time. They had been born and raised in the natural way by human parents, but then entered Eden to start a new, special life with God.

The idea that God might have a special calling for two individuals, a calling that involves the start of a new work on the earth, is a theme that is repeated multiple times in the Bible. Noah and his family were pulled out of the population of humans to restart the human race. Abram and his family were called out of paganism to start a new relationship with God and to provide an example to the rest of humanity. Similar stories of God starting something new can be found with Samson, Gideon, and Jesus' twelve disciples. So, if God was starting something new among humanity with Adam and Eve, this would be consistent with, and actually prefigure, how God operated on many occasions afterwards.

Once Adam and Eve sinned and were sent out of Eden, there would have been an opportunity to have contact once again with other humans. It's not difficult to imagine that some of Adam's descendents could have married other humans that were not part of Adam's lineage. This could solve another dilemma in the Genesis story wherein Cain, after murdering his only sibling and being driven by God out into the wilderness, fears others who will hurt him. If Cain and his parents were the only humans on earth, there would be no one else for Cain to fear. Also, the fact that Cain eventually finds a wife can also be explained by the fact that other humans existed at the same time.

The idea that Adam and Even were not the only humans on earth would also address the issue described under Approach #1 concerning genetic mutation rates. If all humans alive today descended from two individuals that lived about 6,000 years ago, the genetic mutation rate would have needed to have been extremely high to produce all the variation that exists among humans today. However, if Adam and Eve were not the only humans on earth 6,000 years ago, then Adam and Eve are not necessarily in the lineage of every person that exists today, and there is no longer a problem with the mutation rate.

Approach #4: *Adam and Eve were not real individuals, but instead figuratively represent humanity.*

The fourth approach is the greatest departure from a literal reading of Genesis, but has nevertheless been proposed by some Christian scholars based on recent comparisons of the Genesis story with stories from other cultures and traditions. In this approach, Adam and Eve are merely metaphorical representatives of all humanity, or some subset of humanity with which God is beginning a new work on earth. Some have even proposed that Adam and Eve represent a sort of "proto-Israel," the first of many occasions in which God calls his people to a life of obedience but his people disobey and are punished.

This approach requires considerably more creativity in constructing a plausible narrative for how sin entered the picture. After all, if Adam and Eve were not real, specific individuals, then Eden was probably not a real, physical location either. And if there was no Eden, then the tree of the knowledge of good and evil was not a real, physical tree. In this scenario that is so different from the one that the Bible describes, how would humanity have disobeyed a direct and specific prohibition from God, resulting in the introduction of sin into the world?

This is an extremely thorny problem that I'm in no position to address as it treats the whole creation story in Genesis 1-3 as entirely metaphorical. However, it is interesting to note that much of what God calls us to - self-sacrifice, loving our enemies, patience, generosity, helping those in need - are exactly the sorts of things that are atypical under the Organic Paradigm, for humans and for other creatures as well. In nature, every organism must compete to survive. Aggression and selfishness pay dividends in terms of prolonging an organism's life and enabling it to reproduce. In short, outcompeting your neighbor is the name of the game. Is it possible that God's intention when he first began relating to humans was to draw them out of this "natural" way of living, this code of self-preservation and self-promotion that is fundamental to the theory of evolution? After all, if we have a God to rely on, there is no longer a need to rely on ourselves to ensure our well-being. With God we can rise above the natural laws that govern the rest of nature and live in ways that the evolutionary process could never produce.

This is heady stuff, I know. Heady and dangerous. I myself don't know where I stand on it. But I do know that sincere, scholarly Christians have been considering ideas such as these, and this book wouldn't be truly even-handed if I didn't include them.

Chapter 17

Why Noah's Ark Is Important

For many in the Theistic Paradigm, the primary alternative to evolution is the story of Noah's ark in Genesis 6 - 8. While the Bible says nothing about fossils, the great Noachian Flood (which apparently is easier to pronounce than "Noahian Flood") is believed to be the mechanism through which all fossils were created. Since every creature that was not on the ark died, and the turbulent churning of water would have kicked up lots of mud, the bodies of those animals would have settled to the bottom of the worldwide ocean in that mud. In other words, all fossils were formed at the same time in sediments deposited by a single worldwide flood. As the waters receded and collected in modern day oceans, the mud dried out and the animals became fossilized. The same retreating waters are also believed to be the source of the Grand Canyon and many other natural formations we have today.

There are a number of fossil observations that give credence to the Noachian Flood story. For instance, many fossils of what are clearly aquatic creatures have been found in places where there is no water currently, like deserts. There are even fossils of trilobites, ancient bottom-dwelling sea creatures, at the top of Mount Everest. If a worldwide flood churned up the water, it makes sense that some dead creatures could be deposited in mud far from where they normally lived, especially since the Bible says that the floodwaters covered even the highest mountains.

There have also been some creative ways of explaining why fossil deposits seem to follow a trend from invertebrates and marine creatures in the lowest rock layers, amphibians and small reptiles in the middles layers, and land mammals in the highest layers as described in Chapter 13. As the flood began and churned up the existing lakes and seas into a muddy soup, marine creatures would have died. The most delicate, slow-moving invertebrates would have died first, followed by fish who would be able to escape the muddiest waters for a time before also succumbing. As the waters rose, land animals began to die. The larger and more capable land animals and birds would have fled to higher ground as the floodwaters rose, so they would have been buried in the uppermost levels of mud as the floodwaters eventually claimed them as well.

Aligning the flood story described in the Bible with some of what has been found in the studies of geology and paleontology works reasonably well if you take a broad, generalist approach to the issue. If you look more closely at some of the details, however, problems arise. For instance, it is known from experimentation that the formation of rock from mud deposited at the bottom of a lake or river requires enormous pressures. Merely drying out those sedimentary deposits will never produce rocks no matter how long you wait. So, how did the rocks at the top of Mount Everest, the ones containing fossils of trilobites, form? Unless you assume that God miraculously turned that mud into rock Himself, the only other possibility is that, at some point in time after the mud was deposited by some body of water, that mud must have been buried miles underground. Only at those depths would the pressures be great enough to squeeze the water out of the mud and cement the individual particles together into rocks, encasing the dead trilobites within. Later geological upheavals would then have been required to force those rocks and fossils back up to the surface. If the Noachian Flood was responsible for depositing trilobite fossils on the top of Mount Everest, it seems some divine intervention would also have been required.

There is also evidence that sedimentary deposits containing fossils were not all produced at the same time from the same body of water. In some locations there are multiple layers of sediment, one on top of the other. In addition to being different colors, the layers appear to have been deposited at different times because of a characteristic of sedimentation: the largest particles will always fall to the bottom of a body of water before the smallest particles (pebbles drop before sand, sand before clay, etc). It's reasonable to expect that this natural particle sorting would be preserved even after the sediment is slowly compressed into rock. Thus in a given layer of sedimentary rock, geologists typically observe that the particles at the bottom of the layer tend to be larger than the particles at the top. Where multiple layers are present, you can see a pattern consisting of large particles, then small particles, then large particles, then small particles, and so on. The average geologist wouldn't expect this pattern if all the sediment was deposited at the same time. If such a pattern was truly produced by a single flood, the physical mechanism through which it would have occurred is a mystery.

The idea that the Noachian Flood carved out the Grand Canyon as the water retreated into modern day oceans suggests that the walls of the Canyon were made of mud when this occurred. After all, they are made entirely of sedimentary rock, and under the Theistic Paradigm all sedimentary rock was produced by the Noachian Flood. However, the walls of the Grand Canyon are very steep, much too steep to have remained upright if they were made of mud when the floodwaters were receded and the canyon was formed. Again, unless God intervened to turn the wall of mud into rock before the water receded, the only alternative is that the sedimentary rock was there before the water even started flowing. In other words, the sedimentary rock forming the walls of the Grand Canyon must have been formed sometime before the Noachian Flood, not by it. Moreover, those walls consist of many separate sedimentary layers which can be identified by different compositions, grain size, and even color. Multiple layers suggests that they were produced at different times rather than all at once.

Finally, the idea that organisms differed in their ability to escape the flood, leading to different types of fossils in different layers of sediment, is difficult to align with what paleontologists actually see in the fossil record. While it's true that invertebrates and fish are found in the lowest rock layers, they are also found in all other layers as well. If invertebrates and fish died before all other animals, they should only be found in the lowest rock layers. Similarly, reptiles and amphibians are found in the middle rock layers, but they are also found in the highest rock layers. If they all died before the largest land animals and birds, their fossils should not be found in the highest rock layers.

So if some of the basic observations in geology and paleontology seem to contradict what we might expect from a global flood, what are we to make of the Biblical story?

One option is to treat the story of Noah and the ark as a parable that was not intended to be taken literally, but which instead was intended only to demonstrate God's judgment of the wicked and His mercy on the righteous. But this would require some extravagant reinterpretation of scripture given that Noah is treated as a real person in both the books of Ezekiel and Hebrews, and Noah is also listed in Jesus's genealogy. Jesus Himself talks about the Noachian Flood as if it was a real event.

And then there is the fact that there are hundreds of ancient flood stories from cultures all around the world. While most of these stories might be more easily ascribed to local tsunamis or ice dam failures, three of these stories stand out as being particularly similar to the Biblical story. These stories are commonly referred to as Eridu Genesis, The Epic of Atrahasis, and the Epic of Gilgamesh. Not only were they authored in the Mesopotamian region around Babylon and Ur, Abram's hometown, but all three stories follow the same general pattern of events:

- A divine decision is made to wipe out humans using a flood

- A righteous hero figure is warned about the coming flood and is told to build a large boat

- The hero loads a small number of people and lots of animals onto the boat

- When the flood comes, all others die but those on the boat survive

- After the flood, the hero, his family, and all the animals repopulate the earth

The Epic of Gilgamesh also includes several additional features that are extraordinarily similar to the Noachian Flood:

- The boat is sealed with pitch and has only one door

- The hero searches for dry land by releasing birds

- The boat comes to rest on a mountain

- The hero makes animal sacrifices to give thanks for his salvation

Naturally, there are also some differences between these other Mesopotamian flood stories and the Biblical story. For instance, they include multiple gods, the names are all different, and the period of the flooding is 7 days instead of 40. Nevertheless, the similarities leave us with only two options:

1. The Mesopotamian stories and the Biblical story were independently authored descriptions of the same event

2. The more recently written flood stories were modified versions of the oldest flood stories

In general, the Theistic Paradigm prefers conclusion #1 and the Organic Paradigm prefers conclusion #2. Regardless of which one is correct, the very existence of other flood stories lends credence to the idea that the Noachian Flood was a real event.

The next question that arises is then: was it a global flood or a local one?

If you add up all the water in all the world's oceans, rivers, lakes, and underground springs, as well as all the water that exists as water vapor, you could indeed cover the entire face of an earth-size planet to a depth of well over a mile. I say "earth-sized planet" because the only way this could happen on Earth is if Earth was shaped like a perfectly smooth ball with no mountains and no valleys. In fact, all ground that is currently above sea level would need to have been an average of more than a mile lower. The deepest part of the Pacific Ocean, which is over six miles deep, would need to have been about five miles higher. In other words, the earth would have to have been mostly flat prior to the flood, with just enough highlands for people to live. At the time of the flood, great earthquakes would have caused the land levels to drop and the floor of the oceans to rise. This would have forced water from the oceans to flood over all dry land. After the flood, the earthquakes would have had to switch directions, causing land to rise again and the floor of the oceans to drop. The water would then have drained away from the rising landscape back into the oceans.

Since there is no evidence of this sort of worldwide rising and falling of landmasses, and no known mechanism by which it might have occurred, another idea that has been proposed is that much of the water that caused the flood was actually hanging in the air as water vapor. At just the right time, some sort of trigger would have caused all this water to rain down on the Earth. The main problem with that much water vapor is that the resulting air pressure would kill all living things. Alternatively, the water might have been orbiting the earth just like the rings of Saturn. Again, something would have had to cause all that water to suddenly fall to earth.

Since there are significant technical problems with every one of these scenarios for a worldwide flood, the idea of a local flood has gained a lot of traction. Interestingly, the Bible story itself hints that the flood may have been a local event. After the ark comes to rest on a mountain, Noah releases a dove. When it returns to him, it has an olive branch in its beak. Where did it get the olive branch? Somewhere there was an olive tree. But only 232 days had passed since the rain stopped, and there had been dry ground for considerably less time. All olive trees would have died in the flood, and it is unlikely that a new olive tree could have grow from a seed in that short amount of time. A reasonable solution to this conundrum is that the olive tree was simply in some area that had not experienced flooding.

If the Noachian Flood was local, it would most likely have occurred somewhere in Mesopotamia. Coincidentally (or maybe not), there is a long history of major floods in the area between Baghdad and the Persian Gulf, along the Tigris and Euphrates Rivers. As recently as 1954 a flood covered hundreds of miles of this area. There is also a theory that the Noachian Flood may have been in the region of the Black Sea, North of Mesopotamia. Some geologists believe that the Black Sea flooded as a result of rising water levels in the Mediterranean Sea.

As an alternative to the theory of evolution, the Noachian Flood itself is only half of the story. The other half has to do with the ark and the animals that were on it. Putting aside for the moment the idea of a local flood, the Theistic Paradigm views the ark as the means through which God repopulated the entire earth after the flood destroyed everything else. Under this view, every person living today can count Noah as his ancestor, and every animal that exists today is a descendant of the animals that were on the ark. There is no denying that the Bible says (or at least strongly implies) exactly this. However, from a practical point of view it is difficult to see how so many animals could have fit on the ark.

The Bible is clearly describes the basic structure of the ark. At about 450 feet long, it was a bit shorter than the Titanic. It was 75 feet wide and 45 feet high, and had three separate decks. I don't know how Noah and his three sons managed to build it by themselves, but if they had 50 - 75 years to do it (which isn't out of the question given the ambiguity in the Bible), maybe it just took persistence.

The total volume of the ark was about 1.5 million cubic feet. If we assume that one-third of that space was devoted to food and water storage, passageways, and scaffolding and braces for structural support, and if you assume that animal cages could be stacked on top of one another to use up all the remaining space, you could have a total of 8,000 cages, each of which was 5 feet by 5 feet by 5 feet.

Unfortunately, 8,000 cages isn't quite enough. If we assume that Noah did not take any aquatic animals nor any insects, but instead only took mammals, reptiles, amphibians, and birds, he would have needed space for about 30,000 different species that are alive today. If you assume that the ark also held every kind of animal that has ever lived, the total number of species could easily be ten times more.

And don't forget that this includes the dinosaurs, some of which were absolutely huge. Ornithocheirus was an aircraft-sized reptilian flyer, and Argentinosaurus was the heaviest of all dinosaurs at 90 tons and would have filled one-quarter of the length of the ark. Then there was Gigantosaurus which was the largest land predator of all time, larger even than the famed Tyrannosaurus Rex. Just a few of these huge beasts would have completely filled the ark.

One solution that has been proposed for the problem of large animals is that Noah would only have taken juveniles on board the ark. There would also be a lot of variation in the sizes of the cages. For instance, most amphibians and birds would not need cages as big as 5 x 5 x 5 feet. Smaller cages for them would allow for larger cages for some of the dinosaurs and mammals. But it still leaves the bigger problem that there would simply have been too many different species.

The key to solving this dilemma is the Bible's use of the word "kind" instead of "species," as in "every kind of animal." If we assume that "kind" refers not to species, but instead to some higher taxonomic rank such as genus or family, then the number of animals that would need to be on the ark would be significantly reduced. Again, assuming the Noah only loaded mammals, reptiles, amphibians, and birds on the ark, the 30,000 species that are alive today can be grouped into a few thousand genera, which can be further grouped into just a few hundred families. Even if you added in all species that have gone extinct, it might just be possible for a representative of every animal family to be on the ark.

Of course, this solution creates another problem. Once those animals left the ark, they would need to diversify into all the species we have today. In other words, you would need to assume at least some limited form of evolution. As an example, the mammal family Muridae contains 260 genera and 1150 species.

This is the animal group representing all rats, mice, voles, gerbils, hamsters, and the like. If there was only one pair of "muridae rodents" on the ark, then after leaving the ark that pair would become the source of all of the 1150 different species that exist today. Since we know that the genotypes of all 1150 species are different, the process of diversifying the first muridae rodents would require a phenomenally fast rate of genetic mutations, not to mention quickly changing environments to drive natural selection. The alternative, of course, is that God could have intervened to drive the diversification of the single pair of muridae rodents into 1150 different species.

Assuming that the ark could indeed hold 8,000 animal pairs and that these animals were sufficient to repopulate the earth with all known species, consider what it would have taken to care for them. There are only eight people on board the ark. If every one of them worked 16 hours a day, and every animal pair was only fed twice per week, every person would be feeding an animal pair every 4 minutes. They would also have needed to clean out cages at least occasionally. Noah's 600 year old back must have been killing him.

One the flood was over and the animals left the ark, they would have had to reach all places on earth that now have animals. This would have included places where, at least with modern geography, can only be reached by crossing an ocean, something difficult to do for most land animals. One possible solution to this problem is an accelerated rate of plate tectonic movement. Currently continents move at a rate of about 1-2 inches per year relative to one another, and thus have been in essentially the same position for all of human history. But if continents moved much faster immediately after the Noachian Flood ended, it might have been possible for the animals to get to places as far away as South America by simply walking on land (since, for instance, South America and Africa are believed to have once been one land mass). However, there is no evidence that continents ever moved faster than they do today, and significantly faster movement would very likely cause the number of earthquakes and volcanic eruptions to also increase dramatically. The resulting impacts on the land could easily make earth uninhabitable.

Australia is a good example of a place far from Mesopotamia that also has many species that are found no where else in the world. If all animals in Australia are descendants of the animals aboard the ark, then the animals that left the ark must have left no trace of themselves between Mesopotamia and Australia. This means, for instance, that the animals that left the ark must have diversified into the species we know today only after reaching Australia, not before, and could not have left any members of its species in any of the lands along the way.

There is no reason to believe that the Noachian Flood was not a real event, at least locally, and the difficulties of using the Noachian Flood as an alternative to evolution are not insurmountable. But it does require a host of assumptions that do not easily fit with our current understanding of geology and geography, and moreover they bump up against the limits of what is practically feasible. At the same time, we know that with God all things are possible. While some of the problems with the story of Noah's ark and the flood may seem insurmountable, we can't dismiss the possibility that extraordinarily unlikely events actually did occur through divine intervention.

Chapter 18

Is Life Too Complex To Have Evolved?

If you created a list of all the concerns that those in the Theistic Paradigm have with the theory of evolution, many of them would involve specific issues: Was neanderthalensis a human or not? Are atomic decay rates truly constant? Do the nubs on either side of a horse's toe represent the vestiges of additional side toes?

But one of the more general concerns that folks in the Theistic Paradigm have, one that touches all aspects of the theory of evolution, is whether evolution can bring about increases in biological complexity. It's one thing to theorize that an organism might go through changes to help it adapt to its environment. Those changes don't necessarily need to result in an increase in complexity. But if a single-celled organism is going to evolve into a giraffe, there must be an increase in complexity somewhere along the line, and a dramatic one at that. If the theory of evolution cannot explain the development of more complex organisms from less complex ones, then it loses much of its punch.

Recall that a decent summary definition of evolution is:

Natural selection acting on variations in phenotype brought about through random mutations in genotype

The concern regarding biological complexity is not so much with these inner workings of the theory of evolution as it is with the outcome: simple organisms turning into more and more complex

237

organisms over time. Many in the Theistic Paradigm have a visceral reaction to the idea that the complexity and diversity of life might have evolved through the unguided, unconscious, unintentional operation of simple physics and chemistry. This sort of reaction can be driven by the dramatic visual of a single-celled organism evolving into, say, a giraffe. How, any reasonable person might wonder, could such a thing just happen, all by itself? So, before getting into the issue of complexity, let me first break the issue down into something more manageable.

Henrietta the Giraffe lives in Niger, Africa. Biologically speaking, she's as complex a creature as any on earth. According to the theory of evolution, she evolved from a single-celled organism that lived 2+ billion years ago. Single-celled organisms are actually rather complex, but not nearly as complex as a giraffe, so there's an enormous gap that the theory of evolution needs to explain.

Henrietta has an ancestor that lived 10,000 years ago. His name is Jake, and he is Henrietta's great^{2,000}-grandfather. That is, there are 2,000 generations between Jake and Henrietta. To the casual observer, Jake would have looked exactly like Henrietta. But if you studied his DNA, you would discover that he is only 99.99% the same as Henrietta. There is something slightly different about his metabolism, or the width of his pelvis, or something else that wouldn't be obvious without an extremely detailed study of his physiology. Jake and Henrietta may in fact be the same species.

Under the theory of evolution, Jake's descendents evolved to produce Henrietta. But of course very little evolution needed to occur, since Jake's genotype was almost (but not quite) the same as Henrietta's. Over the course of 2,000 generations, the process of natural selection acting on variations in phenotype brought about through random genetic mutations only needed to change 0.01% of Jake's DNA. This small amount of change occurring over such a long period of time does not sound as problematic as a single-celled organism evolving into a giraffe. Certainly there was some sort of increase in complexity occurring between Jake and Henrietta, but it would be very difficult to identify and measure. After all, if Jake's pelvis were slightly wider than Henrietta's pelvis, would we say that Henrietta was really more complex than Jake?

Jake also had an ancestor that lived 10,000 years before him, 20,000 years before Henrietta. Her name was Darla, and she was Henrietta's great^{4,000}-grandmother. Again, Darla looked more or less like both Henrietta and Jake, but her DNA differed from them both. Darla's DNA was 99.98% the same as Henrietta's and 99.99% the same as Jake's. Darla's descendants evolved over 2,000 generations to produce Jake, and Jake's descendents evolved over another 2,000 generations to produce Henrietta. As a result, Henrietta is very slightly more complex than Jake, and Jake is very slightly more complex than Darla.

I could of course go on and on, further and further back in time, with each ancestor differing by only a very small amount from its descendents. I could go all the way back to the single-celled organism that started it all. The point is that the theory of evolution is primarily concerned with these very small changes occurring over very long periods of time. From the point of view of those in the Organic Paradigm, the theory of evolution does not need to explain the increase in complexity between a single-celled organism and Henrietta the giraffe. It only needs to explain the tiny increase in complexity between Jake and Henrietta, or between Darla and Jake.

For some in the Theistic Paradigm, the concern about increasing biological complexity is less troublesome given that the theory of evolution proposes very small increases in complexity occurring over long periods of time. But for others, this fact is irrelevant - any increase in complexity that is posited to have occurred through purely natural processes runs afoul of everything we know about how the universe works.

The Second Law of Thermodynamics

At the heart of most arguments against increases in biological complexity is an appeal, either explicitly or implicitly, to the Second Law of Thermodynamics. The Second Law does not address complexity, at least not directly. Instead, it addresses organization. Complexity and organization are related, and both are important to the question of whether biological life could have evolved naturally. But whereas complexity is a measure of the number of parts in an object and their interactions with one another, organization refers to the arrangement of the parts, such as whether they are in a particular sequence or pattern. This distinction will become a bit clearer in a moment. But first you need to understand what the Second Law of Thermodynamics says, and what it doesn't say, before you can really understand the arguments that make use of it.

The Second Law of Thermodynamics is a principle that describes how the universe behaves with regard to changes in how it is organized over time. In the context of thermodynamics, the definition generally involves references to heat pumps, transformation of heat into work, and heady concepts like Carnot cycles and system irreversibility. But in the context of evolution, a much simpler definition will suffice. Here are two versions that I dug up:

The universe is increasing in disorder over time.

The universe is steadily becoming less organized, more random, and more chaotic.

Or, to sound a bit more scientific:

Entropy (a measure of randomness) in a closed system can never decrease.

A good example of the Second Law would be my teenage sons' rooms. We generally keep the doors shut so we can maintain the illusion that our home is neat and orderly.

If you hold up the Second Law against evolution, they seem to be at odds with one another. Evolution seems to suggest that a bunch of chemicals, randomly bouncing around and looking nothing at all like life, got together and created living organisms. Then those organisms continued to gain order and complexity over time. In short, order arose naturally and spontaneously out of chaos. But if the Second Law is true, then evolution must be false. The universe is always trending towards more disorder, not more order.

There are several common misunderstandings about the Second Law of Thermodynamics. First, it's not really a law about what can and cannot happen. It's more of a description of what's most likely and what's improbable, and it's based more on statistics than on science. For instance, if you blow up a balloon, the air inside the balloon is going to be distributed evenly throughout the space inside the balloon. As a result, the molecules press equally on all sides of the balloon, keeping it in a (roughly) round shape. You would not expect the air molecules inside the balloon to organize themselves and, say, all clump together on one side of the balloon. Such an increase in organization would seem to violate the Second Law of Thermodynamics, but technically it doesn't. Believe it or not, there is actually a chance, a very very small chance, that the air molecules would indeed clump together on one side of the balloon all by themselves. To see why, we look at all possible arrangements of the particles, and then calculate the probability that one particular arrangement that we call "orderly" will occur.

Start with two air molecules in a balloon. Those two molecules would both be found on the same side of the balloon 50% of the time. The reason is that there are only four possible arrangements, and two of those involve both molecules being on the same side at the same time.

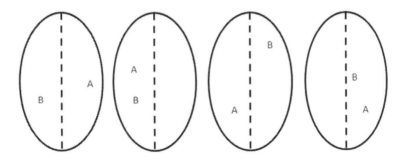

The chances of seeing all the molecules on one side of the balloon shrink as you add more molecules. For instance, if you increase the number of molecules to three, all three will be found on one side of the balloon 25% of the time because there are eight possible arrangements, of which only two involve all molecules being on one side.

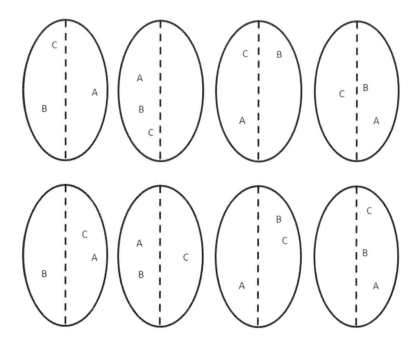

For a balloon holding ten molecules, the chances that all molecules will be on one side shrink to 0.2%. For twenty molecules, the chances are 0.00019%. And for 100 molecules, the chances are 0.00000000000000000000000000000016%.

So how many molecules are typically in a balloon? Way, way more than 100. It's something on the order of a hundred billion trillion. With this many molecules, the odds of all of them being on one side of the balloon at any given moment would be ...

OK, how do I describe this number? It's really really super duper small. If I had to write it out in terms of a percentage like I did above, there would not be enough paper in this book to fit it all.

In fact, there are so many zeros in this number that the number could not fit into all the books that have ever existed in all of earthly history. It is mindbogglingly small.

So, the first important thing to know about the Second Law is that it is really just a description of the probability that an ordered system will arise naturally and spontaneously out of a chaotic system. Depending on the specific system, the likelihood that this will happen could be vanishingly small. But that's not the same as saying it's impossible.

You might think that that's the end of the story. Biological systems have many, many molecules, and thus the probability that they could spontaneously increase in order and complexity is essentially zero. Unfortunately, the application of the Second Law to evolution is complicated by the fact that molecules have certain properties that can, on occasion, make them act in ways that seem contrary to the Second Law. To see why, consider a hexagonal grid with 163 holes:

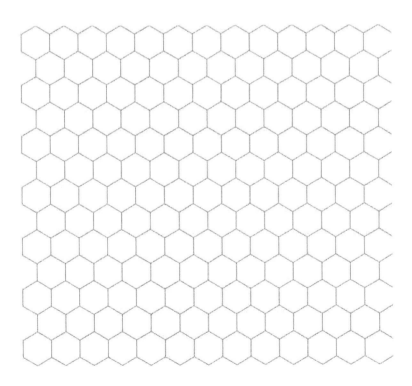

Now imagine that you have 43 hexagonal dice. You drop them all into this grid, shake it and let the dice fall where they will (like a Boggle™ game). You will very likely end up with something random-looking, such as this:

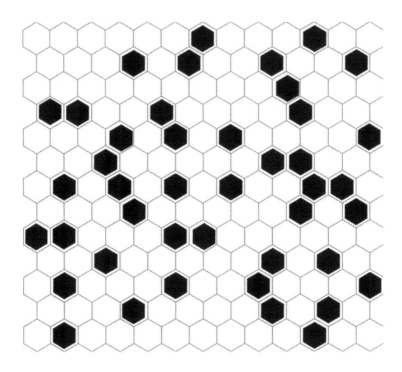

You can calculate the number of different ways that 43 dice can be arranged in a grid containing 163 holes. I won't bother you with the math, but the number of possible arrangements is:

4,959,572,206,997,890,000,000,000,000,000,000,000,000

The vast majority of these arrangements will appear to have no order whatsoever. So, you might be very surprised if you gave the tray a good shake and ended up with an arrangement that looked like this:

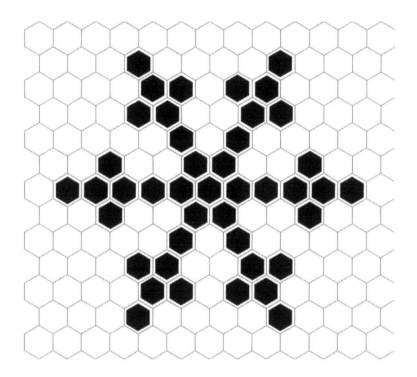

The odds of 43 dice accidentally arranging themselves into this shape is extremely unlikely statistically speaking, and yet it occurs all the time in the real world. This is the shape of a snowflake. Under specific conditions of temperature and pressure, water molecules in the atmosphere will spontaneously bind together into the familiar snowflake pattern. And when you are talking about snowflakes, you aren't just talking about 163 water molecules. No, you're talking about a million million million water molecules. Statistically, the odds of this many water molecules accidentally self-organizing into a six-pointed star are effectively zero.

So how can it be that snowflakes are so common if the odds of them forming are so small?

The answer is that real molecules don't behave merely as dice in a tray. That is, they don't merely follow the mathematics of probability. Molecules interact with one another according to fundamental physical laws that are themselves functions of the properties of the specific atoms of which they are composed. In the case of water molecules, under certain conditions they have a tendency to line up in a hexagonal pattern. Like ice, all crystals have a specific, repeatable arrangement of molecules that appears to defy the Second Law of Thermodynamics. This is the reason that minerals, which are crystals, are thought by some in the Organic Paradigm to be the template on which the first forms of life arose (see Chapter 19 for more on this idea).

The orderly arrangement of molecules in crystals is just one example of how something orderly can arise naturally out of a chaotic system in apparent contradiction to the Second Law of Thermodynamics. If you believe that the universe arose out of the Big Bang rather than having been created instantly by God in its current form, then the structure of celestial bodies is another example. Galaxies, stars, and planets all have orderly structures, at least at large scales, that appear to have arisen naturally out of the chaotic plasma soup produced by the Big Bang. You can also sometimes see orderly arrangements in things like straight rows of clouds or the ripples in sand at the edge of a lake. Pebbles can get sorted by wind or water, with the largest at the bottom and the smallest at the top. Highly structured tornados form spontaneously out of chaotic swirls of moist air. There are also examples of structure occurring at the molecular level apart from crystals. For instance, the Beloussov-Zhabotinsky reaction is an obscure chemical reaction that actually produces a target pattern where concentric rings travel outward from random centers. The resulting patterns have a distinctly biological appearance even though no biological life is involved.

Given that there are examples of order arising naturally out of disorder in non-biological systems, the obvious question is how such things fit with the Second Law of Thermodynamics. The technical answer is that the Second Law only tells you how the total order within an isolated system will change over time. It does not tell you how part of an isolated system will change, nor does it tell you how the order within a non-isolated system will change.

These concepts are a bit abstract, and unless you have been schooled in thermodynamics they may not be easy to grasp. So, below are several examples intended to illustrate how order can increase in apparent contradiction to the Second Law.

When you build a house, you are converting a pile of disorderly lumber and nails into a considerably more orderly structure. The order associated with the lumber and nails has certainly increased, but somehow the Second Law of Thermodynamics must still be true: total order must have decreased. The reason there seems to be a conflict is because it is common to think of order as residing only in the organization of physical objects (including molecules). In reality, order is also a function of energy. In order to convert the disorderly lumber and nails into a more orderly house, a bunch of people, or robots, or people using power tools, had to expend energy. In the case of people, the energy comes in the form of food, while in the case of robots or power tools, the energy comes in the form of electricity from burning coal. The transfer of energy from either food or electricity into the work required to assemble the house is actually quite inefficient, thermodynamically speaking. This means that, for every five units of energy expended, only one actually does some useful work. The rest gets lost as useless heat, and that heat loss actually represents and increase in disorder, thermodynamically speaking. Thus, even though the lumber and nails increased in order, a lot of energy was expended in the process, and the total amount of order in the world actually decreased.

The same process is true for a newly fertilized human egg. Compared to a newborn infant, the egg is biologically less complex. Thus, the biological order increases over the span of only nine months. It is true that the DNA inside the fertilized egg directed the increase in complexity over the course of that nine months, but that fact is actually irrelevant when it comes to the Second Law of Thermodynamics. DNA is just the plan of assembly of a human being, just as a blueprint is the plan of assembly of a house. In order for the Second Law to be satisfied with the growing human fetus, there needs to be an increase in disorder somewhere, and that disorder comes through the expenditure of energy. Mom eats lots of hamburgers and ice cream[32], and this provides the chemical energy that the fetus needs

---

[32] Sometimes all at once.

to increase in biological complexity. Just as for the house, much of the food energy consumed by mom actually gets released as heat from the body. The combination of the increasing order of the fetus plus the decreasing order of the food that has been converted to heat results in an overall increase in disorder.

One more example.

The hydraulic ram is a device that is used to pump water uphill. It has no external power source, but instead is simply a collection of tubes, tanks, and valves. The "power" that drives the pump is water flowing under the force of gravity.

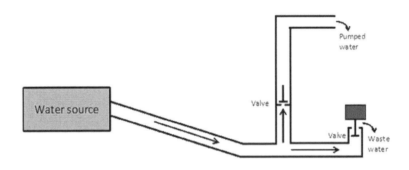

As flowing water moves down from the original water source under the force of gravity, it has a tendency first to flow through the waste valve. Because of the design of this valve, the movement of the water actually forces the valve to close. When it does, the water descending from the original water source "rams" into the newly closed waste water valve, and the pressure in the pipe jumps up slightly. When this sudden pressure spike occurs, some water is forced upwards through the vertical pipe and out the top. You've just pumped a tiny bit of water uphill.

But the operation of the hydraulic ram doesn't stop there. The vertical movement of water causes the pressure in the whole system to drop. The water in the vertical pipe would naturally fall back down, but a one-way valve stops it from doing so. However, since the pressure in the system has dropped, water can once again escape through the waste valve, and the whole cycle starts again. As the water pressures and water flows oscillate between the two valves, water is pumped out through the top pipe.

It's not voodoo. This is a real system that actually works. In fact, a well-constructed hydraulic ram with an unlimited supply of feed water (such as a river) can run more or less indefinitely.

It would be tempting to think of a hydraulic ram as a device that gives you something for nothing, in essence increasing the order of the universe without any energy input. After all, it would have taken work for you to haul buckets of water up a hill, but the device seems to make it happen without any work. In this case, instead of energy coming from food or coal, the energy actually comes from gravity. As the water flows down from the original water source under the influence of gravity, it gains kinetic energy - momentum. Some of that momentum is used to push some of the water uphill, and other portions of the momentum get lost as heat as the water pressure oscillates and valves snap open and shut. The water exiting through the waste valve has almost no momentum at all. For the system as a whole, disorder has increased even though some water (the water exiting the top of the pump) has actually gained some order (in this case, in the form of potential energy).

The hydraulic ram demonstrates how one part of a system can gain order at the expense of another part - order can indeed increase in one place so long as it is decreasing somewhere else. But it's not a good example of how this might occur spontaneously in nature. After all, somebody built the hydraulic ram. Snowflakes, on the other hand, do arise spontaneously, and through a similar process: heat moves out of local area of the atmosphere into the surrounding areas. The reduction in heat energy causes the water molecules to form well-ordered snowflakes. However, the movement of heat energy to another location actually causes an overall increase in disorder for the atmosphere as a whole.

While snowflakes are good examples of how order can arise spontaneously out of chaos in apparent (but only apparent) contradiction to the Second Law of Thermodynamics, that's about as far as you can go with them as far as evolution is concerned. Snowflakes are highly improbable, statistically speaking, but they are also very simple structures, many orders of magnitude less complex than even the simplest single-celled organism. So we are back to the question of whether the biological complexity that the theory of evolution purports to explain is really possible.

Mathematics in nature

If increases in biological complexity were indeed the result of purely natural processes, you would expect to find some sort of law or laws based in physics or chemistry that would drive the process: something in the fabric of matter and energy itself, some property of the way that atoms and molecules interact with one another, some fundamental mechanism whose activities could be described mathematically.

To date, no one has identified such a law or a collection of laws that drive evolution. We have mathematical descriptions of rotational dynamics, gravitation, fluid mechanics, sound, heat conduction, electromagnetic waves, magnetic fields, electrical circuits, optics, and quantum mechanics, but we have never come close to generating a mathematical description of whatever fundamental laws are responsible for increasing complexity in biological organisms through the evolutionary process.

To some in the Theistic Paradigm, the fact that no fundamental laws responsible for driving evolution have been found is evidence that none exist. It may be, however, that such laws simply have not yet been identified. For all the understanding that scientists have of biochemistry, it remains an incredibly complicated subject area and there is much yet to be studied. Maybe fundamental laws responsible for evolution will eventually be identified, maybe they won't.

Scientists have, however, identified some properties of biological organisms that do seem to follow some mathematical functions. These functions hint at deeper fundamental laws operating at the molecular level, though what those deeper laws might be remains elusive.

For instance, many organisms contain structures that follow the

Fibonacci sequence, which follows this formula:

$$N_i = N_{i-1} + N_{i-2}$$

Beginning with the sequence 1, 1, all subsequent numbers in the sequence are simply the sum of the previous two:

$$1, 1, 2, 3, 5, 8, 13, 21, 34, 55...$$

The Fibonacci sequence shows up in the arrangement of leaves around stems, seeds in a sunflower, petals on a rose, seashell spirals, and the patterns of pine cones and pineapples. Other types of spirals that also appear regularly in nature can be described by logarithmic functions. Clearly the DNA of these organisms contains the directions that result in these mathematically-based structures, but no one has yet been able to discern how - or why - the Fibonacci sequence appears out of those instructions.

Similarly, fractal geometry appears to play an important part in the development of many different forms of life. One of the most fascinating approaches to fractals involves the use of mathematical functions that are based on complex numbers that include "real" and "imaginary" components. These functions can be very simple and yet produce extremely complex patterns that have distinctly biological looks to them. I have created a few fractals of my own using free software, and the patterns are both unpredictable and beautiful:

Many structures in biological organisms appear to be based on fractal geometries, including tree branches, the shape of broccoli, bird feathers, the color patterns on animals, the structure of the neural, lymphatic, and circulatory systems, and even the folding of DNA itself. But once again, no one is really sure how it is that the mathematics of fractals are woven into the physical laws that must drive evolution if evolution is a purely natural process.

Some scientists have also observed certain patterns in how organisms are structured that can be described with simple mathematics. For instance, it has long been known that large animals process energy more efficiently than smaller animals. The relationship has even been quantified: an animal's metabolic rate is proportional to its mass raised to the ¾ power. This mathematical relation is thought to be a consequence of the physics and geometry of animal circulatory systems, which as I said above are based on fractals. There are other mathematical relations that have been identified for the relationship between an animal's mass and the concentration of its muscle fibers and the characteristics of its locomotion. To put it in more general terms, the laws of physics seem to dictate, at least in part, how organisms are structured and how they operate.

Empirical results such as these have led some scientists to see biological evolution not in terms of increasing complexity, but instead in terms of increasing thermodynamic efficiency. In this view, evolution isn't driving organisms to be more complex, but instead is reducing the amount of energy required by organisms to function. Since all systems tend to migrate towards the lowest energy state (in fact this is one corollary of the Second Law of Thermodynamics), it's not difficult to imagine that increases in thermodynamic efficiency may be the force behind increases in biological complexity. But the exact mechanism connecting the evolutionary process to thermodynamics has not been identified.

Has life been designed?

The Second Law of Thermodynamics is not an impediment to evolution, and the appearance of some mathematical relations in nature suggests that there are some fundamental but as-yet unidentified physical laws at work driving the process. Even so, life has the appearance of having been designed. Even those in the Organic Paradigm will concede that the machinery of biochemistry, cells, tissues, and organs, not to mention the complexity of interactions between individual organisms and with their environments, looks as if it were assembled and set into motion intentionally. Those in the Theistic Paradigm can legitimately say that, since everyone agrees that life appears to have been designed, it is up to those in the Organic Paradigm to prove that it wasn't. In other words, it would be illogical to assume that life has not been designed when on the surface it appears that it has been.

Some in the Theistic Paradigm take this a step further and point to specific structures or biochemical processes that do not merely appear to have been designed, but are composed of such well-matched, interacting parts that there is no conceivable way that the structure could have come about through a purely natural process involving numerous, successive, slight modifications to a previous structure. Such structures are sometimes called "irreducibly complex". The most commonly cited examples of such structures and processes are:

- The eye
- Bacterial flagellum
- Echolocation in bats and dolphins
- The immune system
- Photosynthesis
- Blood coagulation
- The explosive defense mechanism of the bombardier beetle

The primary flaw in the argument for irreducible complexity is that in essence it claims that since no specific evolutionary mechanism can currently be conceived for certain biological structures, none will ever be discovered. As described in Chapter 5, there is a long history of science uncovering the underlying mechanisms for all sorts of things that had previously been thought to be inexplicable. It might be more appropriate to think of irreducible complexity as a way of highlighting one of the challenges that the theory of evolution has yet to overcome.

At the heart of irreducible complexity are three fundamental ideas:

1. If you remove a single part from a structure composed of many parts, it ceases to function.

2. All parts and all structures must have a useful function at all times. Evolution does not produce parts or structures that have no function now, but might have a useful

function later.

3. Evolution generally devises new uses for existing structures rather than generating a brand new structure from scratch.

To see the problem presented by irreducible complexity, you begin with any structure composed of multiple parts that all work together, and ask the question: What did the immediate precursor to this structure look like? Or alternatively, what was evolution's last step before arriving at the final structure? If you can't create a plausible narrative within the context of the three constraints listed above, you might wonder how the structure in question could have come about through purely natural processes.

Imagine that you have a device containing five interacting gears that together perform some function:

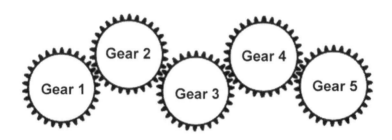

If you spin gear 1, gear 5 will also spin. If you remove any gear from the system, it will no longer work at all. If this five-gear system had evolved, what would have been its immediate precursor?

The very last step in the evolutionary process that created this five-gear system could not have been adding the final gear to a collection of four pre-existing gears, because the pre-existing gears would not have been able to function without the last part. Evolution would not have created a structure that is four-fifths complete but has zero functionality. As described in Chapter 10, if a structure (or part or molecule) has function and thus no adaptive value, natural selection can't select for it, so it shouldn't exit.

The last step in the evolutionary process that created the five-gear system could also not have been the entire five-gear structure popping into existence all at once. Notwithstanding the discussion of the Second Law of Thermodynamics above, the odds are strongly against a collection of random genetic mutations all occurring at the same time that create the five parts (or many more in the case of some biological systems) all at once, and assembled into the proper structure, in such a way that a distinct adaptive advantage is provided and natural selection can choose it.

Finally, the last step in the evolutionary process that created the five-gear system could not have involved five pre-existing but separate gears coming together all at the same time to create a new combined structure with a new function. Prior to being assembled in a single five-gear structure, all the individual gears must have had individual functions of their own that provided an adaptive advantage, or they would not have been present to begin with. But bringing them all together to create a new function is very likely to mean that their old, individual functions disappear. It is difficult to imagine an organism gaining an overall adaptive advantage with the sudden appearance of one new function and the simultaneous loss of many other functions. Moreover, the multiple random genetic changes required to assemble the existing five gears into a single new system with a new function are extraordinarily unlikely.

The idea of irreducible complexity posits that these are the only three possibilities for how the structure could have evolved. Since they each present apparently insurmountable problems, the only reasonable conclusion is that the structure must have been designed by Someone rather than arising through purely natural processes.

When it comes to debate over whether life was designed or not, the classic example is the evolution of the eye. Ironically, the evolution of the eye has been used by both those in the Theistic Paradigm and those in the Organic Paradigm to support their views.

The Organic Paradigm's view of the eye goes like this:

All vertebrates that exist today have light-sensitive photoreceptor cells that can detect light, and many non-vertebrates have the ability to detect light as well. Moreover, there is a wide variety of structures used. This is a good thing because eyes by and large don't fossilize well, so it is difficult to use the fossil record to establish the evolutionary history of the eye.

The table below shows a progression from the simplest to the most complex eyes among organisms that exist today.

Type of eye	Example organism
Spot of light-sensitive pigment that can detect light and dark	Single-celled Euglena
Flat collection of light-sensitive cells. Multiple cells provide more powerful light detection.	Limpet Patella
Light-sensitive cells forming a shallow cup (i.e. having a concave surface). The shallow cup provide a means for roughly determining the direction of light.	Flatworm Planarian
Light-sensitive cells forming a deep cup, providing more accurate detection of the direction of light.	Mollusk Pleurotomaria
Light-sensitive cells form the inside of a sphere (the retina), with only a tiny hole (the pupil) permitting light to enter the sphere. This structure is similar to a pinhole camera, and permits a crude image to be cast on the retina.	Mollusk nautilus
The sphere is totally enclosed, with semi-transparent cells forming a covering over the pupil (a rudimentary cornea). A semi-viscous jelly acts as a simple lens between the pupil and the retina. Images cast onto the retina are clearer than without such a lens.	Marine snail Murex
The lens is a flexible solid whose curvature is adjustable through the movement of attached muscles. An iris adjusts the size of the hole to permit more or less light to enter.	Octopus, moneys, humans

Under the Organic Paradigm, the wide variety of eye types exhibited among organisms that exist today is evidence that evolution could have produced the most complex eye structure through a series of small steps, each of which is only slightly different than the one before. Indeed, when laid out side-by-side, diagrams of different types of eyes exhibited among living organisms do seem to show a progression from simple to complex. It's not difficult to see why many in the Organic Paradigm use such a series of pictures to create a plausible narrative for the evolution of the eye. As additional support for such a narrative, some even point to eyes among mollusks (which includes squid, snails, slugs, clams, etc) which exhibit essentially all types and complexities of eyes in a single family.

With regard to concerns about irreducible complexity, folks in the Organic Paradigm would say that there is no need for each part of the most complex eye to be added one by one. Instead, each part starts out as a poorly functioning modification of a previous structure, but which nevertheless provides some adaptive advantage. Improvements are then made in tiny increments, not large jumps.

Despite the plausible narrative illustrated by the many different eye types among living organisms, there remain some fundamental problems for which there are no clear answers. For instance, it is true that there is no need for the sudden appearance of an enclosed sphere containing the retina; we can all picture a patch of light-sensitive cells bending inwards to form a shallow depression, then a deep cup, then an enclosed sphere. But other parts of the eye do seem to appear suddenly, such as the first lens. The viscous jelly comprising the first simple lens would only have provided an adaptive advantage if it was large enough to focus light coming in through the pupil. If the jelly blob was too small, it would either float around uselessly inside of the sphere, or would simply be too small to focus an image. In other words, it would seem that even the most rudimentary lens would need to pop into existence instantly and fully formed in order for it to be useful. Without a clear mechanism through which a lens would arise slowly over time, the lens, and thus the eye, may indeed be irreducibly complex.

Then there are the muscles that control the focal length of the lens and the muscles that control the size of the pupil in more advanced eyes. There is a certain minimum size for these muscles to be useful. The first appearance of just a few muscle cells would hardly be sufficient to adjust the lens or pupil, and yet such cells would need to provide some sort of useful function if they were to remain as part of the eye under the pressure of natural selection. With no plausible narrative for how these muscles could have arisen slowly through small changes in previous structures, it would seem that they too would fall under the category of irreducibly complex.

While eventually it may be possible to design plausible narratives for how all parts of the eye came into being through a slow evolutionary process, a bigger hurdle is in identifying the specific biochemicals that would need to come into play for these new structures. Further, for a truly complete evolutionary picture, we would also need to identify the genetic mutations that would need to occur, and in what order, that would produce the necessary biochemicals and the associated structures. While you can count the major components of even the most complex eye using just your fingers and toes, there are many thousands of different types of molecules involved not just in their structure, but also in the signaling pathways that actually make vision work. Scientists have yet to identify which genes control the formation, placement, and functionality of each type of molecule used in the eye, let alone demonstrate how a series of individual genetic mutations could have brought them all about in such a way that every step, and every type of molecule, provided an adaptive advantage to the organism on the way to producing a fully functioning eye.

This is not to say that scientists won't be able to do this someday. Indeed there are a number of other biochemical processes and structures for which plausible narratives have been generated. Examples include:

- Evolution of fibrinogen, a protein involved in blood clotting, from previous types of molecules

- Development of flagella from a symbiosis between bacterial spirochetes and eukaryotic cells

- Gene duplication as the source for new molecules used in

the immune system

- Origin of the Krebs metabolic pathway from simpler pathways used in amino acid biosynthesis

- Origin of insect wings from gill-like appendages in aquatic ancestors

In general, however, the evolutionary steps described in these situations are simpler than the case of the eye and rarely include the individual genetic mutational steps that would have been required. In some cases the description of how a biochemical process or structure evolved has been based on computer simulations, while in other cases it has been based on the similarities and differences between the functions of the same biochemicals in related organisms.

In addition to concerns about the ability of the theory of evolution to explain the appearance of the lens and control muscles in eyes, some in the Theistic Paradigm point to the broad variation in complexity of eyes found in nature and ask why there is such a prevalence of simpler eyes. Surely being able to see better would confer an advantage to any organism living in a lighted environment. The nautilus, for instance, has a pinhole camera-type eye with no lens, but has existed long enough to have evolved a more complex eye like its mollusk cousin the octopus. Is it possible that a better-seeing, more complex eye would not have been beneficial to the nautilus? Maybe, but it's difficult to imagine how.

In the Theistic Paradigm, the idea of irreducible complexity has been used to argue that, in the absence of plausible narratives, at least some structures could not have arisen through a purely natural evolutionary process. The alternative, then, is that they must have been designed by Someone. But there is a counterpart idea in the Organic Paradigm that turns the idea of irreducible complexity on its head: poor design. In short, it asks how there can be a Designer when so many organic structures seem to have been designed with flaws?

For instance, the retina in humans (but not, interestingly, in mollusks) actually seems to have been "designed" backwards, with the photoreceptor cells pointing away from the incoming light, not towards it. The nerve that leaves each photoreceptor cell actually extends into the inner part of the eye rather than toward the outer, back part of the eyeball like you might expect. In addition to being seemingly backwards, this organization also forces all the nerves from all the photoreceptor cells to gather together at one location at the back of the eye and burrow through the retina to form the optic nerve that travels to the brain. The location of this bundle of nerves forms the "blind spot" on the retina where we cannot see anything. This all seems like such a poor design, especially given that the eyes of other organisms do not have such flaws. It is difficult to understand why a Designer would have created structures that seem so poorly designed.

The argument for poor design is sometimes extended to other structures as well. For instance, the knee is a hinge joint that moves only in one direction, but the hip and ankle joints are ball-and-socket joints that can move in any direction. This configuration means that the knee is prone to injury due to awkward twisting. Again, the argument from the Organic Paradigm is that this is evidence of evolution at work, since presumably a Designer would have created only perfectly functioning structures. On the other hand, no one has yet proposed an alternative combination of joints in the leg that would serve us better, leaving open the possibility that the knee as we know it is in fact the best of all possible designs.

Finally, some in the Organic Paradigm take issue with using the eye as an example of a designed structure because it seems to have been hand-picked to promote not just complexity, but also beauty. There are plenty of other structures that are ugly, or whose purposes are downright distasteful, and yet are exquisitely designed structures for which there is no plausible narrative for how an evolutionary process may have produced them. Consider the Ichneumon wasp. It has a long ovipositor (looks like a very long stinger) that it uses to pierce and lay its eggs inside a live caterpillar. The wasp's young then feed on the live caterpillar until they are ready to pupate, at which time the caterpillar dies. This is a very efficient design, and one could use it to make the same arguments about the existence of a Designer. But then you would have to struggle with the question of why God would create such a cruel creature. The only way to resolve this dilemma would be to propose some sort of "sin-induced evolution" which occurred after sin had entered the world. In this narrative[33], the Ichneumon wasp either did not exist before sin entered the world, or did exist but laid its eggs strictly on plants. The biochemistry of the wasp's young would have needed to be radically different to consume plant material instead of a caterpillar's innards. When sin entered the world, some sort of evolution took over, either to produce the Ichneumon wasp from scratch, or to change it from one that lays eggs on plants to one that lays eggs inside caterpillars.

---

[33] Plausible or not, I don't know.

Chapter 19

The Origin Of Life

The theory of evolution is not primarily concerned with how life began, but rather how it changed over time. The origin of life is a nearly independent field of study where the primary expertise of value is organic and inorganic chemistry. The fields of expertise that are most relevant in the study of evolution - paleontology, geology, molecular biology, ecology, and genetics - are considerably less useful. Moreover, scientists studying the origin of life are forced to spend all their time in a chemistry laboratory testing out various theories because there is essentially no record of what the very first life forms may have looked like.

In order to determine what the first life form might have looked like, a logical place to start is to identify the characteristics that are common to all forms of life that we know. It turns out that the list is relatively short:

- Highly organized set of structures and processes. This includes being composed of one or more cells.

- Self-regulation to maintain a particular state in the face of changing environmental conditions, including the ability to adapt to those conditions.

- Metabolism: Conversion of chemicals and energy from the environment into cellular components and energy useful to the organism.

- Growth

- Reproduction

Some people also throw an ability to evolve into the definition of life. Since this book is intended to remain neutral with respect to the theory of evolution, I have excluded it from the definition of life. Nevertheless, if life did arise spontaneously out of a soup of chemicals, then even this process would have required some form of selection acting on variation within chemicals, not unlike evolution. But more on that in a moment.

Every form of life that we know is composed of four basic types of organic molecules: carbohydrates, lipids, proteins, and nucleic acids. A summary of these four groups is given in the table below.

	Purpose	Examples	Basic building block
Carbohydrates	Energy storage and transfer	Sugar, starch	Mono-saccharide
Lipids	Cell structure, energy storage	Fat, steroids	Fatty acid
Proteins	Cell structure, promoting chemical reactions, fighting infection	Hemoglobin, collagen, antibodies	Amino acid
Nucleic acids	Storing hereditary information, map for creating proteins	Deoxyribo-nucleic acid (DNA), ribonucleic acid (RNA)	Nucleotide

In the far right hand column of this table, you will see a description of the "building blocks" for each category. The building blocks are relatively simple molecules that must be linked together in very particular ways in order to form the molecules described in the far left column. For instance, a chain of monosaccharides forms a carbohydrate, a chain of amino acids forms a protein, and so on. Any theory of the origin of life must explain not only the origin of the four types of building blocks, but also how DNA appeared to direct the assembly of those building blocks into the carbohydrates, lipids, proteins, and nucleic acids that are part of every known form of life.

Scientists studying the origin of life have coined a term for the organism that is the greatest-great-grandfather of all life on earth: the Last Universal Common Ancestor, or LUCA for short. It's called "last" rather than first because we are counting backwards from today. It sounds backwards to me, but I wasn't consulted.

So what did LUCA look like?

As a starting point, it would be reasonable to assume that LUCA was composed of a single cell. All plants and animals that exist today are composed of cells called eukaryotes that have similar structure. Inside some sort of membrane or wall, these cells are full of things having snazzy names like nucleus, cytoplasm, ribosomes, mitochondria, endoplasmic reticulum, lysosomes, and the Golgi apparatus. Even many single-celled organisms are eukaryotes, such as the amoeba and the paramecium. Pond scum is full of these things, and as a kid I remember collecting samples from the swamp behind our house to examine through an old microscope that my father had brought home from work. Nevertheless, because eukaryotes are actually very advanced types of cells, they are generally assumed to be poor candidates for the first form of life. Considerably simpler are the prokaryotes, otherwise known as bacteria.

Most of us think of bacteria as the things that cause disease and that cause dead plants and animals to decompose. But some bacteria are used to make industrial chemicals, and others are used to make cheese. Bacteria in your gut help you digest your food. Bacteria are an absolutely critical component of Earthly life as we know it, so it's natural to think that the first critters would look basically like bacteria. In fact the oldest fossil record of life on earth is from stromatolites, rocks formed in shallow water from aggregates of blue-green algae, technically known as cyanobacteria. Stromatolites also grow in various places around the earth today, providing a good point of comparison for the structure and growth patterns of the ancient stromatolites.

Bacterial cells are typically about a tenth the size of an animal or plant cell, and don't have all the internal structures that plant and animal cells have. But while these microorganisms are certainly the simplest form of life we know, they are by no means simple.

They still do the same sorts of things that any other living thing does: metabolism, growth, reproduction, etc. Even the bacterium with the smallest genome identified to date, Tremblaya, has about 140 thousand base pairs in its DNA. As discussed in Chapter 9, there are four different types of nucleotides that make up each base pair. You can calculate the odds that a soup consisting of these four nucleotides would spontaneously come together to form the specific DNA of Tremblaya. It's $(1/4)^{140,000}$, which is about $1 \times 10^{-84,000}$. To get an idea of how unlikely this is. consider this: If all earth's oceans were made of nucleotides instead of water, and they randomly reconfigured themselves into DNA strands 140,000 units long trillions of times every second, it would still take many times the age of the universe to end up with just a single Tremblaya genome. Given the odds against such a thing happening, most researchers think that bacteria are not in fact a very good example of what the first form of life must have looked like.

This presents a problem for scientists, because there is no simpler form of life than bacteria. They have been forced to hypothesize a much simpler form of life that got things started, then disappeared from the biological record. Why such a life form would have disappeared is itself a mystery, since there exists today an example of every other form of life that has ever existed. The dinosaurs are gone, but we still have crocodiles and (if you believe they were descended from dinosaurs) birds. The invertebrates of the Cambrian period are gone, but we still have horseshoe crabs and jawless fish today. The ammonites are gone, but we still have the nautilus which is very similar. And while bacteria may have been one of the earliest forms of life, all sorts of bacteria still exist today. So why don't we find an example of the very first, super-simple life form still living today? The answer depends on your point of view: If you tend towards the Theistic Paradigm, the answer is that there was no simpler life form. God created the first bacteria-like life forms, and life evolved from there. If, on the other hand, you tend towards the Organic Paradigm, the answer is that conditions on the earth 3+ billion years ago were dramatically different, so that the first, super-simple life form simply died out as the earth's climate and chemistry changed, and more complex life forms took over.

Regardless, scientists studying the origin of life have turned to other sources in nature for inspiration. One of these sources is viruses. Most people would classify viruses as pseudo-life, not quite alive but not quite not alive. Viruses have no machinery for self-regulation, metabolism, or growth. They are composed merely of a capsule made of proteins which contains DNA or its simpler cousin RNA.[34] They are basically just a box with blueprints. The DNA/RNA provides the instructions for duplication, but viruses do not have the means to duplicate themselves. In order to reproduce, they must hijack a prokaryotic or eukaryotic cell. Once inside the cell, the DNA/RNA from the virus directs the cell's enzymes to assemble more viruses using the proteins and lipids from the cell as the building blocks of the new viruses. In many cases, production of new viruses continues until the cell is completely full of them, at which time the cell bursts open and sends the new viruses out into the environment.

In a very real sense, viruses don't do anything except reproduce, and even then they can't do it by themselves. So it would seem obvious that the first life form could not have been a virus. But some scientists study them nonetheless because of some unique properties that they have. One of those properties is the simple fact that all they really do is reproduce. If you had to pick the single most important characteristic of life, in a biological sense it would be the ability to reproduce. In fact, if you ever found something like a virus that could reproduce on its own, without the need for hijacking another cell, we would very likely call it alive even if it did nothing else.

Viruses have another property that makes them interesting: they have very crystal-like geometries such as icosahedrons, dodecahedrons, and the like. This fact makes them seem more chemical than biological. As I discuss more below, the very first form of life has been hypothesized to have started out growing on the crystalline structure of minerals in rocks. If so, it would make sense that the first forms of life would likewise have a crystalline structure, like viruses have.

---

[34] RNA is similar to DNA but is a single strand rather than a double-helix

Recently some very large viruses have been discovered that still need the machinery of other cells to reproduce, but nevertheless contain genes coding for DNA repair and production of certain types of proteins. This is very unusual for a virus, who's DNA/RNA really only needs to provide the instructions to make more of itself, not other typically cell-like machinery. This finding suggests to some that modern day viruses are actually devolved versions of more complex precursors from the distant past.

Nevertheless, even viruses appear to be too complex to represent LUCA. Viral DNA/RNA contains the instructions for using a cell's machinery to duplicate both the DNA/RNA and also the capsule that houses the DNA/RNA. Most scientists do not believe that LUCA had a capsule, since the odds of both self-replication and capsule formation spontaneously appearing together seems very low. Moreover, the genome of the smallest virus is about 2,000 nucleotides long which, while much smaller than that of any know life form, is still considered by most scientists to be too long for LUCA.

The next step down the ladder of life is the viroids, which are similar to viruses in that they must infect a eukaryotic or prokaryotic cell to reproduce, but viroids have an even smaller genome than viruses and they have no protective capsule. Viroids are composed only of a single loop of RNA that is only a few hundred nucleotides long, significantly shorter than even the smallest virus. This loop of RNA does not need to provide blueprints for proteins, since viroids do not have a protein-based capsule. The only thing that viroid RNA needs to code for is the reproduction of itself. Essentially, they are a blueprint for creating more blueprints. Unfortunately, to reproduce viroids must use RNA polymerase that is produced by the organism that they have infected - the viroid can't produce RNA polymerase itself. As described in Chapter 9, the RNA polymerase is a special enzyme that "reads" the sequence of nucleotides in a strand of DNA (or in this case, RNA), and then builds a duplicate strand of RNA using nucleotides that are floating around. Scientists have actually created their own short strands of RNA and have gotten them to duplicate themselves, but only if some RNA polymerase is added to the mix. Since no RNA polymerase would have been available when LUCA first appeared, viroids are not candidates for LUCA.

This exhausts all of the forms of life and pseudo-life that we know of. As a result, most scientists have hypothesized that LUCA was a special form of RNA, the likes of which no one has ever seen in nature. Instead of requiring a cell's machinery or RNA polymerase to reproduce, LUCA would have been able to act as its own polymerase, catalyzing its own replication. While this might seem like a too-convenient exit from the problem of having no RNA polymerase around, there is actually a scientific basis for this idea. In Chapter 9 I discussed the role of "messenger RNA" in the production of proteins. The messenger RNA attaches to a structure inside a cell called a ribosome. The ribosome "reads" the messenger RNA and then assembles amino acids into a specific type of protein based on the blueprint of the messenger RNA. But it turns out that ribosomes and RNA have a very similar molecular structure. In fact, the "ribo-" in ribosome stands for the monosaccharide ribose, which is exactly the same molecule that forms the basis of RNA (ribonucleic acid). So it should not be surprising that some origin of life scientists are looking for a way that a strand of RNA might also act like a ribosome that would catalyze the production of new RNA strands instead of proteins. Ribozymes (an enzyme based on ribose) have been produced in the laboratory that are both RNA-like and also catalyze a broad range of reactions, though replication of itself is not yet one of those functions. It is these ribozymes that are the focus of much of the current scientific work.

There are two possible ways for LUCA to act as a ribozyme for its own replication. The first is that a single molecule of LUCA would be able to read itself and make a copy of itself. This would require one part of LUCA to act as the ribozyme enzyme, and that the "ribozyme part" would read another part of LUCA and make a duplicate of it. The problem here is that the ribozyme part of LUCA also needs to be duplicated, and there is no straightforward way for that to happen. The second way for LUCA to act as ribozyme for its own replication is for two LUCA molecules to interact. Although the two LUCA molecules would be identical, one would act as ribozyme for the replication of the other.

Of course to make this two-molecule system work, the two initial LUCAs, the great grandma and grandpa of life as it were, would have had to have been independently and spontaneously created, and yet identical to each other. Based on simple probabilities, it has already been demonstrated that it is very unlikely that a soup of chemicals would produce LUCA once, let alone twice. So where would the initial LUCA have come from?

This is where crystals come in. A crystal is any substance that forms very repeatable, orderly patterns at the molecular level. For pure crystals that are large enough to see, the patterns at the molecular level produce recognizable geometric shapes at the macro level, such as cubes, octahedra, hexagonal prisms, and the like. And it turns out that crystals are much more common than most people realize. Every rock you have ever seen is actually composed of minerals, and all minerals are crystals. Most rocks don't look like crystals only because rocks are generally not made of a single type of mineral, but instead are conglomerates of many different types of minerals. But at the molecular level the crystal structure of rocks is clear.

Crystals are thought by some to have played a role in producing LUCA for two reasons: 1) they represent the only clear source of order in the otherwise chaotic environment of early earth, and 2) crystals have a surprising ability to cause other molecules that happen to be in the vicinity to arrange themselves into orderly patterns. When simple organic molecules come into contact with certain types of crystals, those organic molecules tend to stick to the crystal and to arrange themselves according to the crystal's molecular pattern. With rows of organic molecules held in close proximity to one another, those organic molecules have an opportunity to react with one another to form long chains.

It has been proven in a laboratory that crystals can indeed cause free-floating nucleotides to string together into RNA chains. To date none of those RNA chains has exhibited the ability to act as its own ribozyme and self-replicate, nor do anything else of note. But the fact that modern ribosomes themselves have a crystalline structure has convinced some that the crystalline properties of minerals played a role in the emergence of life.

If scientists were successful in creating a self-replicating molecule of RNA, the problem of the first form of life would still be far from being solved. In order to truly solve the puzzle, all the steps between such a self-replicating RNA molecule and the simplest bacterium would need to be explained. For instance, the RNA would need to start coding for the production of some sort of capsule or membrane to enclose the RNA. Most scientists think that this would need to occur before the RNA could start coding for the production of molecules involved in metabolism (for example, carbohydrates, lipids, and proteins). Otherwise, any useful molecules that the RNA produced would float away before it got a chance to do anything useful, and it would quickly be destroyed through interactions with many other molecules in the environment. A membrane or capsule would be critical to providing an enclosed and protected space within which carbohydrates, lipids, and proteins could be produced and begin carrying out the many functions that we associate with life.

So how would the first RNA have "learned" to produce a membrane around itself?

One intriguing possibility is that the membrane occurred first, arising spontaneously from lipids floating in the water, and the RNA molecule simply adopted it. There is some evidence that this might have happened. Once fatty acids form, they have a tendency to self-organize into bubble-like structures if they are put into water. This tendency is due to the fact that one end of a fatty acid molecule is attracted to water while the other end is repelled by water. In the presence of water, fatty acids will line up with their water-loving ends pointed outward and their water-hating ends pointing inwards. The result is a "lipid bilayer" that is remarkably similar to the membrane around all cells. If such bubble-like lipid bilayers were to form in the same vicinity as self-replicating RNA molecules, it is not unthinkable that some of the RNA would find itself inside some of the lipid bilayer bubbles, and the stage would be set for more complex chemistry to occur inside that bubble.

Having an RNA molecule replicating inside of a lipid bilayer bubble certainly has the appearance of the first cell, but it is still a long way off. The RNA would eventually need to be able to code for the production of lipid bilayers itself rather than relying on the generosity of the surrounding soup of chemicals. That lipid bilayer would also need to develop additional protein-based structures within it to do all the things that cell membranes do: control the passage of specific chemicals from inside to outside and vice-versa, identify the conditions of the surrounding chemical environment, recognize other cells, etc. Scientists only have a faint idea of how RNA would have begun to do this.

Similarly, the RNA would need to begin coding for the production of all of the basic building blocks of life - monosaccharides, amino acids, fatty acids, and nucleotides - from other raw materials in its environment, and then direct the assembly of those building blocks into the larger molecules that form the actual machinery of life. Since this would require a dramatic leap in the function of the RNA, most origin of life researchers think that the basic building blocks of life must already have been present in LUCA's surroundings, and that LUCA would have made use of them without having to create them. Certainly there would have had to have been nucleotides from which the first RNA molecules was formed, and lipids to form the first lipid bilayer bubble to surround the RNA. But if LUCA was going to start metabolizing and self-regulating, it would also have had to first make use of amino acids and carbohydrates already in its surroundings. So where did all these organic molecules come from?

If theories about earth's formation and early conditions are correct, there would have been no way that any organic compounds could have existed during the first few hundred million years. It was simply too hot and violent, and any organic molecules that did happen to appear would be instantly destroyed. But the earth was also too hot for any water to exist either. Theories for how water ended up on earth have also provided possibilities for how organic molecules may have ended up here as well.

Other than earth itself, the only other large source of water that we know of is asteroids. We now know that many asteroids are composed of not just rocks, but a large amount of ice. Studies of the moon and other planets suggest that there was a period early in the life of the earth, but after it had cooled substantially, when it was bombarded regularly by asteroids. If so, then this could have been the source of all the water now on earth. While it may seem like an awful lot of asteroids would have had to hit the earth to supply all the water in our oceans, it's actually not that much in comparison to the size of the earth. For instance, if the earth was the size of a basketball, the deepest ocean would be less than 1/100th of an inch thick. That's about the thickness of two sheets of paper. You would barely notice your finger getting wet if you touched it.

The idea that all our water came from asteroids opens up the possibility that those same asteroids might have delivered the first organic building blocks to earth. This isn't just a fanciful idea. It turns out that many meteorites[35] have been analyzed and found to contain organic molecules, including amino acids, sugars, lipids, and nucleotides. Unfortunately, those organic molecules are bound up inside the rock of the meteorites. If they were released during the violent entry into earth's atmosphere when much of the asteroid would have vaporized, or during the impact with the ground, they would most likely have been destroyed by the intense heat. The alternative is that meteorites that made it to the surface of earth intact could have been broken down slowly through erosion and geologic forces. However, it is not clear that this much slower process would have provided a sufficient abundance of organic molecules to get life started. Moreover, organic molecules are not very robust. Once they do enter rivers and oceans, they will eventually be destroyed if they are not used in building RNA, proteins, or cell membranes. Thus they would need to be replenished regularly. So, while the idea of simple organic molecules being delivered to earth by asteroids is intriguing, it's difficult to imagine how they could have played a role in the emergence of life.

The alternative source of organic molecules is through chemical reactions that could have occurred naturally using non-organic

---

[35] Meteorites are asteroids that made it to the surface of earth without being completely vaporized during the passage through earth's atmosphere.

molecules common on early earth. A significant amount of experimental research has gone into this possibility. The first step is making educated guesses about the conditions of early earth, including not just the chemicals that might have been available, but also likely temperatures, sunlight, cosmic radiation, and the prevalence of lightening. Based on studies of volcanic activity and the conditions of other planets, scientists surmise that the early earth's atmosphere was composed primarily of the following:

- Carbon dioxide
- Nitrogen
- Sulfur dioxide
- Hydrogen sulfide
- Methane
- Carbon monoxide

Stanley Miller's original 1953 experiments, which produced amino acids and launched many others into experimental work to find the origin of life, assumed that early earth's atmosphere had lots of methane and ammonia. While scientists today think that this is unlikely, nevertheless many other experiments have been done demonstrating that organic molecules can indeed be produced from the simple chemicals listed above under the right combinations of heat from volcanoes, lightening, and ultraviolet radiation. However, those organic molecules are generally mixed with lots of other molecules that would not have been useful as building blocks for the first forms of life. How it is that this messy mix of chemicals separated itself molecules that formed the first form of life and those that didn't is still quite murky.

In summary, most folks in the Organic Paradigm would concede that theories of the origin of life are considerably less well developed than the theory of evolution. In large part this is because the origin of life is concerned with specific chemical steps, while the theory of evolution is considerably more general in nature and only in rare instances includes descriptions of specific chemical steps. To see just how much work there is to do on origin of life research, consider all the steps that would need to be described and demonstrated experimentally in order to establish the process through which life arose on earth:

- Organic molecules forming from inorganic chemicals, and being replenished regularly as older molecules are destroyed

- A sufficiently high abundance and concentration of organic molecules to permit them to interact with one another

- A mechanism, such as crystals as templates, through which nucleotides could string together to form molecules of RNA

- Appearance of an RNA molecule that can self-replicate

- RNA molecules self-replicating within a protective lipid bilayer bubble

- RNA molecules evolving to manufacture their own nucleotides and fatty acids, and the use of these building blocks for both self-replication and cell division

- RNA molecules evolving to manufacture their own amino acids and monosaccharides

- RNA molecules evolving to organize organic building blocks into larger molecules of lipids, carbohydrates, and proteins having specific functions related to metabolism and growth.

- Transition of RNA into DNA

While none of these steps has been demonstrated unequivocally in the laboratory, scientists have tantalizing clues for how they may have come about. That said, if a full picture of the origin of life is attainable, it will likely require decades of more research.

Chapter 20

Does It Matter?

Soon after I became a Christian, I lived for a summer in a household of college guys that included a Catholic priest. Older and wiser than the rest of us, he had a wealth of experience and fascinating stories that regularly landed him in the center of group discussions.

One day, don't ask me how, the subject of evolution came up. It was a rather freewheeling discussion, each of us tossing into the mix what few factoids we had picked up on the subject. And then, in what seemed to me a rather abrupt and incongruous way, my priest friend blurted out, "But does it really matter?"

That caught our attention fast. Everyone shut up.

"What matters is that there was some kind of falling away, something that happened that broke our relationship with God, and we are in need of a Savior."

Although I hadn't yet formed any particular opinions about evolution, I knew the standard Christian view: evolution was inconsistent with the Bible, and so could not be true. But here was a Christian - a *professional* Christian - who had just sidestepped the whole issue. His approach seemed to be both a deviation from typical Christian views and also more genuinely Christian than those views.

In the 20+ years since that time, I've come to appreciate that view more and more. Many of us Christians have gotten hung up on what the right answer is with regard to evolution, and seem to miss the fact that it has little, if anything, to do with our relationship with God. There's nothing in the sinner's prayer about how the world and all life was created. Neither does the topic show up in the so-called four spiritual laws, or the Apostle's Creed, or the Nicene Creed. Jesus never talked about it, other than to refer to the fact that God made man and woman, and one reference to Noah and the ark. Except for the creation account in Genesis, there are little more than passing references in all of the Bible to the fact that God created the world. It's merely stated as a fact, without any explanation or details.

As I've said before, I'm no theologian, but I do not believe that your view of evolution has any particular bearing on your salvation. That doesn't mean the subject isn't relevant. For one thing, it's always an advantage to believe what is true and not believe what is false. Believing that the earth is flat might not prevent me from getting to heaven, but it might prevent me from travelling too far for fear of falling off the edge of the world. Likewise having at least a healthy respect for some of the basic proposed mechanisms underlying the theory of evolution can help you in the real world. For instance, the antibiotics you probably have used owe their existence to the application of evolutionary theory to bacteria. But in regards to salvation, the truth or falsity of the theory of evolution doesn't seem to carry the same kind of weight.

I know that some in the Theistic Paradigm object to my belief that one's views of evolution and one's salvation are not directly connected. Certainly it is possible to point to individuals who have "deconverted" from a belief in God after learning of or studying evolution, as I said in Chapter 3. A more commonly cited concern, however, is the impact that believing in evolution may have on how one treats the Bible as a whole. The concern goes something like this:

- To whatever degree you are deviating from a literal reading of the creation story in Genesis, you are inserting your own (or someone else's) ideas and prejudices into

God's inspired Word, diluting both its truth and its power.

- Once you open the door to a non-literal reading of Genesis, there is no reason not to also read other parts of the Bible in a non-literal way.

- Less literal interpretations of Jesus' words makes them seem like mere suggestions rather than commands, optional rather than mandatory.

- If Adam and Eve are read to be symbolic rather than real individuals, then there is no reason not the think of Jesus in the same way.

- If Jesus was not a real individual, then there was no real crucifixion and no real resurrection. The foundation of the Christian faith disappears.

While I sympathize with this concern, it's important to recognize that all Christians, including Christian leaders, regularly make decisions about what parts of the Bible must be interpreted literally versus those parts that are better interpreted figuratively. The book of Revelation has been the source of many such debates. Other examples are listed below.

And if your hand causes you to sin, cut it off (Mark 9:43)

"If anyone comes to me and does not hate his own father and mother and wife and children and brothers and sisters, yes, and even his own life, he cannot be my disciple. (Luke 14:26)

I am the door. If anyone enters by me, he will be saved and will go in and out and find pasture (John 10:9)

And in every matter of wisdom and understanding about which the king inquired of them, he found them ten times better than all the magicians and enchanters that were in all his kingdom. (Daniel 1:20)

For in death there is no remembrance of you; in Sheol who will give you praise? (Psalm 6:5)

Do not withhold discipline from a child; if you strike him with a rod, he will not die (Proverbs 23:13)

Clearly it's not possible to take every single part of the Bible absolutely literally. Is the only proper way to discipline our children to beat them with a rod? Are we commanded to hate our parents? Do dead people forget about God? Since even Christian scholars sometimes disagree over what should be taken literally versus figuratively, those of us who are not scholars will be better off if our aim is focused more on a sincere pursuit of truth, and reliance on God's mercy for those things we get wrong.

Whatever your position on evolution, it is also important to treat it, as well as the opinions of others, with a large dose of humility. God's most fundamental concern is relationships, not facts and concepts. If you ever have an opportunity to discuss evolution with someone, odds are very good that you won't have exactly the same views even if you are both Christian. If you fight too hard for your view, even if your view is absolutely spot-on correct, you might win the argument but lose the relationship. "Love does not insist on its own way." (1 Cor 13:5)

As I took great pains to say in the introduction, I didn't write this book to argue for or against the theory of evolution. I wrote it for inquisitive minds that like to wrestle with issues and come to their own conclusions. I wrote it for people who value the pursuit of truth, regardless of where the pursuit leads them. And I wrote it for people who can approach complicated issues like this one with a healthy dose of humility, because evolution is one of those topics that provides fertile ground for changing your mind over and over again.

Next time you are discussing evolution with someone, be quick to listen and slow to speak. Try to learn something you didn't know before. Offer what you've learned, but look for new insights and perspectives that others can offer. You are going to disagree about something, guaranteed, so make it your primary goal to be an example for Christ in His attitude and approach.

Bibliography

Books

Andrews, Roy Chapman. A Remarkable Case of External Hind Limbs in a Humpback Whale. American Museum of Natural History, New York City, June 3, 1921.

Atlas, Ronald. Basic and Practical Microbiology. Macmillan Publishing Company, 1986.

Bebej, Ryan Matthew. Functional Morphology of the Vertebral Column in Remingtonocetus (Mammalia, Cetacea) and the Evolution of Aquatic Locomotion in Early Archaeocetes. A dissertation submitted in partial fulfillment of the requirements for the degree of Doctor of Philosophy (Ecology and Evolutionary Biology) in The University of Michigan. 2011.

Behe, Michael. Darwin's Black Box. Free Press, 2006.

Bowler, Peter. Monkey Trials and Gorilla Sermons: Evolution and Christianity from Darwin to Intelligent Design. Harvard University Press, May 20, 2009.

Carroll, Sean. The Making of the Fittest: DNA and the Ultimate Forensic Record of Evolution. W. W. Norton & Company, September 17, 2007.

Darwin, Charles. The Origin of Species. W W Norton and Company, 1975.

Dawkins, Richard. The Blind Watchmaker. W. W. Norton & Company, 1996.

DeYoung, Don. Thousands...Not Billions. Master Books, 2005.

Enns, Peter. The Evolution of Adam. Brazos Press, 2012.

Fodor, Jerry. What Darwin Got Wrong. Picador, March 1, 2011.

Giberson, Karl. Saving Darwin. HarperOne, 2008.

Godfrey, Laurie. Scientists Confront Creationism. W. W. Norton & Company, April 17, 1984.

Gould, Stephen Jay. The Structure of Evolutionary Theory. Belknap Press, 2002.

Gribbin, John. Alone in the Universe. John Wiley & Sons, Inc, 2011.

Haines, Tim. The Complete Guide to Prehistoric Life. Firefly Books, 2006.

Hazen, Robert. The Story of Earth. The Penguin Group Inc. 2012

Hunt, Kathleen. Horse Evolution. Godslasteraar.org

Kirschner, Marc. The Plausibility of Life: Resolving Darwin's Dilemma. Yale University Press, November 15, 2006.

Klinghoffer, David. Signature of Controversy. Discovery Institute Press, 2010.

Krukonis, Greg. Evolution for Dummies. Wiley Publishing, Inc. 2008.

MacDougall, Doug. Nature's Clocks. University of California Press, 2008.

McWhorter, John. The Power of Babel: A Natural History of Language. Harper Perennial, January 7, 2003.

Miller, Kenneth. Finding Darwin's God: A Scientist's Search for Common Ground Between God and Evolution. Harper Perennial,

April 3, 2007.

Montgomery, David. <u>The Rocks Don't Lie: A Geologist Investigates Noah's Flood</u>. W. W. Norton & Company, 2013

Morris, Desmond. <u>The Naked Ape</u>. Dell Publishing Company, 1967.

Pruthero, Donald. <u>Evolution: What the Fossils Say and Why It Matters</u>. Columbia University Press, 2007.

Psihoyos, Louie. <u>Hunting Dinosaurs</u>. Random House, 1994

Sloan, Christopher. <u>How Dinosaurs Took Flight</u>. National Geographic, 2005.

Switek, Brian. <u>Written in Stone: Evolution, the Fossil Record, and Our Place in Nature</u>. Bellevue Literary Press, 2010

Sykes, Bryan. <u>The Seven Daughters of Eve</u>. W W Norton and Company, 2001.

Tattersall, Ian. <u>The Last Neanderthal</u>. Westview Press, 1999.

Tattersall, Ian. <u>Masters of the Planet</u>. Palgrave MacMillan, 2012.

Films

<u>Dinosaurs Decoded</u>. Dan Levitt, 2009.

<u>Expelled: No Intelligence Allowed</u>. Premise Media Corporation, 2008.

<u>The Human Family Tree</u>. National Geographic, 2009.

<u>Journey to 10,000 BC</u>. David Padrusch, 2008.

The Search for the Ultimate Survivor. John Rubin, 2005.

Unlocking the Mystery of Life. Illustra Media, 2003.

Walking with Monsters: Before the Dinosaurs. Impossible Pictures, 2005.

Magazines

Daley, Jason. "Humans Had Mastered Fire by 1,000,000 B.C." Discovery magazine. January-February 2013 issue.

Jones, Dan et al. "Riddles of our Past." New Scientist. Volume 2013, Number 2857. Pages 34 - 42.

McGowan, Kat. "Most Mutations in the Human Genome are Recent and Probably Harmful." Discovery magazine. July-August 2013 issue.

Various authors. Discover Magazine Presents Evolution. Summer 2011.

Various authors. Scientific American, Special Collector's Edition. "What Makes Us Human." Volume 22, Number 1, Winter 2013.

Wong, Kate. "First of our Kind." Scientific American. Volume 306, Number 4. April 2012. Page 30 - 39.

Yong, Ed. "Study Decodes DNA's True Meaning." Discovery magazine.January-February 2013 issue.

Journal articles

Adams, Dean. "Amphibians Do Not Follow Bergmann's Rule."

The Society for the Study of Evolution. Evolution 62-2: 413-420. February 2008.

Ashton, Kyle et al. "Bergmann's Rule In Nonavian Reptiles: Turtles Follow It, Lizards And Snakes Reverse It." The Society for the Study of Evolution. Evolution, 57(5), 2003, pp. 1151-1163.

Austin, Steven A. "Excess Argon within Mineral Concentrates from the New Dacite Lava Dome at Mount St. Helens Volcano." Creation Ex Nihilo Technical Journal, Vol. 10, no. 3, pp. 335-343, 1996.

Blackburn, Elizabeth H. "Switching and Signaling at the Telomere." Cell, Vol. 106, 661-673, September 21, 2001.

Brady, John B. "Diffusion Data for Silicate Minerals, Glasses, and Liquids." American Geophysical Union. 1995.

Callahan, Michael P. et al "Carbonaceous meteorites contain a wide range of extraterrestrial nucleobases." Proceedings of the National Academy of Sciences.
www.pnas.org/cgi/doi/10.1073/pnas.1106493108

Ewert W, Dembski WA, Gauger AK, Marks II RJ (2012) "Time and information in evolution." BIO-Complexity 2012 (4):1-7. doi:10.5048/BIO-C.2012.4.

Foster, Colin. "Creationism as a Misconception: Socio-cognitive conflict in the teaching of evolution." International Journal of Science Education, Vol. 34, No. 14, September 2012, pp. 2171-2180.

Frost, Darrel et al. "The Amphibian Tree of Life". Bulletin of the American Museum of Natural History. March 15, 2006.

Gatesy, John et al. "A phylogenetic blueprint for a modern whale." Mol. Phylogenet. Evol. (2012).
http://dx.doi.org/10.1016/j.ympev.2012.10.012

Hauffe, Heidi C. "Chromosomal Heterozygosity and Fertility in House Mice (Mus musculus domesticus) From Northern Italy." Genetics 150: 1143-1154 (November 1998).

Holmquist, Gerald P. "Telomere replication, kinetochore organizers, and satellite DNA evolution." Proc. Nati. Acad. Sci. USA, Vol. 76, No. 9, pp. 4566-4570, September 1979.

IJdo, J. W. et al. "Origin of human chromosome 2: An ancestral telomere-telomere fusion." Proc. Nadl. Acad. Sci. USA. Vol. 88, pp. 9051-9055, October 1991.

Joyce, Gerald F. "The antiquity of RNA-based evolution." Nature Publishing Group. Vol 418, July 11, 2002. www.nature.com/nature

Joyce, Gerald F. "Biology 'From Scratch'." The Skaggs Institute for Chemical Biology, The Scripps Research Institute, La Jolla, California.

Kumar, Sudhir et al. "Placing confidence limits on the molecular age of the human-chimpanzee divergence." Proceedings of the National Academy of Sciences. December 27, 2005. www.pnas.org/cgi/doi/10.1073/pnas.0509585102

Laugen, Ane. "Do common frogs (Rana temporaria) follow Bergmann's rule?" Evolutionary Ecology Research, 2005, 7: 717-731.

Libby, Willard F. "Radiocarbon dating." Nobel Lecture, December 12, 1960.

Meiri, Shai. "On the validity of Bergmann's rule." Journal of Biogeography, 30, 331-351. 2003.

Meléndez-Hevia, Enrique et al. "The Puzzle of the Krebs Citric Acid Cycle: Assembling the Pieces of Chemically Feasible Reactions, and Opportunism in the Design of Metabolic Pathways During Evolution." J Mol Evol (1996) 43:293-303.

Molteni, L. et al "A new centric fusion translocation in cattle."
Hereditas 129: 177-180 (1998).

Orlando, Ludovic et al. "Revising the recent evolutionary history
of equids using ancient DNA." Proceedings of the National
Academy of Sciences. October 20, 2009.
www.pnas.org/cgi/doi/10.1073/pnas.0903672106

Petrash, Daniel A. et al. "Dynamic controls on accretion and
lithification of modern gypsum-dominated thrombolites, Los
Roques, Venezuela." Sedimentary Geology 245-246 (2012) 29-47.

Robertson, Michael. "The Origins of the RNA World." Cold
Spring Harbor Laboratory Press, April 28, 2010. Cold Spring
Harb Perspect Biol 2012; doi:10.1101/cshperspect.a003608.
http://cshperspectives.cshlp.org/

Sepkoski, J. John Jr. "Rates of speciation in the fossil record."
The Royal Society. Phil.Trans. R. Soc. Lond. B (1998) 353, 315-
326.

Simões-Lopes, Paulo C. "Notes On The Anatomy, Positioning
And Homology Of The Pelvic Bones In Small Cetaceans (Cetacea,
Delphinidae, Pontoporiidae)." LAJAM 3(2): 157-162,
July/December 2004.

Uhen, Mark D. "The Origin(s) of Whales." Annu. Rev. Earth
Planet. Sci. 2010. 38:189-219.

Websites

http://creation.com
http://creationwiki.org/
http://dinosaurs.about.com/od/thedinobirdconnection/a/dinobirds.h
tm
http://dinosaurs.about.com/od/typesofdinosaurs/u/dinotypes.htm

http://discovery.org/csc/
http://fossilworks.org
http://humanorigins.si.edu/evidence/human-evolution-timeline-interactive
http://periodictable.com/
http://pigeonchess.com/2010/01/24/epic-horse-exhaust/
http://waxingapocalyptic.com/2010/09/30/the-evolution-of-the-eye/
http://www.answersingenesis.org/
http://www.bradshawfoundation.com/origins/
http://www.dhushara.com/book/unraveltree/unravel.htm
http://www.dissentfromdarwin.org/
http://www.enchantedlearning.com/subjects/mammals/classification/index.shtml
http://www.indiana.edu/~geol105/1425chap5.htm
http://www.intelligentdesign.org/
http://www.livius.org/fa-fn/flood/flood1.html
http://www.macroevolution.net
http://www.oldearth.org/
http://www.spec2000.net/05-mineralprops.htm
http://www.talkorigins.org
http://www.trueauthority.com/cvse/main.htm
http://www.wikipedia.org/
http://www-personal.umich.edu/~gingeric/PDGwhales/Whales.htm

Brown, David. "Discovery helps scientists junk theory of 'useless DNA'." September 7, 2012.
http://www.theage.com.au/technology/sci-tech/discovery-helps-scientists-junk-theory-of-useless-dna-20120906-25hf3.html

Landau, Elizabeth. "DNA project interprets 'book of life'."
http://www.cnn.com/2012/09/05/health/encode-human-genome/index.html?hpt=hp_bn12. September 5, 2012.

Luskin, Casey. "Darwinian Philosophy: Darwinian Natural Selection is the Only Process that could Produce the Appearance of Purpose." August 17, 2012.
http://www.evolutionnews.org/2012/08/blind_darwinian063311.html

Martinez del Rio, Carlos. "Body Size and Temperature: Why They Matter." Nature Education Knowledge 3(10):10. http://www.nature.com/scitable/knowledge/library/body-size-and-temperature-why-they-matter-15157011

Millman, Jenna, et al. "Evidence Noah's Biblical Flood Happened, Says Robert Ballard" http://abcnews.go.com/Technology/evidence-suggests-biblical-great-flood-noahs-time-happened/story?id=17884533

shCherbak, Vladimir I. "The "Wow! signal" of the terrestrial genetic code." http://www.sciencedirect.com/science/article/pii/S0019103513000791

Surtees, Marc. "Did Birds Evolve from Dinosaurs?" http://www.truthinscience.org.uk/tis2/index.php/component/content/article/231.html

Yeoman, Barry. "Schweitzer's Dangerous Discovery." Thursday, April 27, 2006. http://discovermagazine.com/2006/apr/dinosaur-dna

Made in the USA
San Bernardino, CA
30 November 2014